U0937956

世界名牌大全

第2版

创想外语研发团队 编著

中国纺织出版社

图书在版编目（CIP）数据

世界名牌大全／创想外语研发团队编著. --2版. --北京：中国纺织出版社，2019.1

ISBN 978-7-5180-4989-9

Ⅰ.①世… Ⅱ.①创… Ⅲ.①名牌－商品－介绍－世界 Ⅳ.①F760.5

中国版本图书馆CIP数据核字（2018）第096085号

责任编辑：汤　浩　　责任校对：寇晨晨　　**责任印制**：储志伟

中国纺织出版社出版发行

地址：北京市朝阳区百子湾东里A407号楼　**邮政编码**：100124

销售电话：010—67004422　**传真**：010-87155801

http://www.c-textilep.com

E-mail:faxing@c-textilep.com

中国纺织出版社天猫旗舰店

官方微博http://weibo.com/2119887771

三河市延风印装有限公司印刷　各地新华书店经销

2014年10月第1版　2019年1月第2版第2次印刷

开本：880×1230　1/32　**印张**：8.5

字数：220千字　**定价**：45.00元

前言 Preface

当今，商品琳琅满目，品牌也不胜枚举，但令人们始终津津乐道的是那些名牌以及它们的经典之作。什么是名牌？有的人说，天价之物是名牌；有的人说，家喻户晓的是名牌；有的人说，品质精良的是名牌。哈布斯堡公爵曾评价世界名表宝玑：“宝玑是欧洲文化遗产的组成部分，它的座右铭是文化！”而顶级名表百达翡丽的传统是“品质、美丽、可靠”。虽然名牌至今还没有真正的定义，但不难看出，名牌意味着高品质，名牌意味着高品位，名牌意味着经典。

人们一直在追求高品质、品位独特的生活，讲究健康、舒适、时尚，还要求简单、安全、快捷。世界顶级名品正是契合人们的生活追求，并把人们的这些追求在作品中发挥得淋漓尽致。爱马仕珍品，是集思想深邃、品位高尚、内涵丰富、力求完美、工艺精湛于一体的艺术品；香奈儿的时装、香水永远演绎着舒适与高雅、简洁与典雅、精致与高贵的经典；名表百达翡丽尊崇“完美的复杂性”与“完美的精确性”结合，追求精确、独特、卓越与高贵的极致；贵族名流钟爱的梵克雅宝珠宝是法国时尚艺术的极致，高贵与典雅无人能及；皮具之王的铁狮东尼优雅独特，用料精良，手工精巧，是现代追求时尚的高品位人士争相入囊之物；轩尼诗OX干邑有如雨后翠林般的清香，香醇回味无穷的口感，如丝绸般润滑的丰厚质感，是由百余种非凡的“生命之水”陈酿而成的世界顶级干邑；豪车玛莎拉蒂在外观造型、机械性能、舒适安全性等方面力争完美，并极具现代感与力求创新突破。任何一个追求高品质、高品位的人，都不会错过这些力求完美、追求卓越的世界名牌。

世界顶级名品都经历了长时间的锤炼，是文化沉淀的精华，比如路易·威登，比如宝玑，比如蒂芙尼……它们无不历经沧海桑田，一路完善与创新，最终创造传奇。每一个世界名牌都极力打造高端卓越品质，这是品牌成长的“生命之源”；每一个世界名牌都有自身的文化价值追求，各经典产品的品位和风格就是她们文化的象征；同时，每一个世界名牌都通过工艺与美学创新推出经典之作，有的经过工艺改良与创新完善产品，有的从颜色、线条组合获得设计灵感，有的从大自然获得启发，进行美学创新。这些不禁让人思考，谁是这些顶级名牌的创始人？他们经历了什么样的风风雨雨？这些名牌成长的道路上有什么样的传奇？这些问题的答案就在本书中。我们如果能够仔细阅读和思考，还能从其中获得许多关于学习、创业或工作、生活等方面的启发与感悟。

《世界名牌大全》是中英文对照白金版本，不仅给读者展现原汁原味的世界名牌，而且在领略名牌风采的同时能提高读者的英语水平和生活品质。

本书根据中国人的喜好先介绍了世界尖端品牌，然后挑选了世界名表、品牌服装、珠宝首饰、皮具、豪车等知名品牌，呈现给读者。

这些世界名牌，每部分分为“品牌名片”和“品牌阅读”并附核心词汇。“品牌名片”一目了然，列举了名牌的品类、标志风格、创始人、诞生地以及诞生时间；“品牌阅读”详细叙述名牌传奇、名牌经典之作等。

本书的主要篇幅为英文，词语精练儒雅，句式严谨，每一篇都是原汁原味的美文佳作，并配以完整恰当的中文译文，是真正的中英饕餮大餐。

编者

2017年8月

目 录 Contents

Part 1 尖端品牌

1.（法国）路易·威登 Louis Vuitton

品牌名片

品　　类：箱包、成衣、腕表、珠宝

标志风格：时尚、高雅

创 始 人：路易·威登（Louis Vuitton）

诞 生 地：法国

诞生时间：1854年

百年历史的路易·威登，旅行箱超凡脱俗，定制的皮革时装高雅独特，成为享誉全球的品牌。

品牌阅读

Louis Vuitton's heritage as a trunk maker preceded even the founding of the company. It was in 1837 that a 16-year-old Louis Vuitton arrived in Paris by foot and started apprenticing for Monsieur Marechal. At the time, horse-drawn carriages, boats and trains were the main modes of transportation, and baggage was handled roughly. Travelers called upon craftsmen to pack and protect their individual objects. Louis Vuitton quickly became a valued craftsman at the Parisian atelier of Monsieur Marechal. These were the roots of his highly specialized trade, the beginnings of his career in an **artisanal** industry that called upon skills to custom design boxes and, later, trunks according to clients' wishes. Louis Vuitton stayed for 17 years before opening his own workshop at 4 Rue Neuve-Capucines near the Place Vendome.

The early success of Louis Vuitton meant he had to expand his operations. This led to the 1859 opening of his **atelier** in Asnieres,

just northeast of the center of Paris. The workshop started with 20 employees. In 1900, there were nearly 100 people and by 1914 there were 225. The original atelier has been expanded throughout the decade including the addition of the Vuitton family residence-but it is still where products are crafted today. While the family home has been preserved and is part of a private museum, 170 craftsmen work in the Asnieres workshop, designing and creating leather goods and special orders for clients around the world.

At that time, travelers carried all their essentials inside wardrobes and flat trunks, which, unfortunately, often attracted burglars. Master trunk maker, Louis Vuitton sought to help his clients protect the goods inside their travel pieces.

In 1886, father and son, Georges, adopted a single lock system with two spring buckles. After several years of development, George patented this revolutionary system. It was so effective that he challenged Harry Houdini, the great American escape artist, in a public newspaper to escape from a Vuitton box and lock. Houdini didn't rise to the challenge, but the lock's effectiveness is **indisputable**. It is still used today.

To celebrate 100th anniversary of the Monogram canvas in 1996, Louis Vuitton invited designers to create unique pieces of luggage. The resulting collection was then exhibited in the world's great capitals, bringing the brand's spirit of innovation and collaboration to fashion lovers across the globe.

artisanal ['ɑːtɪzənəl] adj. 手工艺性的

atelier ['ætəliei] n. 工作室

indisputable [ˌindis'pju:təbl] adj. 无争议的

路易·威登在尚未成立公司之前，便因制作旅行箱而为人所熟知。1837年，年仅十六岁的路易·威登徒步前往巴黎，并当上马雷复尔先生的学徒。当时，马车、轮船和火车是主要的交通工具，行李因经常受到碰撞而磨损。因此，不少旅客要求工匠将行李打包以保护他们的个人物品。路易·威登很快便成为马雷复尔先生位于巴黎工作坊的一名重要工匠。这不仅为他日后专注于硬箱制造奠定了基础，更成为他传奇事业的开始。他凭借精湛的技艺，最初为顾客定制旅行箱，继而按顾客需求制作出各式各样的硬箱。路易·威登在此工作了17年后，在芳登广场附近的Neuve-Capucines大道四号开设了首间工作室。

路易·威登取得成功后，遂着手扩充业务，并于1859年在巴黎市中心东北方向的Asnieres开设了首间工厂。Asnieres工厂初期聘请了20名员工。1900年，工厂的工匠接近100人，至1914年便达到了225人。Asnieres工厂在过去数十年不断扩展，当中包括附加的威登家族的宅第部分，但工厂仍然是路易·威登产品的生产基地。家族大宅现已保留成为博物馆的一部分，170名工匠继续驻守工作坊，为世界各地的顾客设计并制作皮革制品及特别定制产品。

那时，旅客都会将所有必需品置于行李箱中，但这经常引来鼠窃之辈的垂涎。于是，拥有超凡制箱技艺的路易·威登便寻求方法，帮助顾客保护行李内的财物。

1886年，路易·威登和儿子乔治合力研发出一套配备两个弹簧扣的单锁系统。经过数年的发展，乔治为这个革命性的系统申请了专利，并公开在报纸上挑战美国脱逃大师哈利·胡迪尼，要他从路易·威登的箱子和箱锁系统中逃脱。胡迪尼并没有接受挑战，但这套系统的效用却是毋庸置疑的，时至今天仍然被广泛使用。

为庆祝Monogram帆布系列诞生一百周年，路易·威登于1996年诚邀设计师创作独一无二的旅行箱包。各大师的作品于世界各国的首都巡回展出，与全球时装爱好者一同分享品牌的创新和合作精神。

2.（法国）香奈儿 Chanel

品牌名片

品　　类：时装、成衣、化妆品、配饰、鞋

标志风格：高贵、高雅

创 始 人：嘉柏丽尔·香奈儿（Gabrielle Chanel）

诞 生 地：法国

诞生时间：1913年

当今香奈儿已成为时尚引领先锋，产品包括服饰、化妆品、珠宝等。

品牌阅读

Gabrielle Chanel was born in Saumur (France) on August 19th 1883 under the sign of Leo to parents of a modest background. In 1910, she opened her first shop at 21 rue Cambon in Paris, creating hats under the name "CHANEL Modes". Favored by the most famous French actresses of the time, her designs helped to establish her reputation. Gabrielle Chanel's simple elegant style of dress created a sensation, and was soon imitated by all of Paris.

Gabrielle Chanel opened a new boutique in Deauville, France in 1913, and introduced a collection of sportswear. Her line of jersey garments proved revolutionary and changed women's relationships with their bodies and their ways of life. It was an immediate success. In 1915, Her reputation was now firmly established and Mademoiselle Chanel opened her first Couture House in Biarritz, France.

In 1921, Mademoiselle Chanel unveiled her first fragrance, the iconic CHANEL N°5. Created by Ernest Beaux, former perfumer to the Czars, N°5 was so called because it was the fifth scent presented to Mademoiselle Chanel. A truly timeless classic, N°5 remains the ultimate symbol of **femininity**. In 1924, CHANEL presented the first makeup collection, featuring lip colours and face powders. In the same year, the "Société des Parfums CHANEL" was founded and was dedicated to creating unique fragrances and beauty products.

In 1940s, Gabrielle Chanel was **at the height of** her fame. She employed 4,000 workers and owned five boutiques on rue Cambon in Paris. But when the World War II broke out, the House of CHANEL was compelled to closure. Among the five boutiques on rue Cambon, only one remained open: the store at number 31, where perfumes and accessories continued to be in high demand among Parisians and American soldiers alike.

At the age of 71, Gabrielle Chanel staged the grand re-opening of her Couture House. Tired of the fashions of the time, she inspired a second fashion revolution with her original creations.

In February of 1955, Gabrielle Chanel launched the iconic 2.55 quilted handbag, naming the style after the date of its creation. Combining leather and gold chain, she invented a supple new style of shoulder strap that was uniquely strong and light, and that allowed a woman's hands to remain free.

The fascination with CHANEL grew, as the most celebrated stars of the time—Elizabeth Taylor, Jane Fonda, Jackie Kennedy, Grace Kelly and Jeanne Moreau—wore the latest fashions from CHANEL.

The House of CHANEL expanded with the introduction of its first Ready-to-Wear collection and the worldwide distribution of its line of iconic accessories in 1978.

In 1987, the first line of CHANEL Watches was launched with the

creation of the PREMIÈRE watch, designed by Jacques Helleu. The dial of the watch recalled the shape of both place Vendôme and the stopper of the iconic N°5 bottle.

In 1993, a milestone was reached with the launch of the first CHANEL Fine Jewelry collection in the heart of the place Vendôme in Paris. In 1997, CHANEL established 18 place Vendôme as the home of CHANEL Fine Jewelry.

In 2002, CHANEL acquired eight Parisian speciality ateliers to establish PARAFFECTION, a company consisting of Desrues (metalworker), Lemarié (flower and feather craftsmen), Maison Michel (milliner), Maison Lesage (embroiderer), Massaro (shoemaker), Goossens (goldsmith), Guillet (floral accessory expert) and Atelier Montex (embroiderer). In doing so, CHANEL supported the historic arts, and preserved the unique **expertise** of fashion's traditional craftsmen.

femininity [,femə'ninəti] *n.* 温柔；柔弱性；女子本性

at the height of 在……的顶峰或鼎盛时期

expertise [,ekspə:'ti:z] *n.* 专门技术

嘉柏丽尔·香奈儿于1883年8月19日出生于法国索缪一个寒微的家庭，狮子座。1910年，她在巴黎康朋街21号开设了自己的第一家女帽店，以“香奈儿时尚”为名，制作帽子。她的设计受到当时最著名的法国女演员的垂青，也为她带来了美誉。嘉柏丽尔·香奈儿简洁优雅的着装风格引起轰动，很快被整个巴黎竞相效仿。

1913年，嘉柏丽尔·香奈儿在法国杜维埃开设了一家服饰店，推出运动服饰系列。她设计的针织服装具有革命性的意义，改变了女性与自己的身体以及生活方式的关系，并立即大获成功。1915年，声誉卓著的香奈儿在法国比亚利兹开设了自己的第一家个人品

牌时装屋。

1921年，香奈儿推出自己的第一款香水，标志性的“香奈儿N° 5”。香奈儿N° 5由前沙皇宫廷调香师恩尼斯·鲍调制，之所以叫做5号，是因为这是他呈给香奈儿女士的第5款香水。香奈儿N° 5是永恒经典的象征，至今仍是女性之美的极致标志。1924年，香奈儿推出第一个化妆品系列，以唇彩和蜜粉为主打。同年成立“香奈儿香水公司”，致力于生产独一无二的香水和美容用品。

20世纪40年代，嘉柏丽尔·香奈儿的声誉达到鼎盛期。她雇用了4000名工人，在巴黎康朋街拥有5家精品店。而随着第二次世界大战爆发，香奈儿公司被迫关闭。康朋街的5家店中，只有康朋街31号仍继续营业，因为巴黎人和美国士兵仍然对香水和配饰有大量的需求。

71岁时，香奈儿重返高级女装界。对当时的时尚潮流倍感厌倦的她，用自己独创的作品掀起了第二次时装革命。

1955年2月，嘉柏丽尔·香奈儿推出标志性的2.55菱格纹手袋，并以诞生的年月为其命名。她将皮革与金色链带相结合，发明了一种全新风格的柔韧肩带，既结实又轻巧，可以将女性的双手解放出来。

随着当时最著名的明星——伊丽莎白·泰勒、简·方达、杰奎琳·肯尼迪、格蕾丝·凯利和让娜·莫罗纷纷穿上香奈儿的最新时装，人们对香奈儿的迷恋也与日俱增。

1978年，高级成衣诞生。香奈儿品牌拓展业务，推出第一个高级成衣系列，并进一步向全球推广标志性的配饰系列。

1987年，香奈儿推出第一款腕表系列PREMIÈRE ，由贾克·海卢设计。表盘形似芳登广场以及标志性的香奈儿N° 5香水瓶瓶盖的轮廓。

1993年，香奈儿迎来全新里程碑，在巴黎芳登广场核心地带推出第一个香奈儿高级珠宝系列。1997年，香奈儿在芳登广场18号设

立高级珠宝总店。

2002年，香奈儿将八家巴黎高级手工坊收入旗下，成立了PARAFFECTION子公司，包括：Desrues服饰珠宝坊，Lemarié山茶花及羽饰坊，Michel制帽坊，Lesage刺绣坊，Massaro鞋履坊，Goossens金银饰坊，Guillet花饰坊，以及Montex刺绣坊。通过这一方法，香奈儿不仅为传统的手工艺提供了支持，同时也保存了传统工匠的独特技术。

读书笔记

3.（法国）爱马仕 Hermes

品牌名片

品　　类：皮具、服装、香水、饰品

标志风格：奢侈、尊贵

创 始 人：蒂埃利·爱马仕（Thierry Hermes）

诞 生 地：法国

诞生时间：1837年

爱马仕品牌标志最上方是以马车马夫与马的形象呈现，由于爱马仕最早期的时候是以制造高端马具起家，所以这点也看出爱马仕一直保持着初衷。标志设计整体采用橙色，温暖并且时尚。

品牌阅读

Hermes is a world famous luxury brand, founded in 1837 by Thierry Hermes in Paris, France. In the early years, it made advanced harness. Today it specializes in leather, lifestyle accessories, perfumery, luxury goods and ready-to-wear. So far, it has had a history of 180 years.

Born in Krefeld (Germany), Thierry Hermes was the son of a French man and a German woman. The family moved to France in 1828. In 1837, Thierry Hermes first established Hermes as a harness workshop on the Grands Boulevards quarter of Paris, dedicating to serving European noblemen. He created some of the finest wrought harnesses and bridles for the carriage trade. Monsieur Hermes earned citations, including the first-class medal in 1867 at the Expositions Universelles in Paris.

In the 1970s, the watch subsidiary, La Montre Hermès, was

established in Bienne, Switzerland. Then, throughout the 1980s, Dumas strengthened the company's hold on its suppliers, resulting in Hermès gaining great stakes in prominent French glassware, silverware and venerable tableware manufacturers such as Puiforcat, St. Louis and Périgord.

From the 1980s, tableware became a strong segment of the firm. And, overall, the collection of Hermès goods expanded in 1990 to over 30,000 pieces. New materials used in the collection included porcelain and crystal.

By the late 1990s, Hermes continued extensively to diminish the number of franchised stores, buying them up and opening more company-operated boutiques.

Today, Hermes has 17 product divisions encompassing leather, scarves, ties, men's wear, women's fashion, perfume, watches, stationery, footwear, accessories, harness supplies, household series, tableware and jewelry.

爱马仕是世界著名的奢侈品品牌，1837年由蒂埃利·爱马仕创立于法国巴黎，早年以制造高级马具起家，如今专门从事皮革、生活配饰、香水、奢侈品、成衣生产。迄今已有180年的悠久历史。

出生于德国克雷菲尔德，蒂埃利·爱马仕的父亲是法国人，母亲是德国人。1828年，举家搬往法国。1837年，蒂埃利·爱马仕在巴黎的Grands Boulevards创建了马具车间，他决定服务于欧洲贵族。他为上流社会创造精致的马具和缰绳。爱马仕先生赢得了大家的褒奖，包括1867年在巴黎举行的世界博览会中，赢得一级荣誉奖章。

在20世纪70年代，制表子公司La Montre Hermès在瑞士比尔市成立。后来，在整个80年代，爱马仕先生的女婿Dumes加强了对其供应商的管理，这使得爱马仕从著名的法国玻璃器皿、银器餐具制造商那里获得了大量的资助，比如Puiforcat, St. Louis以及Périgord。

从80年代开始，餐具成为公司的一个主打产品。总的来说，爱马仕的产品在1990年扩展到30000多件。产品系列中运用了新材料，包括瓷器和水晶。

到20世纪90年代后期，爱马仕大量减少专卖店的数量，买断专卖店，并开设更多直营精品店。

时至今日，爱马仕旗下共有十七种产品系列：皮革、丝巾、领带、男女时装、香水、腕表、文化用品、鞋类、配饰、马具用品、家居生活系列、餐具及珠宝首饰等。

读书笔记

4.（法国）纪梵希 Givenchy

品牌名片

品　　类：香水、化妆品、服装、配饰

标志风格：华贵、典雅

创 始 人：休伯特·德·纪梵希（Hubert de Givenchy）

诞 生 地：法国

诞生时间：1952年

纪梵希的品牌标志是4个“G”的变形组合黑体字GIVENCHY字样，堪称Givenchy的金字招牌。

品牌阅读

Givenchy is a luxury French brand of clothing, accessories, perfumes and cosmetics with Parfums Givenchy.

The house of Givenchy was founded in 1952 by designer Hubert de Givenchy. It is owned by luxury goods behemoth LVMH and in 1993 achieved a total sales of $176 million, making it the second largest apparel division of LVMH after Dior.

During his reign as the designer, Hubert de Givenchy was known for his modern, ladylike styles, which earned him many loyal clients. The most famous ambassador of the brand was Audrey Hepburn. His other famous patrons included Empress Farah Pahlavi and Marella Agnelli, as well as the Guinness, Grimaldi and Kennedy families, who famously wore Givenchy clothes to the **funeral** of John F. Kennedy. Hubert de Givenchy retired in 1995.

John Galliano succeeded Givenchy upon his retirement. In 2001, designer Julien Macdonald was appointed Artistic Director for the women's lines, which consist of haute couture and ready-to-wear.

Givenchy designs have been worn by a number of celebrities on red carpet occasions, including Rooney Mara at the 2012 **Academy Award**.

funeral ['fju:nərəl] *n.* 葬礼

Academy Award 奥斯卡金像奖

纪梵希是一个集服装、配饰、香水和具有纪梵希香氛的化妆品于一体的法国奢侈品品牌。

纪梵希诞生于1952年，其创始人是设计师休伯特·德·纪梵希。它是奢侈品巨头LVMH（西名悦·轩尼诗—路易·威登集团）旗下的公司，1993年总销售额达到了1.76亿美元，使其成为继迪奥之后LVMH的第二大服装部门。

在担任设计师期间，休伯特·德·纪梵希因其摩登、淑女风格而闻名，这为他赢得了许多忠实的客户。最著名的品牌大使是奥黛丽·赫本。还包括Empress Farah Pahlavi和Marella Agnelli以及Guinness, Grimaldi 和 Kennedy家族，他们曾穿着纪梵希的服装参加了 John F. Kennedy的葬礼。纪梵希于1995年退休。

休伯特·德·纪梵希退休后，John Galliano 接管了纪梵希。2001年，设计师 Julien Macdonald被任命为艺术总监，专门为女性设计，包括高级时装和成衣。

许多名人都穿着纪梵希设计的服装走上了红地毯，包括参加2012年奥斯卡颁奖典礼的Rooney Mara。

5.（意大利）范思哲 Versace

品牌名片

品　　类：时装、皮具、化妆品

标志风格：时尚、魅力、性感

创 始 人：詹尼·范思哲（Gianni Versace）

诞 生 地：意大利

诞生时间：1978年

范思哲的品牌标志采用神话中蛇妖美杜莎的造型作为精神象征所在，汲取古希腊、埃及、印度等国家的瑰丽文化打造而成。美杜莎代表着致命的吸引力，它象征着范思哲不仅有着超脱歌剧式的华丽，还因极强的先锋潮流艺术特征受到世人的追捧。

品牌阅读

The Versace myth is what makes the Versace name world famous. It is centered on the idea of a world of fashion, glamour and sexiness. The myth dates back to 1978, when the brand was created by the founder, Gianni Versace. Gianni Versace became world famous as an innovative fashion designer. Gianni Versace was essentially the architect of modern fashion's place in popular culture. He redefined what a fashion house was by combining fashion with rock'n'roll, art, celebrity, theatre and ballet.

At the age of 25 Gianni Versace moved to Milan. He designed his first collections for Callaghan, Genny and Complice.

In 1979, Gianni Versace collaborates with Richard Avedon for his first fashion photography campaign. This was the beginning of many Versace **campaigns** by Avedon.

In 1982, Versace's Oroton – a metal chainmail invented by Versace – was launched in his collection presented at the Paris Opera. Gianni Versace began an ongoing collaboration with La Scala Theatre, Milan, designing costumes for Josephs Legende (Richard Strauss, directed by Pier Luigi Veronesi). Versace's costumes were featured in stage events worldwide such as: Donizetti's Don Pasquale (1984), Bob Wilson's Salome (1987) and Doktor Faust (1989), and several Béjart ballets, including Dionysos (1984), Leda and the Swan (1987), Malraux ou la Métamorphose des Dieux (1986) and Chaka Zulu (1989).

In 1985, Gianni Versace's first exhibition in the UK was held at the Victoria and Albert Museum. Gianni Versace was awarded the Silver Mask Award for his contribution to theatre. In 1986, the Versace first decade of creativity **retrospective** exhibition was held at the National Field Museum of Chicago Gianni Versace; Fashion Lens exhibition was held at Musee de la Mode, Paris. The exhibition illustrated Versace's collaborations with international photographers including Avedon, Newton, Weber Penn, and Barbieri. Gianni Versace was awarded "Grande Medaille de Vermeil de la Ville de Paris" by Jacques Chirac. This was the first time the award was given to a designer.

Gianni Versace launched his first couture collection in Paris and opened Atelier Versace. Versace's 'Dresses for Thought' exhibition on the Gianni Versace's 25 years in fashion and theatre was held at the Sforzesco Castle in Milan.

In 1991, The Supermodel phenomenon was born when Gianni Versace sent all the top models down the runway for his Autumn/Winter 1991/1992 collection. In 1992, Gianni Versace designed stage costumes for Elton John's World Tour and album cover. "Versace

Signatures" exhibition was shown at the Fashion Institute of New York. Gianni Versace was awarded the first American fashion Oscar by the CFDA in New York in 1993.

Gianni Versace died on July 15, 1997 in Miami, Florida. His sister, Donatella, who started with the design of accessories and went on to create a children's line "Young Versace" in 1993 and subsequently "Versus", a brand aimed at younger fashion enthusiasts, was named Creative Director of the Versace Group. She had successfully taken the DNA of the company and evolved it for the 21st century.

The Versace Group has its own branded luxury stores worldwide. These are created to provide the perfect environment to showcase the Versace collections. There are currently approximately 100 Versace **boutiques** in the most exclusive cities of the world, including Rome, Paris, London, New York, Dubai and Hong Kong. Over the past few years the Versace boutiques have been renovated to keep in line with the modern aesthetic of the brand - there is a chic black and white design code, with a signature use of marble and leather.

retrospective [ˌretrəu'spektiv] adj. 可追溯的

campaign [kæm'pein] n.活动

boutique [bu:'ti:k] n. 精品店

范思哲神话使范思哲这个名字举世闻名。它的核心理念是时尚、魅力和性感。这个神话可以追溯到 1978 年，创始人詹尼·范思哲在这一年创立了范思哲品牌。詹尼·范思哲作为创新时尚设计师闻名于世。在流行文化中，詹尼·范思哲本是流行文化中现代时尚场所建筑师。他将时尚与摇滚、艺术、名人、戏剧和芭蕾舞相结合，重新定义了时装工作室的内涵。

詹尼·范思哲在 25 岁那年前往米兰。他为加勒汉（Callaghan）

公司、珍妮（Genny）公司和康普利斯（Complice）公司设计了他的第一批成装系列。

1979年，詹尼·范思哲与理查得·艾维登（Richard Avedon）合作，第一次举办了时装摄影展活动。这是艾维登参与众多范思哲活动的开端。

1982年，在巴黎剧院举办的范思哲时装系列展示中，范思哲推出了自己独创的“Oroton”金属链时装。詹尼·范思哲开始与米兰的斯卡拉（Scala）剧院长期合作，为 Pier Luigi Veronesi 执导的理查德·施特劳斯（Richard Strauss）作品 Josephs legende 设计舞台服装。范思哲为遍布世界各地的舞台演出设计服装，例如：Donizetti 的 Don Pasquale（1984年）、Bob Wilson 的 Salome（1987年）和 Doktor Faust（1989年）以及数次 Béjart 芭蕾舞剧演出，包括 Dionysos（1984年）、Leda and the Swan（1987年），Malraux ou la Métamorphose des Dieux（1986年）和 Chaka Zulu（1989年）。

1985年，詹尼·范思哲在英国的第一次时装展示在维多利亚与艾博特博物馆（Victoria and Albert Museum）举行。詹尼·范思哲被授予银面具奖（Silver Mask Award），以表彰其对表演艺术的巨大贡献。1986年，范思哲的第一个十年创作精品展在芝加哥的国立菲尔德博物馆（Field Museum）举行。詹尼·范思哲时尚视点展览在巴黎的时装博物馆（Musee de la Mode）举行。在此次展览中，范思哲与多位国际知名摄影家合作，他们是艾维登（Avedon）、牛顿（Newton）、韦伯（Weber）、潘恩（Penn）和巴比亚里（Barbieri）。雅克·希拉克（Jacques Chirac）授予詹尼·范思哲“艺术家巴黎市金质奖章”（Grande Medaille de Vermeil de la Ville de Paris）。这是该奖项首次颁给设计师。

1989年，詹尼·范思哲在巴黎推出他的第一个时装系列，并开设了范思哲高级定制（Atelier Versace）。詹尼·范思哲的时装与剧场 25 年之范思哲“Dresses for Thought”展览在米兰的斯福赛斯克城

堡（Sforzesco Castle）举行。

1991年，在 1991/1992 秋冬系列时装展上，詹尼·范思哲请所有顶级模特走下 T 台，“超级模特现象”从此应运而生。1992年，詹尼·范思哲为埃尔顿·约翰（Elton John）的世界巡回演出和唱片封面设计舞台服装。Versace Signatures 展览在纽约时装学院举办。1993年，CFDA 在纽约为詹尼·范思哲颁发了美国时装奥斯卡奖。

詹尼·范思哲 1997年7月15日在佛罗里达迈阿密市不幸身亡。随后，他的妹妹多娜泰拉·范思哲被任命为范思哲集团的创意总监。多娜泰拉最初是一位配饰设计师，后来转而从事儿童产品的设计工作，并于 1993 年创立了儿童系列“Young Versace”，之后又创立了“Versus”品牌，瞄准更年轻的时装狂热者。

她成功承袭了公司的传统，而且还推动了公司在21世纪的变革。

范思哲集团在世界各地设有自己的品牌店。这些品牌店为展示范思哲系列产品提供了完美的环境。目前在世界众多大城市设有约 100 家范思哲精品店，其中包括罗马、巴黎、伦敦、纽约、迪拜和香港。过去数年中，范思哲品牌店经过重新装潢，统一采用了符合品牌现代审美观的风格——别致的黑白设计典范，标志性的大理石和羽毛装饰。

6.（英国）博柏利 Burberry

品牌名片

品　　类：时装、皮具、香水

标志风格：经典、英伦风

创 始 人：托马斯·博柏利（Thomas Burberry）

诞 生 地：英国

诞生时间：1856年

博柏利品牌标志为骑在战马上的武士手持盾牌，以米色、红色、黑色与白色组成的格纹是其经典标志。

品牌阅读

The Burberry trench coat and perfume are more and more popular in the world. With a traditional design style of Britain, the Burberry has classical plaid and unique cloth and is very elegant. Besides the traditional clothes, the Burberry spreads its design style into other areas, draws the classical factors into them and launchs products like perfume, fur, headscarf, sweater, shoes and so on.

The brand was founded by 21-year-old **dressmaker** Thomas Burberry in 1856.

In 1910, celebrated aviator Claude Grahame-White wore Burberry gabardine. He was the first person to fly between London and Manchester in less than 24 hours.

In 1912, the Tielocken coat was patented, the predecessor to the trench coat. It proved popular among officers during WWI. The coat closed with a single strap and buckle and only one button at the collar.

The Burberry Prorsum label was launched under creative director

Roberto Menichetti. Images from the Burberry Spring/Summer 1998 Campaign featuring British model Neil Fenton, were styled by Carine Roitfeld and photographed by Mario Testino.

The Burberry Autumn/Winter 2004 Campaign featured British model Lily Donaldson, photographed by Mario Testino.

In 2005, Kate Moss was photographed by Mario Testino, wearing a limited edition pink Burberry **trench coat**. Christopher Bailey created the one-off piece to **coincide with** National Breast Cancer Awareness Month.

In 2006, Burberry celebrated 150 years at the Autumn/Winter 2006 womenswear show in Milan.

In 2009, the new Burberry global headquarters opened at Horseferry House in London.

In the 21st century, Burberry quickens its expansive pace in the globe. That was to establish more unique style exclusive shops in some important cities, such as London, Los Angeles, Germany, Spain, Italy and Japan. Today Burberry, the brand of classical style of Britain is well known in the world. Just like a knight in armor, it is protecting the clothing culture of the United Kingdom of Great Britain and Northern Ireland.

dressmaker ['dresmeɪkə] *n.*	裁缝
coincide with	符合；与……相一致
trench coat	军用防水短上衣

博柏利的风衣和香水在世界有很高的知名度。博柏利带有一股英国传统的设计风格，以经典的格子图案、独特的布料、大方优雅为主。除传统服装外，博柏利也将设计触角延伸至其他领域，并将经典元素注入其中，推出香水、皮草、头巾、针织衫及鞋等相关

商品。

1856年，裁缝师托马斯·博柏利（Thomas Burberry）亲手创立了博柏利（Burberry）品牌，此时他21岁。

1910年，著名的飞行家克劳德·格雷厄姆·怀特（Claude Grahame-White）身穿Burberry华达呢外套。他是首位在24小时之内完成伦敦和曼彻斯特之间飞行的飞行员。

1912年，博柏利设计了一款名为“Tielocken”的防雨风衣，它成为了博柏利标志性Trench风衣的前身，风靡第一次世界大战，在军官之间广泛流行。这款风衣仅设搭配扣环的腰部束带，领口处附单颗纽扣。

1998年，创意总监罗伯托·梅尼凯蒂推出“珀松”系列。Burberry 1998春夏广告大片，由英国超模尼尔·芬顿出镜演绎，卡琳·洛菲德（Carine Roitfeld）出任造型总监，并由著名摄影大师马里奥·特斯蒂诺（Mario Testino）掌镜拍摄。

Burberry 2004秋冬广告大片由英国超模莉莉·唐纳森（Lily Donaldson）出镜演绎，马里奥·特斯蒂诺（Mario Testino）掌镜拍摄。

2005年，凯特·摩丝（Kate Moss）穿着由克里斯托弗·贝利（Christopher Bouley)为全国乳腺癌宣传月而设计的限量版粉红色Trench风衣，由著名摄影大师马里奥·特斯蒂诺（Mario Testino）摄影。2006年，博柏利150周年庆典，在米兰举办了2006秋冬女装秀。

2009年，Burberry新环球总部于伦敦Horseferry大厦开业。

21世纪，博柏利加快了其在全球扩张的步伐：在伦敦、洛杉矶、德国、西班牙、意大利、日本的一些重要城市和地区建立起更多独具风格的专卖店。如今，博柏利这个经典英国风格品牌已经在世界上家喻户晓。它就像一个穿着盔甲的武士一样，保护着大不列颠联合王国的服装文化。

7.（意大利）古驰 Gucci

品牌名片

品　　类：服装、皮具、香水

标志风格：高档、性感

创 始 人：古奇欧·古驰（Guccio Gucci）

诞 生 地：意大利

诞生时间：1921年

古驰的品牌标志富有和谐的整体感，下方的图案体现出整个标志的核心，把企业推向了更高的角度。展现出一个更高的层次，一个很多人都想靠近的层次。

品牌阅读

With high fashion, Italian style, Traditional craftsmanship and Global consciousness, Gucci embodies produces exquisitely crafted luxury goods with a thoroughly modern sensibility.

Ever since Guccio Gucci founded the house in Florence in 1921, the brand has been a destination for the world's most discerning men and women. Gucci represents the best of Made in Italy with its inimitable combination of opulence, high artisanry and contemporary glamour.

In 1921, Guccio Gucci opened a leather goods company and small luggage store in his native Florence. Though his vision for the brand was inspired by London and the refined aesthetic of English nobility he had witnessed while working in the Savoy Hotel, his goal on returning to Italy was to ally this classy sensibility with the unique skills of his native Italy. Specifically, with the master craftsmanship of local Tuscan artisans.

Within a few years, the label enjoyed such success the sophisticated international clientele on vacation in Florence thronged to the Gucci's, seeking the equestrian-inspired collection of bags, trunks, gloves, shoes and belts. Many of Guccio's Italian clients were local horse-riding aristocrats, and their demand for riding gear led Gucci to develop its unique Horsebit icon - an enduring symbol of the fashion house and its increasingly innovative design aesthetic.

In 1940s, faced with a shortage of foreign supplies during the difficult years of Fascist dictatorship in Italy, Gucci began experimenting with atypical luxury materials, like hemp, linen and jute. One of its artisans' most subtle innovations was burnishing cane to create the handle of the new Bamboo Bag, which curvy side was inspired by a saddle's shape. An **ingenious** example of "necessity as the mother of invention", the Bamboo Bag became the first of Gucci's many iconic products. A favorite of royalty and celebrities alike, the bag with burnished handle remains a huge favorite today.

During the 1950s, Gucci again found equestrian inspiration with its trademark green-red-green web stripe, derived from a traditional saddle girth. It became an instant success and an instantly recognizable hallmark of the brand. Opening stores in Milan and New York, Gucci started to build its global presence as a symbol of modern luxury. With the passing of Guccio Gucci in 1953, his sons Aldo, Vasco, Ugo and Rodolfo took over the business.

Gucci products quickly became renowned for timeless design and were cherished by iconic movie stars and figures of elegance in the Jet Set era. Jackie Kennedy carried the Gucci shoulder bag, which is known today as the Jackie O. Liz Taylor, Peter Sellers and Samuel

Beckett sported the unstructured **unisex** Hobo Bag. Gucci's classic moccasin with Horsebit hardware became part of the permanent collection at the Costume Institute, Metropolitan Museum of Art in New York. Gucci answered a personal request by Grace Kelly by creating the now famous Flora silk print scarf for the Monaco princess. In the mid-1960s, Gucci adopted the legendary interlocking double G logo, creating yet another chic Gucci visual insignia. Gucci continued its expansion abroad with stores opening in London, Palm Beach, Paris and Beverly Hills.

Gucci continued its global expansion, true to the original aspirations of Aldo, and set its sights on the Far East. Stores opened in Tokyo and Hong Kong. The company developed its first ready-to-wear collections, featuring GG printed shirts or GG buttoned fur-trim coats. The brand became famous for its unique mix of innovative audacity and legendary Italian quality and craftsmanship. Gucci icons were re-invented in new shapes or colors -burning the GG logo through suede and using ever more luxurious materials, like baby crocodile coats with sterling silver snakehead buckles. In 1977, its Beverly Hills flagship was revamped with a private Gucci Gallery, where privileged VIPs like Rita Hayworth or Michael Caine could browse for $10,000 bags with **detachable** gold and diamond chain or platinum fox bed throws.

In 1981, Gucci staged its first ever runway show in Florence. In 1982, Gucci became a public limited company, and leadership passed to Rodolfo's son, Maurizio Gucci, who held 50 percent of the company's shares. In 1987, Investcorp, a Bahrain-based investment company, began buying into Gucci, eventually competing the purchase of all the company's shares in the early Nineties.

Gucci is relaunched to global renown through a **groundbreaking** mix of tradition and innovation. Tom Ford became creative director of Gucci in 1994 and infused the luxury brand with a sense of daring and provocation that resonated with celebrity and the fashion world. The stiletto and silk cutout jersey dresses with metallic hardware details became instant icons of Ford's uniquely glamorous vision. Domenico De Sole was appointed CEO in 1995, and Gucci made the highly successful transformation to a fully public company. Gucci is named "European Company of the year 1998" by the European Business Press Federation for its economic and financial performance, **strategic vision** and management quality. In 1999, Gucci entered into a strategic alliance with Pinault-Printemps-Redoute, transforming itself from a single brand company into a multi-brand luxury group.

Gucci achieved astounding global success and is named the most desirable luxury brand in the world (Nielsen company, 2007). Frida Giannini, formerly Creative Director of accessories, is appointed sole Creative Director in 2006. Exploring Gucci's rich heritage and its incomparable craftsmanship capabilities, Giannini has created a unique vision for Gucci that fuses past and present, history and modernity. Key house icons are reinvented in a fresh new guise, including Flora, La Pelle Guccissima, the New Jackie and the New Bamboo, as the house's tradition for innovation accelerates under Giannini.

ingenious [in'dʒiːnjəs] adj. 有独创性的；精制的

unisex ['juːnɪseks] adj. 男女皆宜的

detachable [dɪ'tætʃəbl] adj. 可分开的；可拆开的

groundbreaking ['graʊndbreɪkɪŋ] adj. 开创性的

strategic vision 战略远景

古驰象征了顶级时尚、传统工艺、意大利风格、全球化意识，以现代的敏锐直觉，创造出凝聚精美工艺的奢华之作。

自1921年创办人古奇欧·古驰在佛罗伦萨创立古驰品牌以来，古驰就一直为全世界最具鉴赏力的男士和女士的心之所系。富贵、精妙工艺与时尚魅力，这一无可比拟的结合，令古驰成为“意大利创作”的顶级象征。

1921 年，古奇欧·古驰在家乡佛罗伦萨创办了一家经营皮具和小型行李箱的店铺。古奇欧·古驰在伦敦瑟佛酒店工作时深受英国贵族优雅审美情趣的影响，其品牌创意的最初灵感便来自伦敦，之后，为了将这种优雅感性与意大利本土的卓越技艺，特别是托斯卡纳皮革工艺大师的精湛技艺相结合，他回到了意大利。

短短数年之间，品牌就取得巨大成功，在佛罗伦萨度假的国内外大批上流社会顾客纷纷涌向古驰的小店，寻找自己钟爱的马术风情提包、箱包、手套、鞋履和皮带。古驰的许多意大利客户都是当地热衷马术的贵族，为了迎合他们对马术装备的需求，古驰设计了独特的马衔扣图案——成为品牌的不朽标志，更是其不断创新的设计美学的成功典范。

20世纪40年代，当时意大利正处于法西斯独裁统治下的艰难岁月中，来自国外的原材料十分匮乏，面对这样的困境，古驰开始尝试使用特殊的材料，如大麻、亚麻和黄麻。工匠最妙不可言的创新之一是用经抛光处理的竹子作为手柄的竹节包，其侧边弯曲的设计灵感则来自马鞍的形状。“竹节包”是古驰众多标志性产品中首批推出的精妙作品之一，体现了“需求是发明之母”的至理真言。这款具有磨光手柄的手袋备受皇室人员和社会名流青睐，至今仍深受人们喜爱。

20 世纪 50 年代，古驰再次从传统马鞍带获得灵感，设计出绿—红—绿条纹织带标识。该设计立即获得成功，并成为古驰品牌最广为人知的标志之一。随着米兰和纽约专卖店的开业，古驰开始建立起享誉全球的时尚奢侈品牌形象。1953 年，古奇欧·古驰去世，他的儿子奥尔多（Aldo）、万斯科（Vasco）、于戈（Ugo）和鲁道夫（Rodolfo）接管了公司业务。

凭借不朽的设计，古驰产品迅速走红，并深受国际知名影星和上流社会优雅人士的青睐。杰奎琳·肯尼迪曾背过的古驰肩背包，正是如今著名的 Jackie O；伊丽莎白·泰勒、彼得·塞勒斯和塞缪尔·贝克特都曾经背过那款休闲中性的Hobo Bag；带马衔扣配饰的古驰经典轻便鞋如今已成为纽约大都会艺术博物馆时装学院的永久收藏。此外，古驰还应摩纳哥王妃格蕾丝·凯丽的个人委托，为她量身打造了如今享誉全球的 Flora 印花真丝丝巾。20世纪60 年代中期，古驰推出了极具传奇色彩的双 G 互扣标识，创造了又一个别致的古驰时尚视觉标志。随着伦敦、棕榈滩、巴黎和贝佛利山专卖店的开业，古驰全球扩张的步伐在不断前进。

古驰继续推动全球业务的扩展，并根据奥尔多的提议开始进军远东市场。东京和香港专卖店相继开业。公司首次推出成衣系列，其中最具特色的是印有 GG 图案的衬衫及带有 GG 纽扣的毛皮镶边外套。品牌以大胆创新与意大利传奇工艺品质的独特结合而闻名。古驰的标识推陈翻新，采用了新的款式及颜色，同时推出了绒面印制的 GG 标志，并采用更豪华的材料，带有纯银蛇头纽扣的小鳄鱼皮外套正是这种奢华品质的体现。1977 年，贝弗利山旗舰店重新翻修，新建了一所 Gucci 私人艺廊，专供像丽塔·海华斯或迈克尔·凯恩这样的高级贵宾鉴赏价值 1 万美元、以黄金和钻石链装饰的皮包，以及浅色狐皮床品等。

1981年，古驰在佛罗伦萨举办了首次时装秀。1982年，古驰成为上市公司，由鲁道夫的儿子毛里西奥·古驰（Maurizio Gucci）接管，他拥有公司 50% 的股权。1987年，巴林的一家投资公司 Investcorp 开始收购 Gucci，最终于90年代初收购了 Gucci 的所有股权。

古驰通过将传统与创新以前所未有的方式完美融合，再次赢得

全球追捧。1994 年，Tom Ford 出任古驰创作总监，为这一奢侈品品牌注入大胆、刺激的全新感觉，在社会名流和时尚人士中引起强烈共鸣。古驰的细高跟女鞋和搭配金属配饰细节的真丝镂空裙装成为体现 Ford 独特视角的经典之作。1995 年，多梅尼科（Domenico De Sole）出任 CEO，而古驰也成功地转型为完全的上市公司。凭借其经济及财务业绩、战略眼光和管理品质获得了欧洲企业新闻联盟授予的“1998 欧洲年度公司”的称号。1999 年，古驰与巴黎春天集团结成战略联盟，从一家单一 品牌公司转变为多品牌奢侈品集团。

古驰在全球范围内获得了惊人的成功，并获得全球最梦寐以求的奢侈品牌称号（Nielsen 公司，2007 年）。2006 年，前配饰创作总监弗里达·詹尼尼（Frida Giannini）被任命为全权创作总监。通过对Gucci丰富的传统积累和无可匹敌的工艺的进一步探索，詹尼尼为古驰创造了将过去和现在、历史与潮流相融合的独特理念。在詹尼尼对公司创新传统的进一步推动下，公司的标志性产品，包括Flora、La Pelle Guccissima、New Jackie 及 New Bamboo 等经过重新诠释，呈现出令人耳目一新的面貌。

读书笔记

读书笔记

Part 2 世界名表

1.（瑞士）浪琴 Longines

品牌名片

品　　类：腕表

标志风格：集传统、优雅和运动于一体

创 始 人：奥古斯特·阿加西（Auguste Agassiz）

诞 生 地：瑞士

诞生时间：1832年

浪琴（Longines）的品牌标志——一个带翅膀的沙漏，是最古老的表类注册商标。浪琴公司属于瑞士斯沃琪集团。浪琴以它的“飞行家”表而著名。

品牌阅读

Based in the Swiss town of St. Imier since 1832. Longines is celebrating its 186th anniversary in 2018. The famous Swiss watchmaker can boast a technical expertise born of tradition, elegance and performance. With many years of experience as a timekeeper for world **championships** in sport or as a partner of international sports federations, Longines – famous for the elegance of its timepieces – is a member of the Swatch Group Ltd, the world's leading manufacturer of horological products. The brand known by its winged **hourglass** logo now has outlets in over 130 countries.

In 1832 Auguste Agassiz entered the world of horology when he joined a trading office established in St. Imier. He soon rose to become the manager and the company took on the name Agassiz & Co. At the time, he was producing timepieces under the "établissage" system, whereby watchmakers worked at home and supplied their products

to the trading offices. Agassiz built up a network of commercial contacts, which enabled him to sell his watches on other continents, in particular in North America. During the 1850s Agassiz's nephew Ernest Francillon took over the running of the office. When Francillon took on this responsibility, he considered ways of perfecting the manufacturing methods used in watchmaking in the area. He concluded that it would be **advantageous** to try to bring together the different stages that go towards making a watch under one roof. Francillon's intention was to set up a factory where he could assemble and finish each watch, introducing a degree of **mechanization**. In order to achieve this, he bought two adjoining pieces of land on the right bank of the River Suze in 1866 , which ran through the St. Imier valley. The site was known locally as Les Longines and he adopted this name for the factory which he built there in 1867. Ernest Francillon took on Jacques David, a young engineer who was also related to him, to help develop the machines needed for perfecting the manufacture of timepieces. During the 1870s, Francillon's choice of industrial options was proved sound and the factory continually expanded until the first third of the 20th century: in 1911, the Longines factory employed over 1,100 workers and sold its products all over the world.

The technical research carried out at Longines was rewarded by various prizes which gradually gave the company its reputation of winning the most awards in international and world exhibitions until the 1929 exhibition in Barcelona, by which Longines had won no fewer than 10 Grand Prix. In 1889, Francillon patented a trademark comprising the name Longines and the now famous winged hourglass. Today, Longines is the oldest trademark or logo still in use in its original form registered with the **World Intellectual**

Property Organization (WIPO). As early as 1867, Longines was using the winged hourglass symbol and the tradename "Longines" as a guarantee of quality in order to combat counterfeit products aimed at taking advantage of the reputation already established by the company.

championship ['tʃæmpiənʃip] n. 锦标赛

hourglass ['auəglɑ:s] n. 沙漏；水漏

advantageous [,ædvən'teidʒəs] adj. 有利的；有益的

mechanization [,mekənai'zeiʃən] n. 机械化；机动化

World Intellectual Property Organization (WIPO)
世界知识产权组织

浪琴表于 1832 年在瑞士的圣耶米（Saint-Imier）创立，截至 2018 年，这一卓越品牌已历经了 186 年的辉煌。这个钟表世家拥有着集传统、典雅及高性能于一身的独特专有技术。作为世界锦标赛的计时员及国际运动联合会的合作伙伴，浪琴表以其典雅的钟表享誉全球，是世界领先钟表制造商 Swatch Group S.A. 公司的旗下一员。浪琴表世家以飞翼沙漏为徽标，业务遍布全球 130 多个国家。

1832 年，奥古斯特·阿加西（Auguste Agassiz）加入圣耶米（Saint-Imier）的一家贸易公司，进入钟表制造界，并迅速成为了阿加西公司（Agassiz & Co）的经理。当时，他依照"établissage"制表方式生产钟表，即制表匠在家中工作，然后供货到贸易公司。Aqqsiz大力拓展商业网络，成功将产品销售到了其他大洲，尤其是北美洲。19 世纪 50 年代，阿加西（Agassiz）的侄子奥内斯特·弗兰西昂（Ernest Francillon）接管了贸易公司的生意。在承担这家著名世家经营责任的同时，他也在思考如何对本地钟表业常用的制造方法进行改良。他准备对原本零星分散的制表步骤进行重组，将其全部整合在一起完成。弗兰西昂（Francillon）想要建立一家工厂，引进机械工艺，实现从组装到完工的各道流程。为了实现设想，

1866 年，他在流经圣耶米山谷（Saint-Imier）的苏士河（Suze）右岸购买了两块毗连的土地。那里在当地被叫做“Les Longines”，于是，他 1867 年建立制造工厂时就以“Les Longines”对其进行了命名。奥内斯特·弗兰西昂（Ernest Francillon）聘请了亲族中一位名叫雅克·大卫（Jacques David）的年轻工程师，协助其开发设备、改良钟表制造工艺及流程。19 世纪 70 年代，弗兰西昂（Francillon）坚持的工业化选择取得了很好的实效，直至 20 世纪前叶，工厂均始终保持着不断发展壮大的强劲势头：1911 年，浪琴表厂的员工已超过 1100 人，钟表产品畅销世界各地。

浪琴表专注技术研究、精益求精，截至 1929 年巴塞罗那展会，已在众多国际及世界博览会上揽获了十次以上的显赫大奖，堪当实至名归的“最荣耀”钟表世家品牌。1889 年，弗兰西昂（Francillon）对浪琴表（Longines）名称及飞翼沙漏图形组成的品牌进行了专利注册。如今，浪琴表（Longines）已经成为世界知识产权组织（WIPO）所有国际注册中历史最为悠久、未经任何修改的品牌。早自 1867 年起，该钟表世家就将“飞翼沙漏”图形及“浪琴表（Longines）”名称作为非凡品质的象征，与那些试图盗用浪琴表声誉牟利的赝品进行着不懈的斗争。

读书笔记

2.（瑞士）天梭 Tissot

品牌名片

品　　类：腕表

标志风格：本色、自然

创 始 人：查理–艾米尔·天梭（Charles–Emile Tissot）

诞 生 地：瑞士力洛克

诞生时间：1853年

天梭表品牌标志上的T是Tissot的首字母，亮丽的“红十字”是国际人道主义保护标志。最下方的“Swiss Watches since 1853”表示天梭表的开创时间。

品牌阅读

From 1853 to the present day, Tissot has continually surprised and delighted customers with its **product innovation**. A relentless pioneering spirit led the company from its foundation in the small Swiss Jura town of Le Locle to a presence in 160 countries. From its first pocket watch with two time-zones in 1853 to its revolutionary touch-screen technology T-Touch watch, Tissot has presented a series of “firsts” in terms of technology, materials and design - even to the extent of creating watches made of rock, wood and pearl.

From day one, Tissot was also dedicated to taking its innovations to destinations well beyond the Swiss borders. In 1858, the founder’s son, Charles-Emile Tissot, left Le Locle for Russia and successfully sold Tissot savonnette pocket watches across this huge and influential empire. International expansion **went from strength to strength** and Tissot is today the leading producer of the traditional Swiss watch

industry in number of units. Being sold by 16,000 Points of Sale across five continents, Tissot products offer a wide selection of watches to suit diverse functional needs and tastes.

Over years many key figures have owned Tissot watches, including actress Sarah Bernhardt, singer Carmen Miranda, Elvis Presley, Grace Kelly and Nelson Mandela.

The proud Tissot Ambassadors of today are:

Danica Patrick - Race car driver

Deepika Padukone - Actress

Barbie Xu - Actress

Nicky Hayden - MotoGP racer

Thomas Lüthi - Moto2 racer

Steven Stamkos - Ice hockey player

Tony Parker - Professional basketball player

Huang Xiaoming - Actor and singer

Although Tissot keeps expanding in order to reach people around the globe, it will always remain faithful to its home country of Switzerland. This is one of the reasons it found such an ideal partner in the Jungfrau Railway and its Centenary Celebration of 2012. The collaboration incorporates strong common values with extremely deep roots. Just like Tissot's hometown of Le Locle, the Jungfrau region is also on the **UNESCO World Heritage list**. Additionally, they both demonstrate ultimate timing and precision to reach the top.

product innovation	产品创新
go from strength to strength	不断壮大
UNESCO World Heritage list	世界遗产名录

从1853年至今，天梭一直致力于能为顾客带来惊喜的产品创

新。锐意进取、不懈创新的精神使天梭走出瑞士侏罗山区的小镇力洛克，足迹遍布全球160多个国家。从1853年推出具有双时区显示功能的怀表，到采用创新触屏技术的T-TOUCH腕表，天梭在技术、材料和设计方面已经创造了诸多的“第一”，甚至利用石头、木头、珍珠做素材来制作手表。

从诞生之日起，天梭就一直专注于将它的创新带到瑞士以外的国家和地区。1858年，天梭创始人之子查理–艾米尔·天梭走出力洛克小镇来到俄罗斯，并成功地将天梭猎手怀表销售到地域辽阔的沙皇俄国。天梭的销售区域在全球不断扩大，今天已成为瑞士传统制表行业中销量第一的品牌。

天梭产品在五大洲有16000多个销售网点，提供广泛的产品选择，以满足顾客对不同功能和品味的需求。时到今日，已有许多人佩戴天梭表，如演员Sarah Bernhardt, 歌手Carmen Miranda, Elvis Presley, Grace Kelly 和Nelson Nlandela。

以下是天梭引以为傲的形象大使：

美国赛车手丹妮卡·帕特里克（Danica Patrick）

印度演员迪碧迦·帕多特尼（Deepika Padukone）

中国台湾知名艺人徐熙媛（Barbie Xu）

美国MotoGP赛车手尼克·海顿（Nicky Hayden）

瑞士Moto2赛车手托马斯·卢斯（Thomas Lüthi）

加拿大冰球运动员史蒂芬·斯塔姆科（Steven Stamkos）

法国职业篮球运动员托尼·帕克（TonyParker）

中国知名演员及歌手黄晓明（Huang Xiaoming）

虽然天梭为了让更多人熟知并持续在全球开拓市场，它却始终忠于自己的家乡瑞士。这也是天梭作为2012年少女峰铁路百年诞辰合作伙伴的重要原因之一。相同的价值观及深厚的历史渊源成就了此次合作。如同天梭的故乡力洛克，少女峰（Jungfrau）地区也被联合国教科文组织列入世界遗产名录。此外，它们都对时间和精确有着严格的要求。

3.（瑞士）伯爵 Piaget

品牌名片

品　　类：腕表

标志风格：华美、精致

创 始 人：乔治·爱德华·伯爵（Georges Edouard Piaget）

诞 生 地：瑞士

诞生时间：1874年

伯爵Piaget的品牌标志是英文单词“piaget”的大写全称，如今伯爵不仅仅只是一个姓氏，而是丰富专业知识的代名词。

品牌阅读

It was in La Côte-aux-Fées, a small village in the Swiss part of the Jura, that Georges Édouard Piaget sketched the first strokes of what, decades later, was to become an **inimitable** signature in the world of luxury and fine watchmaking. In 1874, he started his first workshop on the family farm and devoted himself to making high-precision movements that he soon began supplying to the most **prestigious** brands. The business developed very quickly. Piaget's fame spread far beyond the crests of the mountains around Neuchâtel, increased by demand from those who already recognized his signature on a movement as a mark of seldom-equaled expertise, and his workshop grew.

Georges Édouard's son Timothée Piaget took over the business in 1911, displaying the same passion, demanding for quality and success as his father. Sound and solid foundations had been laid for Piaget.

An enterprising spirit, willingness to take risks and the desire never to rest on its laurels were **indelibly** inscribed on Piaget's DNA. In 1943, the company made a decision that was crucial to its future by registering the brand. From then on, the movement Manufacture for La Côte-aux-Fées watches was signed by and sold under its own name, created with the same close attention to aesthetics and technical performance. This rebirth can be ascribed to Gérald and Valentin Piaget, the founder's grandsons. They also started the brand's geographic expansion and worked to increase its **international recognition**.

Faithful to its pioneering spirit, Piaget began to design and build the **ultra-thin** movements that were to become one of the company's "signatures", making an enduring impression on the watchmaking world. In 1957, the Manufacturer introduced the famous ultra-thin hand-wound Calibre 9P, which was only 2 mm thick. In 1960, Piaget launched the Calibre 12P, the world's thinnest **self-winding** movement. It measured just 2.3 mm thick.

Piaget's supremacy in ultra-thin mechanical movement had earned the brand a special place among the great Swiss watchmakers. By mastering this area of expertise while elevating boldness and creativity to the status of primary values, it was bound to cause sparks to fly. These fireworks opened the doors to international recognition for Piaget and helped the brand make a name for itself in the world of fine watchmaking and precision work. In the 1960s, the company reiterated its desire to achieve ever-increasing control over its production by purchasing several goldsmiths' workshops in Geneva.

These watches were all inspired by the brand's rich historical heritage, which they reinterpret in a forceful and distinctively modern way. Piaget's deep-felt attachment to traditions and its expertise in

movement manufacturing made it a natural choice for the city of Venice as a partner in restoring the Torre dell'Orologio on St. Mark's Square, a legendary monument bearing eloquent testimony to the history of time measurement.

In order to keep pace with its growing success, the company opened the new Manufacture de Haute Horlogerie Piaget in Plan-les-Ouates in 2001 , just outside Geneva. This event consolidated a visionary integration strategy already undertaken by the company in the 1960s. This **high-performance** facility, regrouping both watchmaking and jeweler crafts, complements the historical site in la Côte-aux-Fées where the movements were made. At the same time, Piaget continued to invest in the domain of research and development.

Within barely a decade, almost 30 new movements were to be created, including some of the most prestigious **horological** complications, and notably a tourbillion, a dual time-zone flyback chronograph and a perpetual calendar. Meanwhile, jewelry watches were endowed with innovative concepts adding further sparkle to the natural radiance of diamonds.

All these masterpieces are entirely in line with Piaget's proverbial inventiveness and emphatically reassert the founder's motto: "Always do better than necessary".

inimitable [i'nimitəbl] adj. 独特的；无比的；无法仿效的

prestigious [pre'stidʒəs] adj. 有名望的；享有声望的

indelibly [in'delibli] adv. 不可消除地

international recognition 国际认可

ultra-thin 超薄

self-winding 自动上发条的

high-performance 高性能的，高效能的

horological [ˌhɔrəˈlɔdʒikəl] adj. 钟表的；钟表术的

乔治·爱德华·伯爵（Georges Edouard Piaget）在瑞士侏罗山区的小村庄La Côte-aux-Fées安家立业，这里数十年后成为奢华与精准腕表制造的代名词。1874年，他首先在自家农舍开设了首家机芯制造工作坊，专门为瑞士著名钟表品牌制作性能精准的高质机芯。蒸蒸日上的钟表事业得到迅速发展，而伯爵的声望也远近驰名。出自伯爵之手的钟表机芯，皆以精湛工艺制作而成，倍受各界肯定，工作坊也不断扩大。

1911年提摩太·伯爵（Timothée Piaget）从父亲乔治手中接掌家业，并秉承着其父对钟表业的热情以及对质量的一贯坚持。伯爵表厂自此打下了稳健而坚实的基础。

企业家精神—勇于尝试、永不言败的精神，深植在伯爵家族的血统中。伯爵在1943年决定将伯爵（Piaget）注册为品牌名称，并在La Côte-aux-Fées表芯的正式推出及销售冠上“Piaget”标志。在创办人的孙子杰若德和华伦太·伯爵（Gérald、Valentin Piaget）两人的掌舵下，伯爵品牌在世界各地开疆拓土，知名度与日俱增，展现出脱胎换骨的全新气象。

伯爵坚持先锋精神，投身超薄机芯的设计和制造，在钟表史上写下美丽的篇章。1957年，伯爵表厂推出著名的9P手动超薄机械腕表，厚度仅为2毫米；1960年，伯爵推出的厚度仅有2.3毫米的12P腕表，成为世界最纤薄的自动机械机芯。

伯爵超薄机械机芯的独家技术让品牌在瑞士高级制表业无可争议地享有一席之地。精湛的技术和创新第一的精神激发出创意的火花。伯爵令人目眩神迷的创新设计，为品牌赢得享誉国际的声望，并在奢华腕表与精准性能领域名声鹊起。20世纪60年代，品牌再次显示出扩大生产的雄心，在日内瓦收购了数家金饰车间。

这些表款灵感源于品牌深厚的历史传承，并以浑然有力和极具现代感的方式重新演绎。伯爵对传统的坚持和精湛的机芯制造技术，令其当仁不让被威尼斯市选定为合作伙伴，参加计时历史的传奇见证——威尼斯钟楼的修缮工程。

为顺应企业的蓬勃发展，伯爵表厂在日内瓦的Plan-les-Ouates建立了全新高级制表厂，2001年正式落成启用。制表厂的建立体现了伯爵早在60年代就已制定的富有远见的整体发展战略。在这个效率极高的表厂，同时聚集钟表和珠宝制造部门，与La Côte-aux-Fées表厂的机芯生产业务相互补足。与此同时，伯爵继续投资研发。

短短十余年，表厂已推出近30款新型机芯，其中包括珍贵的复杂功能机芯，特别是一款陀飞轮机芯、一款双时区计时机芯和一款万年历机芯。而珠宝腕表融入非凡创新理念，令散发自然光泽的美钻更加璀璨炫丽。

这些杰作均体现出伯爵家喻户晓的创新原则，更出色地证明了其创立者一贯秉持的格言：“永远比要求的做得更好。”

读书笔记

4.（瑞士）劳力士 Rolex

品牌名片

品　　类：腕表

标志风格：庄重、实用、不显浮华

创 始 人：汉斯 · 韦尔斯多夫（Hans Wilsdorf）

诞 生 地：瑞士

诞生时间：1905年

劳力士Rolex的品牌标志是一顶皇冠，以示其在手表领域中的霸主地位，展现着劳力士在制表业的帝王之气。

品牌阅读

The history of Rolex is **inextricably** linked to the visionary spirit of Hans Wilsdorf, its founder. In 1905, at the age of 24, Hans Wilsdorf founded a company in London specializing in the distribution of timepieces. He began to dream of a watch worn on the wrist. Wrist watches were not very precise at the time, but Hans Wilsdorf foresaw that they could become not only elegant, but also reliable.

Hans Wilsdorf wanted his watches to bear a name that was short, easy to say and remember in any language, and that looked good on watch movements and dials. He said, “I tried combining the letters of the alphabet in every possible way. This gave me some hundred names, but none of them felt quite right. One morning, while I was riding on the upper deck of a horse-drawn omnibus along Cheapside in the City of London, a genie whispered ‘Rolex’ in my ear.”

Four years later, in 1914, Kew Observatory in Great Britain awarded a Rolex wristwatch a class “A” precision certificate, a

distinction which until that point in time had been reserved exclusively for marine **chronometers**. From that date forward, the Rolex wristwatch was synonymous with precision.

In 1926, the creation by Rolex of the first waterproof and **dustproof** wristwatch marked a major step forward. Given the name "Oyster", this watch featured a **hermetically** sealed case which provided optimal protection for the movement. It was one thing to claim a watch was waterproof. It was quite another to prove it. In 1927, a Rolex Oyster crossed the English Channel, worn by a young English swimmer named Mercedes Gleitze. The swim lasted over 10 hours and the watch remained in perfect working order at the end of it.

In 1953, Sir John Hunt's expedition, in which Sir Edmund Hillary and Tenzing Norgay reached the summit of Mount Qomolangma, was equipped with Oyster Perpetuals.

In 1971, Rolex presented the Oyster Perpetual Explorer II, dedicated to polar explorers, speleologists and all those pushing the boundaries of exploration. The watch featured a distinctive 24-hour hand, an invaluable aid around the poles and beneath ground when you can't tell night from day.

On March 26th, 2012, filmmaker and National Geographic Explorer-in-Residence James Cameron **descended into** the Mariana Trench, making the first solo dive into the deepest point on earth and the only dive into the trench since the two-man Trieste expedition of 1960. Only one passenger was on both voyages: a Rolex watch.

In keeping with its history of close ties to motorsports, in 2013 Rolex entered into a long-term partnership with Formula 1 Racing as Official Timekeeper and Official Timepiece.

inextricably [ˌinik'strikəbli] adv.密不可分地	
chronometer [krə'nɒmɪtə] n.精密记时表；高度精确的钟表	
dustproof ['dʌstpru:f] adj. 防尘的	
hermetically [hə:'metikəli] adv. 密封地，不透气地	
descend into 向下行	

劳力士的历史与其富有远见和开拓精神的创办人汉斯·韦尔斯多夫（Hans Wilsdorf）有着密不可分的关系。1905年，年仅24岁的他便在伦敦开设了钟表销售公司。他幻想将表佩戴在腕上。虽然当时的腕表精准度不足，但汉斯·韦尔斯多夫却能预见到，腕表不但可展示优雅风格，而且精准可靠。

汉斯·韦尔斯多夫希望为腕表取一个精简易读的名字，任何语言都容易记得，而且在腕表机芯和表面上美观悦目。他说："我几乎尝遍所有字母组合，最终得出数百个名字，但没有一个让我满意。一天早上，我坐在公共马车的上层，途经伦敦市齐普赛街时，我仿佛听到一个声音在耳边低声说道'劳力士'。"

1914年，英国矫天文台（Kew Observatory）颁授劳力士腕表"A"级证书。当时，此等级一般都是航海精密仪表方能获取的。自那时起，劳力士腕表便成为精准时钟的象征。

1926年，劳力士创制了首款能防水、防尘的腕表，成为制表技术重要的里程碑。这款名为"Oyster"的蚝式腕表配备密闭的表壳，能为机芯提供最佳的保护。要证明腕表能防水，必须能提供真凭实据。1927年，年轻的英国女士梅塞迪丝·吉莉斯（Mercedes Gleitze）佩戴劳力士蚝式腕表成功横渡英吉利海峡。在游了十几小时到达终点之后，她佩戴的腕表依然丝毫无损、运行如常。

1953年，约翰·亨特爵士（Sir John Hunt）、埃德蒙·希拉里（Sir Edmund Hillary）和丹增·诺吉（Tenzing Norgay）都曾佩戴劳力士蚝式恒动腕表，首次成功登上珠穆朗玛峰之巅。

1971年，劳力士推出Oyster Perpetual探索者2代。此款专为探索者及推动极限探索的人所设计。特有的24小时指针对极地周围及地下无法分辨日夜的地方是无可比拟的帮助。

2012年3月26日，在马里亚纳海沟（Mariana Trench）最深处，电影制作人及《国家地理》驻会探险家詹姆斯·卡梅隆（James Cameron）刷新单人深潜纪录，独闯海沟。而在此前，只有在1960年两位探险家驾驶的里雅斯特号（Trieste）征服此处。两次同行，缔造创举，唯有劳力士腕表。

为延续与赛车运动悠久密切的联系，劳力士在2013年成为一级方程式赛车的长期合作伙伴，进行赛事官方计时和比赛用表赞助。

读书笔记

5.（瑞士）百年灵 Breitling

品牌名片

品　　类：腕表

标志风格：融实用性、功能性和多元性为一体

创 始 人：里昂·百年灵（Léon Breitling）

诞 生 地：瑞士

诞生时间：1884年

百年灵的品牌标志由三部分构成。最上面是一双围绕字母B展开的翅膀，寓意百年灵展翅翱翔。中间部分是百年灵的英文大写字母"Breitling"，简洁明了。最下方的1884是百年灵的创建时间。

品牌阅读

Founding his workshop in the Swiss Jura in 1884, Leon Breitling chose to devote himself to an exclusive and demanding field: that of chronographs and timers. These precision instruments were intended for sports, science and industry. Thanks to its high-quality products and its constant quest for innovation, the brand accompanied the boom of competitive sports and of the automobile ,as well as the first feats of the aviation pioneers. In 1915, it **herald**ed the emergence of the wrist chronograph by inventing the first independent chronograph pushpiece. In 1923, it perfected this system by separating the stop/start functions from that of resetting. This patented innovation thereby made it possible to add several successive times without returning the hands to zero - which proved extremely useful both for timing sports competitions and for calculating flight time. In 1934, Breitling set the final touch to the modern face of the chronograph by creating the

second independent reset pushpiece – a decisive breakthrough that was soon adopted by the competition. In 1969, the brand took on one of the greatest 20th century watchmaking challenges by presenting the first self-winding chronograph movement. In 1984, Breitling heralded the rebirth of the mechanical chronograph by launching the famous Chronomat, which has since become its leading model. In 2009, the firm's engineers once again made their mark on the history of the chronograph by creating Caliber 01 – the finest self-winding chronograph movement, entirely developed and manufactured in the workshops of Breitling Chronométrie. A leader in the field of mechanical chronographs, the brand has also established itself in the **vanguard** of electronic watch making by developing an entire range of high-tech instruments first and foremost dedicated to aviation.

It is the authentic partner of aviation. Aviation pioneers needed reliable and efficient instruments and soon took an interest in Breitling's pocket chronographs and later its wrist chronographs. In the early 1930s, building on its reputation for precision and sturdiness, Breitling enriched its range with a "specialty" that would earn it worldwide fame: onboard chronographs intended for aircraft cockpits. These instruments **indispensable** to secure piloting enjoyed great success with the various armed forces, including the Royal Air Force which used them to equip its famous World War II propeller-driven fighter planes. In 1952, Breitling launched its legendary Navitimer wrist chronograph featuring a circular slide rule serving to perform all navigation-related calculations. A cult object for pilots and aviation enthusiasts, it has been continuously manufactured for almost 60 years - making it the world's oldest mechanical chronograph still in production. In 1962, a Navitimer accompanied Scott Carpenter on his orbital flight aboard the Aurora 7 capsule, thus becoming the first space-going wrist chronograph. During the 1950s and 1960s, Breitling played a key role in the boom of commercial aviation, as its onboard chronographs became standard equipment first on the propeller-driven planes and later on the jet aircraft of many airplane manufacturers and airline companies. The brand thus quite naturally earned the status of "official supplier to world aviation". Today Breitling is perpetuating these authentic and privileged ties with aviation by cooperating with the world's elite pilots. Several exceptional teams fly the firm's colors, including the famous Breitling Jet Team with its spectacular **aerobatics**. It is associated with the greatest airshows on the planet, such as the famous Reno Air Races (Nevada/United States). By supporting the restoration of legendary aircraft such as the Breitling Super Constellation, one of the last flightworthy "Super Connies" in the world, the brand with the winged B asserts its determination to preserve the aeronautical legacy - the magnificent adventure with which its own history is so intimately **entwined**.

It doesn't become official supplier to world aviation by chance. As a spccialist of tcchnical watchcs, Brcitling has playcd a crucial role in the development of the wrist chronograph and is a leader in this complication. The firm has shared all the finest moments in the conquest of the skies thanks to its sturdy, reliable and high-performance instruments. The world's only major watch brand to equip all its models with chronometer-certified movements, the ultimate token of precision, Breitling is also one of the rare companies to produce its own mechanical chronograph movement, entirely developed and manufactured in its own workshops. This family business is also one of the last remaining independent Swiss watch

brands.

herald ['herəld] vt. 通报；预示……的来临

vanguard ['vængɑ:d] n. 先锋；前锋；先驱；领导者

indispensable [,indis'pensəbl] adj. 不可缺少的；绝对必要的

aerobatics [eərə'bætɪks] n. 特技飞行

entwine [in'twain] vt. 盘绕

1884年，里昂·百年灵（Léon Breitling）在瑞士汝拉（Jura）建立制表工坊，决心投身于一个独特而又极具挑战性的领域：制造计时码表和计时器。这些精密仪表被广泛应用于体育、科学和工业领域。由于产品的卓越表现和对创新的不懈追求，百年灵得以见证竞技体育、汽车工业的蓬勃发展以及飞行先驱所取得的伟大成就。1915年，百年灵首开计时腕表之先河，并革新性首创了第一枚独立计时按钮，成为现代计时腕表领域的先驱。1923年，百年灵完善了独立计时按钮系统，首次将计时与归零功能分离，实现了分段连续计时的全新计时模式。这项创新在计算体育竞赛和飞行时间方面有着显著的实用价值。1934年，百年灵发明了第二枚独立计时按钮，从而奠定了现代计时腕表的外观——双独立计时按钮。这一革命性的创新，迅速引得同行争相效仿。1969年，百年灵主导推出全球首枚自动上弦计时机芯，引领计时腕表进入自动上弦的全新时代。1984年，百年灵推出享誉全球的机械计时腕表（Chronomat），宣告了机械计时腕表的复兴，成为百年灵的旗舰表款。2009年，百年灵的工程师们在计时腕表史上再次写下辉煌的篇章——推出首枚100%自主研发的自动上弦计时机芯Caliber 11，这枚性能超卓的机芯完全在百年灵精密时计中心（Breitling Chronométrie）研发并生产。百年灵不仅是机械计时腕表领域的领军者，同时也确立了百年灵在电子制表领域的领导地位，开发了一系列高科技仪表，致力于服务世界航空业。

百年灵是航空业值得信赖的伙伴。早期航空业的飞行先驱们需要性能稳定、品质卓越的计时仪器，很快百年灵的计时怀表和之后的计时腕表便受到他们的青睐。20世纪30年代早期，以精密准确和坚固可靠著称的百年灵特别推出了“专业仪表”——专为飞机驾驶舱设计的机载计时设备，从此百年灵名扬四海。这些精密仪器对保障飞行安全起了至关重要的作用，受到多国空军的青睐。“二战”期间，百年灵成为英国皇家空军指定供应商，那些装配百年灵驾驶舱计时器的战斗机在战争中声名鹊起。1952年，传奇的百年灵航空计时腕表（Navitimer）诞生。这款腕表配备环形飞行滑尺，可以轻松快速完成飞行相关的所有运算。这款计时腕表受到飞行员和广大航空爱好者的追捧，至今已连续生产60年，成为全球历史最悠久的在产机械计时腕表。1962年，百年灵宇航员腕表伴随美国宇航员斯科特·卡彭特（Scott Carpenter）少校一起搭乘极光7号（Aurora 7）太空舱绕地球飞行，成为第一枚遨游太空的计时腕表。20世纪50至60年代，百年灵为商用航空的蓬勃发展发挥了重要作用，其驾驶舱计时器起初被用于螺旋桨飞机，后来为众多飞机制造商和航空公司的喷气式飞机广泛使用，成为当时飞机的标配。百年灵因此荣膺“世界航空业官方指定供应商”的殊荣。如今，百年灵还通过与精英飞行员合作，从而与世界航空业继续保持紧密联系。一些飞行大队采用公司的色彩标识，包括著名的百年灵飞行大队和其精湛的飞行特技。百年灵与优秀的飞行表演队合作，如有名的Reno Air Races（内华达/美国）。此外，百年灵还鼎力支持传奇飞机的修复工作，如“百年灵超级星座号”客机（Breitling Super Constellation），它是世界上仅存的几架仍具飞行能力的“超级星座号”飞机之一。以展翅翱翔的字母B作为品牌标志的百年灵将继续保持与世界航空业的紧密联系，成就蓝天上的传奇征程。

百年灵成为“世界航空业官方指定供应商”绝非偶然。作为腕表技术专家，百年灵在计时腕表的发展史上扮演了重要角色，是计

时腕表领域的领导者。百年灵凭借其精准可靠、性能超卓的精密仪表，在人类征服天空的漫漫征程中，见证了无数辉煌时刻。作为全球唯一全系产品机芯均通过瑞士官方天文台认证（COSC）的腕表品牌，百年灵不仅象征着非凡精度，更是为数不多自主研发生产自动上弦计时机芯的腕表品牌之一，这些机芯全部由百年灵精密时计中心生产制造。作为一家家族企业，百年灵也是目前瑞士仅存的几家独立制表商之一。

读书笔记

6.（瑞士）真力时 Zenith

品牌名片

品　　类：腕表

标志风格：精美绝伦、精确精准

创 始 人：查尔斯·维尔莫（Georges-Favre Jacot）

诞 生 地：瑞士

诞生时间：1865年

真力时手表的品牌标志在设计上采用非常简洁的字母，体现了一种庄严的风格。上方的一颗五角星象征真力时手表的星辰始终在天空闪闪发光，它的创始人也在另一个世界关注着企业的发展，为辛勤耕耘的后人祝福。

品牌阅读

In the 19th century in the region of Le Locle, the cradle of Swiss watchmaking, numerous artisans worked in small **scattered** workshops or in their own homes with no particular links between them. Based on the principle that all the parts of a watch are **interdependent**, Zenith founder Georges Favre-Jacot decided to bring together the full range of watchmaking professions under one roof in 1865. This marked the birth of the first ever Manufacture-a term to which only a few watch companies can still lay claim, since it involves in-house mastery of all stages involved in developing and producing movements.

Still located in the premises where it was founded in 1865, the Manufacture Zenith currently houses 80 professions exercised by its 250strong personnel. Whether exponents of the more artistic crafts or of ultra-technical skills, all are engaged in the task undertaken by

Georges Favre-Jacot almost 150 years ago: mastering each gesture in order to enable free-spirited creation of mechanical marvels combining noble watchmaking traditions with avant-garde innovations.

From technical plans to the last polishing and through **prototype-making**, movement ébauches, stamping, tool-making, research on materials, decoration, assembling and casing-up, each step must be executed to perfection. This involves a blend of **dexterity**, patience and rigorous standards. Making a single watch in the El Primero Collection actually entails an average of nine months during which over 2,500 operations are performed by 300 pairs of expert hands.

From Blériot to Felix Baumgartner, Zenith has made its mark on the history of aviation and the discovery of space. By keeping time with the footsteps of Gandhi, the Manufacture has become part of an enduring legend. By equipping a number of explorers, it has contributed to major breakthroughs. These fabulous epics belong to the brand heritage and naturally influence the spirit that continues to guide it.

In the years from 1930 to 1940, the Montre d' Aéronef Zenith Type 20 was fitted in many aircraft, notably the famous Caudron Simoun C635 planes used by the French air force for training purposes and by the Air Bleu postal company on its international and **transatlantic** routes. The years went by, and the Pilot Montre d' Aéronef of today has drawn on the lessons of the past to create a modern-day embodiment of precision and reliability, a timepiece that is able to realize the wildest of dreams.

In **perpetuating** the legacy of its founder, Zenith has begun the mammoth task of renovating the 19 buildings of its Manufacture-a process that was completed in 2015, its 150th anniversary year.

While applying the most advanced technologies, Zenith has chosen to jealously safeguard the site's historical architecture- for it is within these red-brick walls with their large picture windows that the finest chapters of its legend have been written and will continue to be written by many generations to come.

scattered ['skætəd] adj. 分散的

interdependent [,intədi'pendənt] adj. 相互依赖的；互助的

prototype-making 原型制作

dexterity [dek'sterəti] n. 灵巧；敏捷；机敏

transatlantic [trænzæt'læntɪk] adj. 大西洋彼岸的，横渡大西洋的

perpetuating [pə'petʃʊeitiŋ] adj. 永存的；不灭的

19世纪时，在瑞士制表业的摇篮——力洛克地区，许多工匠分散在各处的小工坊甚至在家中工作，各自为政、缺乏联系。鉴于一枚腕表的所有部件息息相关，真力时表厂的创建者乔治-法力·亚各布（Georges-Favre Jacot）在1865年决定，将制表领域所有工种集中在一起。史上第一家表厂诞生了！由于在表厂内部需要掌握设计和制造机芯的所有工序，现如今只有屈指可数的几个制表品牌才够得上“表厂”这个称号。

真力时表厂自1865年创立以来始终位于同一地区，如今表厂拥有80项专业技艺，约250位员工。从艺术技能到技术层面，工匠们仍专注于约150年前乔治-法力·亚各布先生开创的事业中，那就是：熟捻每个手法，以开放的思维，打造出传统工艺制表传统和前卫创新相结合的机械杰作。

从技术图纸到最后抛光，中间还包括打样、草图、冲模、制造工具、研究材质、装饰、组装或嵌合，每个步骤务必精益求精，这集灵巧、耐心和严谨于一身。事实上，EiPrimero系列的任何一枚腕表的

制作过程平均耗时9个月，经300位专业人士之手，共有2500多道工序。

从路易斯·布雷里奥（Blériot）到菲利克斯·鲍加特纳（Felix Baumgartner），真力时在航空和航天领域的历史留下足迹。此外，品牌亦跟着圣雄甘地的脚步名留青史。真力时的钟表作品伴随许多冒险家见证人类历史的重大突破。这些传唱不辍的英雄史诗不仅是品牌历史不可分割的一部分，也是奠立真力时成长进步的重要基石。

在1930年至1940年间，真力时Type 20腕表成为众多的机载仪器，尤其是用作法国空军训练机及Air Bleu邮政公司服务国际和跨大西洋线路的Caudron Simoun C635型飞机。几度流年，而今的飞行员系列腕表从既往经验中汲取精粹，将精准度与可靠性融为一体，缔造出一款令最疯狂的梦想化为现实的卓越计时器。

真力时为延续其创立者的事业，开始大面积翻修表厂内的19幢建筑，工程于2015年表厂150周年华诞时竣工。运用最尖端技术的同时，真力时决定精心保留表厂的原有建筑。因为正是在这些红色砖墙和宽大玻璃窗内，书写了该表厂历史中最美丽的篇章，而且传奇将长久继续下去。

读书笔记

7.（美国）波尔 BALL

品　　类：腕表

标志风格：大方、时尚

创 始 人：Webb C. Ball

诞 生 地：美国

诞生时间：1891年

波尔表品牌标志上的双R图标是Rail Road的意思，代表波尔表的历史：做铁路时钟起家的。

品牌阅读

To a large extent, the development of the watch industry in America can **be attributed to** the advent and **subsequent** development of American railroads.

Prior to the advent of trains as a means of transporting people and goods, there was no real need for precise timekeeping or uniform time. Even after the railroad system in the United States had reached significant proportions following the Civil War, communities continued to maintain their local times.

By the end of 1883, the railroad industry had agreed, at least among themselves, to divide the nation into four time zones and had adopted Standard Time. The public soon followed suit, although it is interesting to note that the Congress did not officially sanction the concept until 1918.

In 1996, Cleveland, Ohio, celebrated the bicentennial of the founding of the city on the lake. During this celebration, many

individuals were remembered and recognized as Cleveland's favorite sons, and their **accomplishments** were reviewed. One Clevelander honored, whose accomplishments reached international acclaim, not only for his civic contributions, but also for his place in horology, was Webster Clay Ball.

Webster Clay Ball was born in Fredericktown, Ohio on October 6th. When Standard Time was adopted in 1883, he was the first jeweler to use time signals, bringing accurate time to Cleveland. On July 19, 1891, the General Superintendent of Lake Shore Lines appointed W.C. Ball as Chief Inspector for the lines. His early **inspection system** was the beginning of the vast Ball network that would encompass 75% of the railroads throughout the country and cover at least 175,000 miles of railroad. W. C. Ball also extended his system into Mexico and Canada.

On April 19, 1891 the Fast Mail train known as No. 4 was coming west on the Lake Shore & Michigan Southern Railroad in Kipton, Ohio. At Elyria, 25 miles from Cleveland, the Engineer and the Conductor of the Accomodation were given orders to let the fast mail train pass them at Kipton, a small station west of Oberlin, the University town.

As the Conductor of Accomodation admitted afterward, from the time the train left Elyria until it collided with the Fast Mail at Kipton, he did not take his watch out of his pocket. He said that he supposed the Engineer would look out for Fast Mail No. 4. But the Engineer's watch stopped for four minutes and then began running again, a little matter of life and death of which he was unconscious. There were several stations between Elyria and Kipton, but the Engineer pounded slowly along in the belief that he had time to spare.

Leaving Oberlin, the Engineer supposed he had seven minutes before reaching the meeting point. Of course he only had three minutes. Had the Conductor looked at his own watch he could have prevented the accident. The trains came together at Kipton, the Fast Mail at full speed and the Accomodation under brakes, because it was nearing the station. The Engineers of both trains were killed, and the dead bodies of nine clerks were taken from the kindling wood and broken iron of the postal cars.

The Kipton Disaster prompted the Lake Shore officials to enlist W. C. Ball to investigate Time and Watch conditions throughout the Lake Shore Line and develop an inspection system for their implementation.

W. C. Ball set about immediately and put in place **fortnightly** checks on the watches worn by all railroad workers. The checks were carried out by approved watchmakers. Ball set strict standards, forbidding variations more than 30 seconds among the watches.

It is important to recognize and applaud W. C. Ball, for his system was the first successful one to be accepted on a broad scale. It was his system that set the standard for railroads; it was his system that helped establish accuracy and uniformity in timekeeping. It was his system that resulted in railroad time and railroad watches being recognized as STANDARD, whenever accuracy in time was required. In general, it became accepted that when the average person asked a railroad man the time, he was assured a correct answer.

Today, BALL Watch is one of the most respected and established watch brands in the United States. It continues to update the product range in the 21st century to keep pace with shifting consumer patterns. But, despite changes in appearance, the founding spirit of the brand -

industrial function - is never compromised.

It is upheld in Ball's original details, such as the watch dial that faithfully follows his design guidelines for the standard railway watch. Every detail, from the shape of the hands to the style of the numerals, was laid down by the founder in his quest for accuracy in timekeeping.

It is a vision that the Ball family remains faithful to. For legions of men and women today whose split-second decisions keep the world ticking, it is a shared commitment.

The focal point of all these presentations remained the same – Since 1891, Accuracy under adverse conditions.

be attributed to 归因于

subsequent ['sʌbsikwənt] adj. 后来的，随后的

accomplishment [ə'kʌmpliʃmənt] n. 成就

fortnightly ['fɔːtnaɪtlɪ] adv. 隔周地；每两星期一次地

美国钟表业的发展，在很大程度上与美国铁路的出现及发展紧密相连。

在火车成为主要客货运输工具之前，并不需要精确计时，亦毋须维持统一的时间。随着美国内战结束，铁路系统渐渐发展成为重要运输工具，但各个地区仍如常按照其当地时间生活。

直至1883年末，铁路行业达成内部协议，将全国分成四个时区，采用标准时间制度。不久，公众亦相继采用有关制度。然而，国会却于1918年才正式采纳此制度。

1996年俄亥俄州克利夫兰市（Cleveland, Ohio）举行该湖上城市创立二百周年庆典，并且表扬克利夫兰市过去功勋卓著、成就显赫的伟人和英雄，细说他们的丰功伟绩。在这些克利夫兰伟人当中，WEBSTER CLAY BALL先生的成就，不单遍惠国民，在钟表制造学上的贡献，亦受世人推崇，蜚声国际。

Webster Clay Ball于1847年10月6日在俄亥俄市费达力镇（Fredericktown）出生。当1883年标准时间制度被采用，W. C. Ball成为克利夫兰首位采用报时信号为克利夫兰发布准确时间的珠宝商。1891年7月19日，湖岸铁路线的总监委派W. C. Ball出任湖岸线首席检察官，他的手表检查系统日后发展成庞大的网络，覆盖全美国75%的铁路，超过175,000英里。之后，系统亦扩展至墨西哥及加拿大。

1891年4月19日，“快邮邮车4号”在俄亥俄州基普顿以西湖岸与密歇根南方铁路上行驶。在距克利夫兰市25英里的艾里利亚火车的工程师及火车司机收到指令，让邮车在大学城奥柏林以西的一个小火车站基普顿超越他们。

火车司机后来承认，火车离开艾里利亚之后及在基普顿与“快邮邮车4号”相撞之前的一段车程，他一直没有拿出手表查看时间。他以为工程师会注视“快邮邮车4号”的动态。但是，工程师的手表曾停顿四分钟，之后又重新运行。而工程师却无法想象这短短四分钟会影响着许多人的生死。在艾里利亚与基普顿之间设有多个火车站，但工程师却认为有充裕时间，便让火车在铁路上慢慢前行。

离开奥柏林，工程师认为距他到汇和地点还有7分钟。当然，他实际只有3分钟。如果火车司机看一下自已的表，他是可以防止事故发生的。两列火车同时到达基普顿。快邮邮车全速驶来，而火车带着刹车，因为它正驶进火车站。两车的工程师都遇难了，9位员工的尸体从邮车上着火的木头和破损的铁皮中抬出。

发生意外后，湖岸铁路的官员立即任命W. C. Ball负责调查湖岸铁路全线的计时系统及时钟运作状况，并制订实施的检查系统。

W. C. Ball也立刻开始行动，并对所有铁路员工佩戴的手表进行隔周检查，所有检查工作都由经过审查的手表制造商来完成。W. C. Ball为此设立了严格的标准，严禁时钟误差超过30秒钟。

W. C. BALL所创立的系统是首个获得广泛接受和称许的成功

铁路计时系统。他的系统为铁路开创标准，协助确立准确及统一的计时方法，亦让铁路计时系统及铁路时钟成为人们心中计时标准典范。总而言之，如果普通市民向铁路员工查问时间，他们都会确信这个时间是准确的。

今天，波尔表是美国最受尊重，历史最悠久的手表品牌之一。21世纪波尔表不断更新产品系列以跟随消费者不断变化的品味。但是不管外表如何改变，品牌建立之初的精神——工业功能——从未改变。

在W. C. Ball最初的详细标准中，包括手表表盘都需要严格遵从他的铁路手表设计原则，每一个细节，从指针的形状到数字的形式，都按他准确计时的要求被制定出来。

这就是波尔家族仍然坚持的精神。对于今天分秒必争的社会，瞬间的决定将会改变世界，这是公认的看法。

所有这些表述均聚焦于同一点：始于1891，在恶劣环境中依然准确无误。

读书笔记

8.（瑞士）豪雅 TAG Heuer

品　　类：腕表

标志风格：创新、前卫

创 始 人：爱德华·豪雅（Edouard Heuer）

诞 生 地：瑞士

诞生时间：1860年

豪雅表的品牌标志是由一个棱角感非常强的图案以及“TAG Heuer”构成。图案中上半部分是绿色的TAG字样，下半部分是红色的Heuer字样。

品牌阅读

In 1860, Edouard Heuer set up a watchmaking workshop in St. Imier in the Swiss Jura region. In 1876, he established a **subsidiary** in London.

Major improvement in the chronograph industry: TAG Heuer invented thc famous “oscillating pinion” for mechanical stopwatches. In 1887, the Oscilating Pinion was patented. It is still used to this day by leading manufacturers in the production of mechanical chronographs and for example in the Calibre 1887, the fourth movement developed and produced in-house by TAG Heuer. In 1889, TAG Heuer won a silver medal at the Universal Exhibition in Paris, for its collection of pocket chronographs. The patent for one of the first **water-resistant** cases for pocket watches was granted in 1895. In 1908, the company obtained a patent for a Pulsometer dial which is still used today by doctors.

The introduction of the brand's first wrist chronographs was in 1914, with a silver case, enamelled dial and **luminous** hands. This large wrist chronograph was fitted with the same mechanics, powered by a pocket watch movement. Its crown and integrated button for start, stop and reset were located at 12 o'clock.

Paris Olympic Games: TAG Heuer split second pocket chronographs were selected as official stopwatches used at the Olympic Games on 3 **consecutive** occasions: Antwerp in 1920, Paris in 1924, and Amsterdam in 1928.

In 1945, General Eisenhower bought a TAG Heuer chronograph with a steel case. In 1957, the 'Ring Master' stopwatch was lauuched-a world first interchangeable rings of scale for timing various sports with readings down to 1/5th of a second, central minute-hand.

In 1962, TAG Heuer became the first Swiss watchmaker to go into space. On February 20, John Glenn made the first manned American space flight, orbiting the Earth three times in five hours. On his wrist was a Heuer stopwatch.

During the 1960's and the 1970's, the legendary "Film-Master'"model was used by Hollywood's most famous movie directors to time film sequences.

In 1995, TAG Heuer invented a prestigious and spectacular campaign based on the world of sports as never before portrayed, creating a firm foundation for the brand's positioning in the luxury sector. This TAG Heuer campaign won 15 of the world's most prestigious advertising awards. Sports figures are no longer seen as merely positive "subjects", but also convey an **up-to-date** image of success.

In 2002, The "Mikrograph F1" won the Watch Design Award

at the Geneva Grand Prix d'Horlogerie. TAG Heuer reinvented the "Mikrograph", the world's first sports stopwatch with 1/100th of a second precision, patented in 1916.

In 2012, the brand launched the TAG Heuer Carrera Mikrogirder, a dual-assortment and ultra high-frequency watch that beats 7.2 million times every hour and has a flying central chronograph hand that rotates 20 times per second. This astounding machine - the first timepiece ever created with neither a balance wheel nor a hairspring, is accurate to an unprecedented 5/10,000 of a second. At the Geneva Watchmaking Grand Prix ceremonies in November 2012, it was singled out as the best overall watch in all categories, taking home the prestigious Aiguille d'Or, the most coveted distinction in the global watch industry. With this 8th Grand Prix de l'Horlogerie de Genève award in just 11 years, TAG Heuer confirms its unrivalled mastery of extremely complex timepieces.

subsidiary [səb'sidiəri] n. 子公司

water-resistant ['wɔ:təri,zistənt] adj. 防水的

luminous ['lju:minəs] adj. 发光的；明亮的

consecutive [kən'sekjutiv] adj. 连贯的；连续不断的

up-to-date 最新的；最近的

1860年，爱德华·豪雅在瑞士汝拉地区的圣耶米创立了一间制表工厂。1876年，于伦敦设立分公司。

计时秒表行业的重大改进：豪雅发明用于机械秒表的"振动齿轮"。1887年，振动齿轮获得专利。这一技术至今仍为机械计时秒表生产领域的顶级制表厂所沿用，豪雅自行研发和生产的第四款机芯Calibre 1887型就是其中一例。1889年，豪雅以其计时怀表系列获得巴黎万国博览会银奖。1895年，豪雅以一款最早的怀表防水表壳

获得专利。1908年，豪雅公司的一款脉搏计表盘获得专利，这款表盘至今仍为医生所用。

1914年，豪雅推出第一款计时腕表，银色表壳，珐琅彩表盘，夜光指针。这款大号计时腕表装配了用怀表机芯驱动的机械装置。12点钟方向设表冠和集成按钮（计时、停止、重置）。

巴黎奥运会：豪雅追针计时怀表连续三次被选为奥运会官方计时秒表：1920年（安特卫普），1924年（巴黎），1928年（阿姆斯特丹）。

1945年，艾森豪威尔将军购买了一枚精钢表壳豪雅计时秒表。1957年，推出“Ring Master”计时秒表，全球首创可更换刻度环，用于各种运动计时，精确度达1/5秒，中央分针。

1962年，豪雅成为第一个进入太空的瑞士制表厂。2月20日，约翰·格伦首次为美国实现载人太空飞行，在5个小时内环绕地球飞行3次。他佩戴的就是豪雅计时腕表。

1960年代和1970年代间，具有传奇色彩的“Film-Master”表被好莱坞众多最著名导演用于电影计时。

1995年，豪雅以前所未有的方式演绎运动世界，推出一系列引人瞩目的广告活动，奠定品牌在奢侈品领域的坚实地位。豪雅的这一广告活动赢得了15个全球最受推崇的广告大奖。运动人士不再仅仅是积极正面的“主体”，同时也传递着成功的最新形象。

2002年，“Mikrograph F1”于日内瓦高级钟表大会赢得腕表设计大奖。豪雅对1916年获得专利的全球首款精确度达到1/100秒的运动计时秒表“Mikrograph”进行了重新设计。

2012年，品牌推出卡莱拉Mikrogirder双调整超高振频腕表，每小时振动720万次，配有每秒旋转20次的飞返中央计时指针。这款令人叹为观止的仪表是史上首款摒弃了平衡齿轮和螺旋形游丝的腕表，能精准测量到前所未有的5/10,000秒。在2012年11月的日内瓦高级钟表大会颁奖典礼上，在所有类别中，它被评选为整体最佳表，并囊括全球制表行业最令人向往的著名“金指针”大奖。这是豪雅在短短11年内第8次荣获日内瓦高级钟表大奖，进一步确立了品牌在极致复杂的钟表制造方面无与伦比的地位。

读书笔记

9.（瑞士）宝玑 Breguet

品牌名片

品　　类：腕表

标志风格：创新、精确

创 始 人：阿伯拉罕-路易·宝玑（A.-L. Breguet）

诞 生 地：巴黎

诞生时间：1775年

宝玑标志由表针和“Breguet”两部分组成。字母的左右设计上也有对称的均衡感，不是重量上的均衡而是形式上的对等。飘逸简洁，有种人间仙物的感觉。

品牌阅读

If Breguet holds a special place in the cultural heritage, it is because of its founder, Abraham-Louis. Breguet (1747-1823), set the standard by which all fine watchmaking has since been judged. Today, his heirs at Breguet still make each watch as a model of supreme horological art.

Abraham-Louis Breguet was born in Neuchâtel, but it was in Paris that he spent most of his productive life. In 1775, A.-L. Breguet set up his own business on Quai de l'Horloge, Ile de la cité in Paris. No aspect of watchmaking escaped his study, and his inventions were as fundamental to horology as they were varied.

His career started with a series of **breakthroughs**: the development of the successful self-winding perpétuelle watches, the introduction of the gongs for repeating watches and the first shock-protection for balance pivots.

Louis XVI and his Queen, Marie-Antoinette, were early enthusiasts of Breguet's watchmaking. Each watch from his workshops demonstrated the latest horological improvements in an original movement, mostly fitted with lever or ruby-cylinder **escapements** that he perfected.

A.-L. Breguet took refuge in Switzerland from the excesses of the French Revolution. He returned to Paris overflowing with the ideas that produced the Breguet balance-spring, his first carriage clock (sold to Bonaparte), the sympathique clock and its dependent watch, the tact watch and finally the tourbillon, patented in 1801.

Breguet became the indispensable watchmaker to the scientific, military, financial and diplomatic elites of the age. His timepieces ruled the courts of Europe. For his most celebrated clients, Breguet designed exceptional timepieces. For Caroline Murat, queen of Naples, he conceived in 1810 the world's very first wrist watch. Honours saluted his enormous contribution to horology. Appointed to the Board of Longitude and as chronometer-maker to the navy, he entered the Academy of Sciences and received the Legion of Honour from the hands of Louis XVIII.

The House of Breguet was privileged to create timepieces for the diplomatic, scientific, military and financial elite. Among its clients, Queen Marie-Antoinette, Napoleon Bonaparte, Talleyrand, the Sultan of the Ottoman Empire, Caroline Murat, Tsar Alexander I of Russia, Queen Victoria, Sir Winston Churchill and Arthur Rubinstein who put their confidence in the taste and artistry of Breguet.

The number of references to Breguet watches in French and foreign literature is an indication of the remarkable reputation enjoyed by both the firm and its founder. Breguet is now so deeply rooted

in European culture that the name is virtually a sine qua non of any depiction of the aristocracy, the **bourgeoisie** or, quite simply, a life of luxury and elegance. Stendhal, Mérimée, Pushkin, Balzac, Alexandre Dumas, Thackeray and Victor Hugo are only some of the writers who have made reference to Breguet in their works, followed closer to our own day by Kuprin, Max Jacob and Patrick O'Brian.

Today more than ever, its capacity to innovate reflects a brand's vitality. Breguet's own creative powers and **ingenuity** have certainly not declined over time. Driven by Nicolas G. Hayek, they have indeed been amplified, resulting in Breguet filing in eight short years a number of patent applications exceeding that of its founder's own inventions.

Manufacture

(1) A single number

Watch enthusiasts agree that each Breguet watch represents an exceptional standard of horological art that deserves to be identified for posterity. Since Breguet's early days, the manufacturing numbers of its watches have enabled collectors to confirm their origin and provenance. In keeping with tradition, the unique production number assigned to each Breguet watch will testify to the talent and the care its manufacture for generations to come.

(2) The secret signature

Their very success soon made Breguet's watches a tempting target for counterfeiters. In 1795, Breguet came up with a countermeasure: the secret signature. Etched into the dial, the signature is all but invisible unless the dial is examined in oblique light. Still a token of authenticity today, the secret signature has remained a feature of most

Breguet dials down to the present.

(3) Engine-turned dials

Around 1786, Breguet began fitting his watches with engine-turned silver or gold dials of his own design. The craft of carving recurring patterns in metal is rare today, but it remains one of the details that identify Breguet watches. Manually engine-turned, their dials are celebrated for the fineness of their patterns, reflecting the regularity of the movements within.

(4) Breguet hands

Breguet watches have featured its founder's celebrated **hollow**, eccentric "moon" tip watch hands for over two centuries now. Designed around 1783, his slim and sleek hands proved an instant success and the expression "Breguet hands" soon became a common watchmaker's term. Simple and easy-to-read, they are found on most Breguet time-pieces and have been widely imitated by others.

(5) Breguet numerals

Some Breguet watches display the **distinctive** numerals that A.-L. Breguet designed. Although he himself was no calligraphist, Breguet's Arabic numerals show his flair for combining function with elegance. Still used today particularly on watches with enamel dials, Breguet numerals first appeared before the French Revolution when they shared the dial with tiny stars to mark the minutes and stylised fleur-de-lys at five-minute intervals. By 1790 they had assumed their definitive form.

(6) Lugs

Although essential only to wristwatches, the lugs that link the strap to the case bear all the hallmarks of authentic Breguet styling. Screw-pins, rather than the more usual sprung bars, hold the strap

between the horns, a solution that is not only better looking but also more secure. The lugs have to be welded onto the caseband as much for the technical reasons of rigidity and strength as for aesthetic consistency. Equally exacting is the drilling of the hole for the winding stem. Only absolute precision ensures a watertight case.

(7) Caseband fluting

The fluting (fine grooves enhanced with double beading) on the caseband of Breguet's watches is another of the **discreet** decorative details that constitute what has become known as the Breguet style. In common with many period Breguet timepieces, most of its modern wristwatches have fluted case bands - one of the features that set them apart from other watches. The fluted pattern is cold-rolled into the caseband then finished by hand on a mechanical workpiece-holder.

breakthrough ['breikθru:] n. 突破；突破性进展
escapement [i'skeipmənt] n. 擒纵机构；棘轮装置
bourgeoisie [ˌbʊəʒwɑː'ziː] n. 资产阶级；中产阶级
ingenuity [ˌindʒi'nju:əti] n. 心灵手巧，独创性
hollow ['hɔləu] n. 中空
distinctive [dis'tiŋktiv] adj. 有特色的，与众不同的
discreet [dis'kri:t] adj. 谨慎的；小心的

宝玑之所以在文化传统中占据特殊地位，均拜其品牌创始人阿伯拉罕–路易·宝玑（1747—1823年）所赐，他制定的制表标准成为整个高级制表业界尊崇的金科玉律。今天，宝玑后人所制作的每款宝玑腕表仍是顶级钟表工艺的典范。

阿伯拉罕–路易·宝玑生于纳沙泰尔，却在巴黎度过其大半制表职业生涯。1775年，宝玑在巴黎的钟表堤岸开始创业。他潜心研究制表工艺的方方面面，而出自他手的各类发明，对钟表业界产生了深远影响。

宝玑的事业始于几项突破性发明：开发大获成功的自动上链怀表、首次在三问表中使用打簧，以及首创平衡摆轮轴防震装置。

法国国王路易十六及其王后玛丽·安托瓦内特是宝玑钟表产品最早的追随者。每一块产自宝玑工作坊的钟表均配备独创机芯，体现当时的最新制表技术。其中大部分钟表产品更配备宝玑精心改良的杠杆式或宝石轴柱擒纵装置。

法国大革命期间，宝玑逃亡至瑞士。战乱平息后，他怀着满腔灵感与创意重返巴黎，先后创制宝玑摆轮游丝、第一座旅行钟（随后售给拿破仑）、自鸣钟及悬垂表、触摸表，最后更创制了陀飞轮，并在1801年注册专利。

宝玑成为当时科学、军事、金融以及外交才俊不可或缺的制表大师。他的钟表大受欧洲王室欢迎。宝玑为其最为尊贵的顾客设计了多款匠心独具的作品，例如，他于1801年就已经为那不勒斯王后卡洛琳·缪拉构想腕表。荣誉随之而至。他得到经度委员会（board of longitude）委任，作为海军的精密计时器制造大师，加入了科学院，并荣获国王路易十八亲授的荣誉勋章（Legion of Honor）。

宝玑一直为众多来自外交、科学、军事和金融界的精英之士打造钟表。其中包括法国王后玛丽·安托瓦内特、拿破仑·波拿巴将军、法国主教塔里兰、奥斯曼帝国苏丹沙林三世、那不勒斯王后卡洛琳·缪拉、俄国沙皇亚历山大一世、英国维多利亚女王、温斯顿·丘吉尔爵士和阿瑟·鲁宾斯坦，他们都对宝玑钟表的工艺和品位给予了充分信赖。

宝玑在法国和外国的文学作品中频频出现，也是宝玑公司及其创始人极高声望的佐证。现在，宝玑已深深扎根于欧洲文化，成为描述贵族、资产阶级或奢华优雅生活时不可或缺的重要代名词。司汤达、梅里美、普希金、巴尔扎克、亚历山大·杜马、萨克雷和维克多·雨果都曾在作品中提及宝玑表，而继其之后，还有现代作家

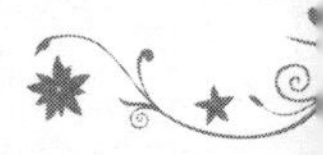

库普林、马克斯·雅各布和派特里克·欧布莱恩等。

如今，创新能力更能显示品牌活力。宝玑所拥有的创造力和聪明才智愈加历久弥新。在尼古拉斯·海耶克的带领下，品牌实力得以大大增强，在短短八年时间里，先后申请多项设计专利，比其创始人更胜一筹。

制表工艺

（1）独立编号

世界各地表迷都认同每块宝玑表均体现一种不同凡响的制表工艺标准，且值得流传后世。宝玑自创始至今，所制作的每块钟表均带有独立编号，可供收藏家确定其真伪与来历。 这项优良传统延续至今。每一块宝玑表均附有独一无二的生产编号，将明证品牌世代相传的制造技艺和心血。

（2）隐蔽签名

宝玑表因大获成功而成为仿冒者的目标。1795年，宝玑采用了一项防伪技术：隐蔽签名。在表盘上蚀刻一个隐蔽签名，只在光线以斜角照射时才显现出来。时至今日，隐蔽签名仍是辨别宝玑表真伪的标记，也是大部分宝玑表表盘的专有特征。

（3）手工镌刻表盘

宝玑约于1786年开始为腕表装配自行设计的手工镌刻银质或金质表盘。在金属表面镌刻重复图案的工艺目前已几近失传，但这却成为鉴别宝玑腕表的重要细节之一。制作精美的手工镌刻表盘以其图案优雅脱俗而闻名于世，与其所搭载的精准机芯相得益彰。

（4）宝玑指针

过去的两个多世纪至今，宝玑一直沿用品牌创始人创制的带镂空偏心“月形”针尖的指针。这款修长雅致的指针约于1783年设计，一面世即大受欢迎。自此，“宝玑指针”便成为制表业的常用专业名词。宝玑指针简洁易读，是每块宝玑表的必备特色，更成为许多其他品牌竞相仿效的对象。

（5）宝玑数字时符

许多宝玑表款仍采用阿伯拉罕–路易·宝玑设计的独特数字符号。尽管宝玑并非书法家，但其所设计的阿拉伯数字却优雅实用，尽显其惊人天赋。数字符号于法国大革命之前就已问世，当时表盘除了饰有阿拉伯数字外，还有小星分针及风格独具的百合花形五分钟刻度，至1790年发展成为今天所见的式样。如今，配以珐琅表盘的宝玑表依然沿用这套原创数字符号。

（6）表耳

尽管仅仅是腕表的组件，把表带与表壳相连的表耳亦体现了百分百的宝玑风格。宝玑以螺丝栓取代常用的弹簧杆，将表带固定于表耳之间，不仅美观，而且稳固。表耳焊接于表框上，确保坚固耐用，令整块腕表更具美感。此外，上链杆的孔眼必须准确钻制，才能确保表壳具有高度防水性能。

（7）表框坑纹

宝玑表框上的坑纹（双排串珠形）是闻名遐迩的品牌标志，展现宝玑设计的含蓄修饰细节。一如以往的经典作品，大部分宝玑现代表款均带有坑纹表框，在众多表款中脱颖而出。工匠把坑纹冷轧到表框上，然后放置在机械夹钳上，手工加工而成。

读书笔记

10.（日本）精工 Seiko

品牌名片

品　　类：腕表

标志风格：创新、精炼

创 始 人：服部金太郎（Kintaro Hattori）

诞 生 地：日本

诞生时间：1881年

Seiko的品牌标志就是一个简单的“SEIKO”，是日本晶振制造商Seiko Instruments Inc.的缩写，也称为SII。

品牌阅读

The story of SEIKO began in 1881, when Kintaro Hattori opened a clock repair shop in central Tokyo. Only after 11 years, the company produced the first clock and produced the first wrist watch in 1895.

SEIKO has launched many **epoch-making** products in the world. SEIKO's cutting edge innovations make it possible to create wonderful world's first products. In 1929, SEIKO pocket watch was appointed as Japan National Railway's official "Railway Watch". In 1964, the world's first portable **quartz** chronometer QC-951 was introduced. This year, SEIKO served as official timer of the 18th Tokyo Olympic Games. It introduced the world's first six-digit LCD quartz watch cal.0614 in 1973 and the world's first TV watch cal. T001 in 1983. It also served as official timer at the 25th Olympic Games held in Barcelona, Spain in 1992. In 2006, it introduced the world's first watch with electrophoresis display module cal. G510.

Technology

SEIKO believes that the wristwatch is an intimate accessory. The best watches live in harmony and interact with the wearer, and their functions offer a reassuring and emotionally satisfying bond. SEIKO's technological development is focused on the creation of 'emotional technologies. Emotional technology creates the interaction between the wearer and the product.

(1) Kinetic

Like mechanical and quartz, Kinetic is a platform. Over the past 20 years, SEIKO has created on this platform a suite of Kinetic movements, each bringing unique features to the consumer.

It was at the 1986 Basel Fair that SEIKO unveiled its first Kinetic prototype. Introduced under the trial name of "AGM", it was the first watch in the world to convert kinetic movement into electrical energy. It was the first step in a development that, 20 years later, has made Kinetic **synonymous with** environmental friendliness, high performance and **long-lasting** convenience to a generation of users worldwide.

In 1998, Kinetic Auto Relay was released, extending the 'at-rest' operating period of the watch to a remarkable 4 years. 1999 saw the launch of the Ultimate Kinetic Chronograph, a masterpiece which fused the very best of SEIKO's mechanical and electronic watchmaking skills, and in 2003 another Kinetic Chronograph was launched. At Baselworld 2005, the Kinetic Perpetual made its first appearance, combining Kinetic convenience and longevity with a perpetual calendar, correct to the year 2100. In 2007, SEIKO's emotional technology Kinetic Direct Drive was introduced.

(2) Mechanical

SEIKO automatic movement 6R20. This high grade caliber is designed to place the SEIKO firmly in the high quality mechanical market. The 6R20 movement is made of parts, all of which except rubies, are produced and assembled by SEIKO Instruments Inc. The movement is **exquisitely** finished with an engraved rotor, polished edges to the bridges and hairline shading on the main surfaces. The high beat (28,800) movement delivers accuracy of -15~+25 seconds a day and the Spron 510* mainspring generates a power reserve of more than 45 hours.

(3) Quartz

With SEIKO's passion, the SEIKO Quartz has brought innovation to the history of watches. The quartz watch, developed in 1969, revolutionized the conventional concept of watches. This is a watch that has a crystal oscillator at its core for accuracy. The crystalline body of a crystal cut to a fixed shape has a characteristic to generate steady vibration if voltage is applied to it. Through the ages, the idea has existed that this crystal-specific electrical property is used for a crystal oscillator to be the standard of timekeeping accuracy of watches. However, to take advantage of quartz crystal, whose excellence had been demonstrated in terms of accuracy, in a small world "watch" there were many barriers that had to be overcome.

In 1969, SEIKO succeeded in resolving all these issues and made available to the world for the first time a commercially viable quartz watch. It was a long ten years since the start of development plan of crystal oscillation watch at Suwa Seikosha. To develop a quartz watch for practical use, unique technologies only available by SEIKO were created. For example, adoption of a crystal oscillator cut in the shape of a tuning-fork and development of an IC and step motor to properly operate signals from a **crystal oscillator** had to be created. Additionally, with a passion to change the future of watches, SEIKO did not pursue **monopolization** on patent rights of those unique technologies and opened them to the world. Later on, many technologies provided by SEIKO became world standards and have contributed to development of present day quartz watches.

epoch-making 划时代的，开创新纪元的
quartz [kwɔ:ts] n. 石英
interact with 与……相互作用
synonymous with 与……同义
long-lasting ['lɔ:ŋla:stiŋ] adj. 持续时间长的
exquisitely [ek'skwizitli] adv. 精致地；精巧地；敏锐地
monopolization [mə,nɔpəlai'zeiʃən] n. 垄断；专卖
crystal oscillator 晶体振荡器

精工的故事始于1881年，当时Kintaro Hattori（服部金太郎）在东京市中心开了一家时钟修理店。仅仅过了11年的时间，这家公司就制造出了第一只时钟，并在1895年制作出第一只腕表。

精工推出过许多开创世界制表新纪元的产品。始终处于最前沿的创新技术保证了精工不断制造出世界第一的产品。1929年，精工制造的怀表被日本国营铁路官方授予“铁路专用表”的称号。1964年，制造出世界上第一只可携带式石英计时器QC-951。这一年，精工还被指定为第十八届东京奥林匹克运动会官方计时器厂商。1973年，推出世界第一只六位数字液晶表Cal. 0614。1983年，推出世界第一只附加电视功能的腕表Cal. T001。1992年，精工还被指定为第25届西班牙巴塞罗那奥运会的官方计时器厂商。2006年，推出世界第一只电子墨水腕表G510。

精湛技术

SEIKO深信腕表是个性化的配饰。最好的腕表应该与佩戴者有契合的默契和互动的感觉，而且腕表所提供的功能让佩戴者感到安心可靠以及情感上的满足。SEIKO（精工）的科技研发就是致力发展“人性化科技”。人性化科技使得腕表产品和佩戴者之间产生了互动的联系。

（1）Kinetic人动电能系统

Kinetic人动电能和机械式、石英式一样，都是动力传送系统的一种。在过去的20年中，精工以 Kinetic人动电能这种动力传送系统为基础，推出了众多的腕表产品，每一款都让消费者体验到它的独特性。

早在1986年瑞士巴塞尔展览会上，精工就推出了 Kinetic人动电能最初的试制品，暂命名“ AGM ”向外推出，这是当时世界上第一款将人体运动转化成为电能的腕表。在迈出了这第一步后，经过二十年的发展，如今对于全世界 Kinetic人动电能的众多用户而言，Kinetic人动电能已经成为了环保、高性能、持久耐用的代名词。

1998年，精工推出 Kinetic Auto Relay（人动电能、智能时控），将腕表“休眠节能”模式的时间延长到了令人吃惊的四年之久，在这四年内可以随时激活腕表，使其自动回复到当前的准确时间。1999年，见证了 Ultimate Kinetic Chronograph（人动电能计时表极限款）的诞生，这款腕表是集精工机械式和电子式制表工艺之大成的杰出作品；2003年又一款 Kinetic Chronograph（人动电能计时表）推出上市。2005年巴塞尔世界展览会上，Kinetic Perpetual（人动电能、万年历）首次亮相，将 Kinetic（人动电能）便利性与至2100年都无需调校的恒久万年历相结合；2007年，精工人性化科技的结晶：Kinetic Direct Drive（人动电能，可手动充电）面世。

（2）机械式系统

精工自动机芯 6R20 使得精工在高品质机械表市场占有稳固的

地位。6R20 运动机芯的所有构成部件，除了红宝石外，都是由精工电子有限公司制造的。机芯的制造工艺精密，包含一个雕刻过的摆陀，自动陀夹板的边沿经过抛光，大部分表面都经过发丝打磨。高转速（28,800转）的机芯能达到每天-15 ~ +25秒的精确度。由 Spron 510* 发条能产生使腕表工作超过45小时的能量储存。

（3）石英石系统

精工对于制表工艺充满热情，其生产的石英表为腕表的发展史带来了伟大的革命。1969年研制推出的石英表颠覆了传统的腕表概念，带来了制表业界中革命性的变革。在这只腕表的核心安装了一个石英晶体震荡器，以确保腕表的精准。对切割成固定形状的水晶施以电压，水晶就会产生稳定的震动。多年来，石英晶体震荡器利用水晶的电能特性以确保时间精确性的标准模式，已经众所周知。但是，要将石英水晶在精确性方面的优势充分地应用到腕表中去，在这条行业道路上还有许多技术问题需要解决。

1969年，精工成功地解决了所有的问题，第一次向全世界推出了它的首款石英腕表产品。从Suwa Seikosha（诹访精工舍）开始石英晶体震荡器研发计划到首款石英腕表面世，整整经历了10年时间。为了研发出实用的石英表，精工创造出了独一无二的技术。例如，将石英晶体切割的形状调整为音叉的样式；通过研发IC（集成电路）和步进马达（时间能一秒一秒地运行）来更好地利用从晶体震荡器中发出的信号并进行准确的运作。除此之外，精工怀着改变腕表未来制造工艺的激情，并没有对自己独一无二技术的专利权进行垄断，而是向全世界公开。不久之后，精工提供的很多技术成为了世界标准，直到今天，这些技术还在为石英表制造业的发展而做着贡献。

11.（意大利）沛纳海Panerai

品牌名片

品　　类：腕表

标志风格：超大表面

创 始 人：乔凡尼·沛纳海（Giovanni Panerai）

诞 生 地：意大利

诞生时间：1860年

沛纳海1860年在佛罗伦萨诞生，自19世纪以来技艺日益精湛，成为意大利海军的测量及精密仪器供应商。品牌定位为运动、休闲领域中的高档腕表。

品牌阅读

Giovanni Panerai opened his watchmaker's shop on Ponte delle Grazie in Florence in 1860: both shop and workshop, and also the city's first watchmaking school. Officine Panerai's history begins here. The shop later moved to its current location in the Palazzo Arcivescovile in Piazza San Giovanni, changing its name to "Orologeria Svizzera" at the beginning of the twentieth century.

To meet the military needs of the Royal Italian Navy, which it had already been supplying with high precision instruments for a number of years, Officine Panerai created Radiomir, a radium-based powder that gave luminosity to the dials of sighting instruments and devices. Reference to the name "Radiomir" was documented in the supplement to the patent filed in France on 23 March 1916. The substance's high visibility and the paint's excellent underwater adhesive qualities immediately made the radium paste a key element in Officine

Panerai's production. The Radiomir patent was the first of the many patents filed to mark Panerai's history of innovation.

On the eve of the Second World War, Panerai created the first prototypes of the model now known as "Radiomir" for the frogman commandos of the First Submarine Group Command of the Royal Italian Navy. Today's Radiomir retains many of the prototype's features: a large and cushion-shaped steel case (47mm), **luminescent** numerals and indices, wire lugs welded to the case, a hand-wound mechanical movement and a water-resistant strap long enough to be worn over a diving suit. The Navy's historical archives record that just ten prototypes were produced in 1936.

In 1943, Officine Panerai presented the prototype of a model specifically designed for deck officers: the Mare Nostrum, a two-counter chronograph. It is thought that only two or three of these watches were ever made, and all that remains of them are some photographs and a single example discovered in 2005. The research and planning for one of the fundamental steps in the Florentine brand's design began in the early 1940s: the crown-protecting device, a sort of steel half-moon designed to prevent infiltrations of water into the case and to protect the crown seal from the stresses of winding.

In 1956, Panerai developed a Radiomir watch known as the "Egiziano" for the Egyptian Navy. It is characterized by its exceptional size (case diameter of 60 millimetres) and strength: it has great water resistance and a marked **bezel** for calculating immersion time. The patent for the crown-protecting bridge, which previously appeared in Panerai prototypes and supply documents provided to the Italian Navy, was filed in the same year, thereby becoming both the distinguishing mark of the Luminor models and of the DNA of the Florentine

company's brand.

Giuseppe Panerai, son of Guido, died in 1972. The management of the family business, along with the Italian Navy supply contracts long covered by military secrecy, passed to engineer Dino Zei, who changed the company name from "G.Panerai & Figlio" to "Officine Panerai S.r.L.", the name that had appeared on the very first models. Another chapter in Officine Panerai's production related to the instruments created for and supplied to the Italian Navy for many years - compasses and wrist depth gauges, as well as pressure compensation underwater torches providing greater resistance **in the depths of** the sea.

The year of 2002 was a milestone for Officine Panerai, with the opening of the Panerai Manufacture in Neuchâtel, Switzerland. Fine Swiss watchmaking, exclusive design and know-how came together in a single location where planning, development and continuous research offered new technical and functional perspectives. Officine Panerai also opened up to the Orient with its first Asian boutique, located in the prestigious Landmark Prince's Building in Hong Kong.

In 2005, Officine Panerai launched its first in-house movement, the P.2002: a hand-wound calibre with GMT function and an eight-day power reserve, as in the Angelus movements used in the 1940s. The calibre took its name from the year in which Officine Panerai inaugurated its production plant, a tribute to the watchmaking art of the Florentine brand.

On the occasion of the 400th anniversary of his first celestial observations, Officine Panerai dedicated a triptych of exceptionally complex models to the Tuscan genius Galileo Galilei: L'Astronomo, Lo Scienziato and the Jupiterium clock. Panerai's Jupiterium model is a planetary clock with perpetual calendar which shows, from a geocentric perspective, the positions in the celestial sphere of the Sun, the Moon and Jupiter with the so-called Galilean Moons, i.e. its four main satellites, now known as Io, Europa, Ganymede and Callisto, observed for the first time by Galileo Galilei in 1610, thanks to the invention of the telescope. Officine Panerai launches the in-house P.999 movement and the first Panerai Composite watch at the Salon International de la Haute Horlogerie.

luminescent [ˌljuːmɪ'nesənt] adj. 夜光的

bezel ['bez(ə)l] n. 宝石的斜面

in the depths of 在……的深处

1860年，乔凡尼·沛纳海（Giovanni Panerai）在佛罗伦萨创立钟表店：这家钟表店身兼店铺和工厂，同时还是城中第一家制表学校。沛纳海的历史由此开始。这家钟表店在20世纪初更名为“Orologeria Svizzera”（瑞士钟表店），之后搬迁至圣乔瓦尼广场的圣芝奥凡尼广场内，至今仍是沛纳海佛罗伦萨总部所在地。

当时沛纳海已成为意大利皇家海军供应商多年，为其提供高精度的计时工具。根据军方的要求，沛纳海创制出Radiomir，一种以镭为基础的发光材质，作为仪器表盘的夜光涂剂之用。有关“Radiomir”这一名称的文献记载见于1916年3月23日在法国填写的专利文件附录中。其高可视性及漆面在水中出色的黏附性立即让这种以镭为基础的涂剂成为沛纳海生产过程中不可或缺的一种材质。Radiomir的专利成为第一批由沛纳海研发的专利技术，由此展开了沛纳海源远流长的创新历史。

第二次世界大战前夕，沛纳海开发出“Radiomir”腕表的首个试用品，供意大利皇家海军第一潜水部队指挥部的蛙人部队使用。这款表的众多特点仍然保留至今：阔大的精钢枕型表壳，夜光数字和

时标，线型表耳与表壳焊接相连，手动上链机械式机芯，加长防水表带，可佩戴于潜水衣之外。海军的历史档案记载在1936年仅生产了10枚原型腕表。

1943年，沛纳海表厂推出特别为海军文职军官所设计的原型表款：Mare Nostrum双表盘计时码表。据说这款腕表当时仅生产了两三枚，如今只能看到它们的一些照片，在2005年发现了其中一枚。沛纳海从20世纪40年代开始初步研发和设计这一表款。半月形钢制表冠防护装置，防止海水渗入表壳，同时保护表冠密封不会因上链应力而受损。

1956年，沛纳海为埃及海军开发了一款名为“Egiziano”（埃及人）的Radiomir腕表。这款腕表体型很大（表壳直径60毫米），坚固耐用：它具备极好的防水性能，同时配备刻度表框以便计算潜水时间。其特有的冠状护桥设计，最早出现在沛纳海原型表款上，同年的意大利海军档案中也有记载，同年申请了专利权，成为了Luminor表款的经典造型，也成为了沛纳海品牌的标志性特征。

1972年，吉赛·沛纳海（Giuseppe Panerai）去世。工程师迪诺·哲（Dino Zei）接手管理沛纳海家族事业，并将公司名称从“G.Panerai & Figlio”改为“Officine Panerai S.r.L.”，该名称曾经出现在最初的几个表款上。在此期间，沛纳海仍然是意大利海军的秘密供应商。为意大利海军长期提供并研发相关仪器，包括在深海中具有极佳防水功能的指南针以及手腕上佩戴的深度计以及压力补偿水下手电筒等，这也为沛纳海公司揭开了新的历史篇章。

2002年，沛纳海于瑞士诺沙泰尔（Neuchâtel）开设表厂：这是对沛纳海来说具有里程碑意义的一年。品牌将精密的瑞士制表工艺、独有设计以及精湛工艺融于一体，依托持续不断的科技研发，沛纳海不断地将新技术与各种功能加入到产品设计中。沛纳海也勇于开拓亚洲市场，在香港的标志性建筑太子大厦开设了亚洲第一家精品店。

2005年，沛纳海研制的首款自制机芯P.2002在国际市场上推出：这款手动上链机芯配备两地时间功能和八日动力储存，类似于20世纪40年代的Angelus机芯。 这款机芯以沛纳海创立自己表厂的年份命名，向这一源自佛罗伦萨的腕表品牌致敬。

2010年，为了向400年前伽利略的第一次重大天文发现致敬，沛纳海发布了三个表款，以纪念这位托斯卡纳的天才：分别是L'Astronomo、Lo Scienziato 以及 the Jupiterium表款。沛纳海的Jupiterium原型表款是一款行星腕表，根据地心引力的原理，其万年历显示了太阳、月亮、土星以及其他伽利略卫星之间的关系，特别是四个主要的卫星：木卫一到木卫四。得益于望远镜的发明，伽利略于1610年发现了伽利略卫星。 沛纳海在国际高级钟表沙龙上发布了其P.999自制机芯，以及首款沛纳海Composite腕表。

读书笔记

12.（瑞士）百达翡丽 Patek Philippe

品牌名片

品　　类：腕表

标志风格：精准、完美

创 始 人：安东尼·百达（Antoine Norbert de Patek）

简·翡丽（Jean-Adrien Philippe）

诞 生 地：瑞士

诞生时间：1839年

百达翡丽品牌标志上的图标由骑士的剑和牧师的十字架组合而成，合在一起便成为庄严与勇敢的象征。这象征代表着百达翡丽的两位创始人安东尼·百达与简·翡丽合作的精神。这个厂标从1857年便开始使用。

品牌阅读

Since 1839 without interruption, Patek Philippe has been perpetuating the tradition of Genevan watchmaking. As the last family-owned independent watch manufacturer in Geneva, it enjoys total creative freedom to entirely design, produce and assemble what experts agree to be the finest timepieces in the world- following the vision of its founders Antoine Norbert de Patek (1839) and Adrien Philippe (1845). Thanks to its exceptional know-how, Patek Philippe maintains a tradition of innovation hailed by an impressive repertoire of more than 80 patents.

Independence, tradition, innovation, quality and craftsmanship, rarity, value, aesthetics, service, emotion and legacy are the fundamental values of the Genevan watchmaker. Patek Philippe has always aimed for perfection by creating timepieces of unrivalled quality and reliability, the uniqueness and exclusiveness of which makes them rare and precious pieces, a unique legacy to be **handed down** from one generation to the next. To achieve this, the company invests in innovation with new materials and leading-edge technologies, while continuing to preserve the tradition of **ancestral** watchmaking know-how, and maintains the industry's strictest quality control standards.

In 2009, Patek Philippe launched its proprietary quality label for mechanical watches. The Patek Philippe Seal attests to the utmost quality of its timepieces, far above and beyond official standards, by integrating all competencies and features of relevance in manufacturing, precision and lifelong maintenance. The Patek Philippe Seal applies to the entire watch and is the only seal of quality that assures lifetime maintenance of the watch, regardless of the date of completion. It is governed by detailed regulations and an independent supervisory body. The Patek Philippe Seal embodies all the company's values and quality standards.

History

On May 1st, 1839 two Polish immigrants, Antoni Patek (Businessman) and François Czapek (Watchmaker) joined forces to found "Patek, Czapek & Cie" in Geneva.

In 1844, Patek met the French watchmaker, Jean-Adrien Philippe in Paris where the latter presented his pioneering stem winding and setting system by the crown.

In 1845, when Czapek decided to leave the company and to continue on his own, the company name changed to "Patek & Cie".

Later, in 1851 when Jean- Adrien Philippe officially became associated with the company, it was renamed "Patek Philippe &

Cie", before changing once more in 1901 to "Ancienne Manufacture d'Horlogerie Patek Philippe & Cie, S.A.".

In 1932, the company was purchased by two brothers, Charles and Jean Stern, owners of a fine dial manufacture in Geneva. Since then, "Patek Philippe S.A." remains a family owned firm.

In 2009, the company presidency was officially transferred from the 3rd to the 4th generation: Thierry Stern became president and his father Philippe Stern, Honorary president.

Patek Philippe watches are timekeeping instruments of a benchmark stature. They are also works of art which beauty reflects their mechanical perfection. To **distill** the best of an era and transform it into a timeless icon is the **infinitely** delicate task of Patek Philippe's design experts. With their designs, they must evoke emotions that are as lasting as the movements themselves. From the first pencil sketch, to the finished watch, the objective is always to find the perfect balance between classicism and modernity. Only a design that is deemed worthy will bear the Patek Philippe signature. The outcome is timeless appeal, as evidenced by the sustained success of Patek Philippe watches at prestigious auctions.

hand down 把……传下去

ancestral [æn'sestrəl] adj. 祖先的；祖传的

distill [dis'til] v. 提取；浓缩

infinitely ['infinitli] adv. 无限地

创立于1839年的百达翡丽，从未间断对日内瓦制表工艺传统的传承。作为日内瓦最后一家独立制表商，百达翡丽在设计、生产直至装配的整个过程中享受着全面的创新自由，打造出令专家交口称赞的全球钟表杰作——谨遵品牌创始人百达先生（Antoine Norbert de

Patek, 1839年）和翡丽先生（Adrien Philippe, 1845年）的卓越远见。凭借超凡的专业技能，秉承创新传统，百达翡丽至今拥有80余项技术专利。

独立自主、尊崇传统、革新创造、品质工艺、珍贵稀有、恒久价值、工艺美学、优质服务、情感传递和承传优质，就是这家日内瓦制表商恪守的基本价值。追求完美是百达翡丽始终不变的理念，其作品拥有无与伦比的品质和可靠性能，它们的独特风格和尊贵气质成就了一枚枚珍奇的腕表杰作，这份独一无二的财富将会世代相传。为此，百达翡丽在锐意创新方面从不吝惜投入，大胆开发并运用新材料和超前技术，在继续延用传统制表技术的同时，采用业界最为严格的质量控制标准。

2009年，百达翡丽宣布了针对机械腕表的全新质量标准。百达翡丽印记证实了其钟表产品的终极品质，融合了这家制表工坊的全部制表工艺和特色、卓越的计时精度和终身保修服务，从而远远超越了官方标准。百达翡丽印记适用于整枚腕表，这也是唯一一枚保证腕表终身保修的印记，并无需考虑该腕表的生产日期。它有着详细的实施规定，并由一家独立监管机构进行管理。百达翡丽印记是公司价值观和品质标准的化身。

品牌历史

1839年5月1日，两名波兰移民，Antoni Patek（商人）和François Czapek（钟表匠）在日内瓦共同成立了“Patek, Czapek & Cie”公司。

1844年，Patek 在巴黎巧遇法国钟表匠 Jean-Adrien Philippe。当时，Philippe 向他展示了利用表冠实现柄轴上弦和设置时间的创新系统。

1845年，Czapek决定离开公司自立门户，公司名称变为 “Patek & Cie”。

到了1851年，Philippe 先生正式加入公司，公司因此更名为“Patek Philippe & Cie”。1901年，公司再次更名为“Ancienne

Manufacture d'Horlogerie Patek Philippe & Cie, S.A."。

1932年，日内瓦一家高档表盘制造厂的Charles Stern和Jean Stern两兄弟收购了该公司。从此之后 "Patek Philippe S.A." 一直是家族企业。

2009年，Thierry Stern先生出任总裁，而其父Philippe Stern先生担任荣誉主席，标志着公司管理权由第三代继承人正式过渡给第四代继承人。

百达翡丽腕表不仅是堪称行业典范的计时仪器，同样是杰出的艺术作品，其高贵优雅尽显机械工艺之美。浓缩时代精华并将其转化为永恒的经典，这就是百达翡丽腕表设计专家孜孜以求的目标。这些设计犹如经典机芯一般恒久流传，让人永难忘怀。从第一幅铅笔草图到完成最后一道工序的成品腕表，目标始终是在经典与现代之间实现完美平衡，而百达翡丽的名字便是卓越设计的保证。正是这一设计理念造就了百达翡丽经典永恒的魅力，成为各大知名拍卖会上长盛不衰的珍宝。

读书笔记

读书笔记

Part 3 品牌服装

1.（意大利）华伦天奴 Valentino

品牌名片

品　　类：时装

标志风格：奢华、高调

创 始 人：瓦伦蒂诺·加拉瓦尼（Valentino Garavani）

诞 生 地：意大利

诞生时间：1960年

华伦天奴是全球高级定制和高级成衣奢侈品牌，代表一种宫廷式的奢华，高调中带着冷静。从20世纪60年代以来一直都是意大利国家级品牌。

品牌阅读

Established in 1960 by legendary fashion designer Valentino Garavani and his business partner Giancarlo Giammetti, Valentino S.p.A. recently celebrated an iconic **cornerstone** - its 50th anniversary - that further consecrates its heritage and success story.

One of the most storied brands in the world, Valentino offers a wide range of luxury products from Haute Couture and Prêt-à-Porter to an extensive accessories collection that includes bags, shoes, small leather goods, belts, eyewear, watches and perfumes.

The brand is available in over 70 countries thanks to a capillary retail network charted out over the decades of over 129 Valentino directly-operated stores located in the most elegant shopping streets in the world as well as in over 1,250 points of sale.

In October 2008, Maria Grazia Chiuri and Pierpaolo Piccioli were named Valentino Creative Directors, a choice that proved to

be fruitful and insightful move as the design duo have been credited with rejuvenating the brand via highly-successful and well-received collections that stayed true to the brand's legacy of half a century while moving the design aesthetic forward with designs that are at once feminine and contemporary.

Maria Grazia Chiuri and Pierpaolo Piccioli, who had worked under Valentino Garavani's for over a decade, contributing to the international success of the fledgling accessories project, displayed all the best assets to thrive an innate sense of leadership, a corporate-centric approach and an extremely talented **in-house** design team.

The duo debuted with their first Haute Couture collection in Paris in January 2009, demonstrating the ability to fully understand and interpret the Valentino world, a vision that was applauded **unanimously**. Hollywood stars, socialites and fashion leaders were immediately wooed by their creations.

Six months later, Maria Grazia Chiuri and Pierpaolo Piccioli consecrated their success with the July 2009 Haute Couture collection, which also fully expressed their vision for the Valentino woman: an unconventional idea of femininity and of extreme elegance that becomes a way of being, a dichotomy of a fragile yet dangerous nature mixed with an element of uniqueness and distinction.

THE COMPANY TODAY

In July 2012, Mayhoola for Investments S.P.C., an investment vehicle backed by a major private investor group from Qatar, entered into an agreement with Red & Black Lux S.a.r.l. (a company indirectly controlled by the Permira Funds in partnership with the Marzotto family) for the acquisition of the entire stake capital of Valentino

Fashion Group S.p.A. (VFG).

Through the acquisition of VFG, Mayhoola for Investments acquired Valentino S.p.A. and the M Missoni license business, while MCS Marlboro Classics was **carved-out** from VFG. Red & Black continues to own a majority stake in Hugo Boss, which was not part of the transaction.

Valentino Haute Couture

Valentino Haute Couture offers a variety of collections that comprise of unique items exclusively handcrafted in the prestigious Roman atelier, where a team of about 40 seamstresses is entirely dedicated to handcrafting precious one-of-a-kind confections.

Valentino Prèt-à-Porter

Valentino Prèt-à-Porter presents sophisticated and exclusive lines for men and women that target a chic young clientele that belongs to the new generation of international jet setters. In January 2012, Chiuri and Piccioli unveiled their first men's wear collection in Florence as Special Guests of Pitti Uomo. The designer tweaked the notion of Italian sartorial tradition and classic attitude with a collection that combined **voluminous** and fitted shapes enriched with playful details.

cornerstone ['kɔːnəstəʊn] n. 奠基石

at the helm of 掌握着

in-house [ɪn haʊs] adj. 内部的

unanimously [ju:'nænɪməslɪ] adv. 全体一致地

carved-out （股权）分离

voluminous [və'lju:minəs] adj. 大量的

具传奇色彩的时装大师瓦伦蒂诺·加拉瓦尼与他的商业伙伴 Giancarlo Giammetti 于 1960 年创立了华伦天奴。最近，Valentino S.p.A. 庆祝其成立五十周年，这无疑是一个具代表性的里程碑，象征着华伦天奴为其成功的品牌故事写下了光辉的一页。

华伦天奴是举世闻名的奢华品牌之一，产品包括：高级定制服、成衣以及一系列配饰，包括手袋、皮鞋、小型皮具、腰带、眼镜、腕表及香水。

经过几十年的零售渠道建设，品牌目前在 70 多个国家设有超过 129 个直营店和1250多个销售点。

自 2008 年 10 月起，Maria Grazia Chiuri和 Pierpaolo Piccioli 成为华伦天奴的创意总监，这一决定富有成果且有远见。他们努力地令品牌年轻化，创造了十分成功和受欢迎的系列。他们的作品不但传承了品牌半个世纪的传奇，同时亦融合女性气质和现代设计的美感。

Chiuri 和 Piccioli 与 Valentino Garavani 共事逾 10 年，这些经验有助他们的配饰系列取得国际上的成功，同时亦展示了二人的领导才能、以企业为中心的方针和极具才华的内部设计团队。

Maria Grazia Chiuri 和 Pierpaolo Piccioli 在 2009 年1月在巴黎首度展示第一个高级定制系列，作品表现了二人充分掌握且能诠释 Valentino 风格特色的能力。不少好莱坞明星、社会名流和时尚名人都十分喜爱他们的作品。

6个月后，Chiuri 和 Piccioli 所创造的新一季2009年7月高级定制系列亦取得成功，系列完美地诠释了他们心中对 Valentino 女士的构思：非传统的女性气质和极度优雅的存在脆弱但危险的特质混合了独特元素的混合体。

今日的华伦天奴

2012年7月，Mayhoola投资公司（卡塔尔私人投资组织背景）

Red&Black Lux S.a.r.l.（由Permira基金与Marzotto家族合伙控股）签署协议获得Valentino Fashion Group S.P.A(VFG)的全部股权。

通过这次的收购,Mayh oola获得了 Valentino S.p.A.（“Valentino”）以及 M Missoni 的控制权。同时，MCS Marlboro Classics 从 VFG 剥离。 Red & Black仍拥有Hugo Boss的多数股权，这部分并不包含在收购交易内。

华伦天奴高级定制服

提供多种款式，各具特色的服装每一件都在享有盛誉的罗马制衣工坊以手工缝制，由一组大约 40 人的精英团队专责打造出最高质量的创作；每一件都是举世唯一，绝无仅有。

华伦天奴高级成衣系列

提供洒脱而自成一格的男女服装，最适宜年轻、优雅而不拘传统的尊贵客户。2012 年 1 月，Chiuri 和 Piccioli 以 Pitti Uomo 的特别嘉宾身份，在佛罗伦萨展示了他们首个男装系列。设计师将意大利裁剪艺术的传统和对经典的态度与其系列相结合，玩味细节造型合身。

读书笔记

2.（意大利）康纳利 Canali

品牌名片

品　　类：时装

标志风格：高贵、优雅

创 始 人：乔瓦尼·康纳利（Giovanni Canali）

　　　　　贾科莫·康纳利（Giacomo Canali）

诞 生 地：意大利

诞生时间：1934年

意大利康纳利公司是世界十大男装品牌，专注于精美优质男士服饰的制作。以完美无瑕的制衣工艺、高档精致的款式、顶级品质的面料著称于世。

品牌阅读

In 1934, the brothers Giovanni Canali and Giacomo Canali founded a tailoring workshop dedicating to the manufacture of clothing. In the 1950s, with the contributions of the family's second generation, sales increased. By the mid 1970s, the firm had opened its doors to foreign buyers. Exports consumed 50 percent of the entire Canali production in 1980.

In 2013, Alec Baldwin wears Canali in the movie *Blue Jasmine*, written and directed by Woody Allen. For Woody Allen's latest film, *Blue Jasmine*, Suzy Benzinger, the costume designer, chose Canali for the character played by Alec Baldwin in the film. Canali suits and other attire were chosen for their elegance, fine tailoring tradition and **premium quality**.

Flagship Store Opening

Canali opened its flagship store in Hong Kong in 2013, the Asian metropolis that manages to achieve a perfect blend of tradition and modernity. A skill the brand has transferred to its suits for almost 80 years now ensures they convey unique emotions.

A store with 260 square meters of retail space at 20 Pedder Street, one of Hong Kong's luxury shopping **thoroughfares**, where the finest materials in contrasting colors provide the backdrop for a sophisticated ambiance with a decisive and authoritative personality.

The statue, in the display window, is an installation created exclusively for the flagship store in Canali's new corporate colors of grey and yellow. The statue's abstract geometrical shape is a reference to the paper patterns used to create tailor made suits and its powerful presence emphasizes the dynamic gestures of a **time-honored** art.

Everything has been designed to express that typically Italian sense of savoir faire and offer a unique experience, including private shopping with the assistance of a personal shopper in a sophisticated VIP room, the brand's SU MISURA service for an exclusive tailor suit and a stunning video wall to replay key moments from the Milan fashion shows.

AUTUMN WINTER 2013

The modern spirit, expressed through the desire to stand out and feel unique, is transformed into a sophisticated but easy-going style. With the essence of the purest elegance, eclectic and suited to every occasion, the waistcoat is the main feature of the new personality portrayed by the suit: the two-button jacket with peak lapels and waist pocket, the color coordinated waistcoat and the non-pleated trousers

with high cuffs create an astonishing balance of form and color. Being the non plus ultra of the art of fine tailoring, the three-piece suit is worn with a precious **astrakhan** scarf for an authoritative and precise style which is a mixture of retro and cutting edge.

premium quality 一流品质，优质
flagship store 旗舰店
thoroughfare ['θʌrəfeə] n. 大道，通路
time-honored ['taim,ɔnəd] adj. 历史悠久的；因古老而受到尊重的
astrakhan [,æstrə'kæn] n. 俄国羊羔皮

1934年，乔瓦尼·康纳利（Giovanni Canali）和贾科莫·康纳利（Giacomo Canali）两兄弟成立了一家制衣工坊。20世纪50年代，家族第二代成员开始经营公司，销售量增加。70年代中期，公司进入国际市场，1980年公司产品的出口占总产量的一半。

2013年，亚力克·鲍德温身穿康纳利西装出演伍迪·艾伦监制执导的《蓝色茉莉》。《蓝色茉莉》是伍迪·艾伦的最新影片。该片的服装设计师Suzy Benzinger为出演电影的亚力克·鲍德温选择了康纳利西装。Suzy选择康纳利西装以及其他服装是因为这些服装的优雅魅力、精致剪裁传统以及非凡质量。

开设旗舰店

2013年，康纳利在香港这座完美融合了传统与现代的亚洲魅力之都开设品牌旗舰店。近八十年来，康纳利亦在其男装产品中充分展现出这种融合理念，确保每件西装传达出独一无二的风格。

这家零售面积高达260平方米的专卖店位于毕打街20号，那里是香港各大奢侈品牌的购物天堂之一。精选的高档装饰材料以及对比鲜明的颜色，烘托出高贵优雅的购物环境以及独树一帜的风格特点。

橱窗展示的雕塑是专为香港旗舰店创作的装饰艺术作品，采用黄色和灰色，即康纳利新的企业颜色。这座雕塑的几何抽象造型从制作定制西装的纸样图案中汲取设计灵感，其强烈风格彰显出经典艺术杰作的动感活力。

每个细节设计均散发着意大利制造的传统韵味，带来独一无二的体验，不论是私人购物顾问提供的私密购物体验，风格优雅的VIP贵宾室，品牌的SU MISURA独家定制服务，还是循环播放康纳利米兰时装发布会精彩片段的宏伟电视墙。

2013秋冬系列

现代男士渴望展现个性、感受不同，康纳利将这种现代精神演绎为一种精致优雅、轻松随性的风格。西装马夹融汇了最纯粹的优雅，设计兼收并蓄，适合各种场合，堪称本季旨在展现全新个性的三件套西装的主打特色。这款两粒扣西装采用戗驳领和腰袋，搭配色彩和谐的西装马夹和无褶翻边西裤，打造出均衡的外形与色彩，令人惊叹。作为高档制衣工艺的登峰造极之作，这款三件套西装搭配珍贵的俄国羔羊毛围巾，展现出高贵而精致的风格，复古中透出时髦。

读书笔记

3.（英国）金鹰 Lyle&Scott

品牌名片

品　　类：服装

标志风格：皇家御用

创 始 人：威廉·莱尔（William Lyle）

沃尔特·斯科特（Water Scott）

诞 生 地：英国

诞生时间：1874年

Lyle&Scott具有独特的金色老鹰标志，象征高贵、典雅并且充满苏格兰风格的现代休闲时尚感。

品牌阅读

In 1874, William Lyle and Walter Scott founded a knitwear company in Hawick, a small town hidden in the Scottish Borders. With a loan of £800, the premise was to meet the demand for high quality **underwear** in Victorian Britain.

In 1926, the brand progressed into the realms of fashion, applying its accomplished woollen skills to **knitted** outerwear; doubling turnover in the space of two years.

Lyle & Scott became a respected name in international fashion overnight when managing director Charles Oliver negotiated a partnership with Christian Dior in 1954 to produce joint branded cashmere. This was the first of many collaborations with luxury fashion houses & department stores including Chanel, Yves Saint Laurent, Liberty, Bergdorf Goodman and Michael Kors.

In the 60s Lyle & Scott launched the golf wear range, a move that coincided with the design of the now iconic Golden Eagle motif. This new relationship with golf brought yet more exposure on the global stage, with charismatic golfers like Gary Player and Tony Jacklin as well as A-list golf fans like Bob Hope and Bing Crosby.

In the 80s the bright colors of Lyle & Scott's golf wear range were then adopted by and introduced to the main **apparel** range, bringing a more contemporary image for the brand.

In 2003, Lyle & Scott expanded the horizons of the brand, attracting a new generation of young, talented music, TV and film stars and the bands like Vampire Weekend, Arctic Monkeys and Bloc Party.

underwear ['ʌndəwɛə] *n.* 内衣物

knitted ['nitid] *adj.* 针织的；编织的

apparel [ə'pærəl] *n.* 服装；衣服

landmark ['lændmɑ:k] *n.* 里程碑；划时代的事

1874年，威廉·莱尔和沃尔特·斯科特在苏格兰霍伊克小镇成立了一家针织公司。贷款800英镑，前提是满足英国维多利亚时代对内衣的高质量要求。

1926年，该品牌进军时尚领域，应用其熟练的毛织技巧编织外衣，两年之内就取得了营业额翻倍的成绩。

1954年，在总经理Charles Oliver的协商下，Lyle & Scott与克里斯汀·迪奥达成合作，生产联合品牌的羊绒衫，这使得Lyle & Scott一夜之间成为国际时尚界一个受人尊敬的名字。这是Lyle & Scott与许多奢华时装公司及百货商店众多合作中的第一次，包括香奈儿、圣罗兰、Liberty、波道夫·古德曼和Michael Kors。

20世纪60年代，Lyle & Scott推出高尔夫服装系列，此举与现在的金鹰图标设计不谋而合。与高尔夫的这一新关系为公司带来了更多在全球舞台上曝光的机会，与具有超凡魅力的高尔夫球手Gary

Player和 Tony Jacklin以及一流的高尔夫球迷Bob Hope和Bing Crosby一起。

20世纪80年代，Lyle & Scott高尔夫服装，明亮的色彩被采纳并引进到主要的服装领域，从而为它带来了一个更具现代性的品牌形象。

2003年，Lyle & Scott扩大了品牌视野，吸引了新一代年轻的、具有天赋的音乐、电视及电影明星，比如Vampire Weekend, Arctic Monkeys及Bloc Party乐队。

读书笔记

4.（法国）浪凡 Lanvin

品牌名片

品　　类：时装、配件、香水

标志风格：优雅、精致

创 始 人：珍妮·浪凡（Jeanne Lanvin）

诞 生 地：法国

诞生时间：1889年

浪凡是法国历史最悠久的高级时装品牌，是法国高级时尚业的代表。在时装、香水、配饰各个方面领导潮流，以简单和利落的剪裁及颜色搭配的功力赢得时尚人士的拥戴。

品牌阅读

Lanvin was the oldest brand of high fashion in France. Its founder, Jeanne Lanvin was active during the first and second world wars. The elegant and delicate style that she created brought a fashion with an accumulation of the deep cultural inside information.

On January 1st, 1867 Jeanne Lanvin was born.

In 1889, Jeanne Lanvin set up a milliner's boutique on the corner of Boissy d' Anglas and Faubourg St Honore. She later created her own House at the same address.

On August 31st , 1897 Jeanne gave birth to a daughter, Marguerite Marie Blanche, who would become Jeanne's muse, her principal source of **inspiration**.

A Child Apparel department was created in 1908 and Departments were opened for Young Ladies and Women in 1909. Jeanne Lanvin joined the Syndicat de la Couture and entered the world of accredited

Fashion Houses.

Between 1920 and 1921, Lanvin Decoration was founded with **renowned** designer Armand- Albert Rateau at 15 Rue du Faubourg St Honore. In 1923, Lanvin Sport was established at 15 Rue du Faubourg St Honore.

In 1926, Lanvin Tailleur/Chemisier was created at 15 Rue du Faubourg St Honore. Lanvin Fourrure and Lanvin Lingerie were also created. Jeanne Lanvin was named Chevalier of the French Legion d'Honneur.

On July 6th , 1946 Jeanne Lanvin died and leaved her daughter **at the helm of** Jeanne Lanvin Lanvin S.A and Lanvin Parfums S.A. Then Marie-Blanche died twelve years later.

Jules-Francois Crahay designed the House's Haute Couture collections from 1964 to 1984. He received three Golden Thimble awards (Autumn-Winter 1977, Spring-Summer 1981 and Autumn-Winter 1984).

Claude Montana presented five Haute Couture Collections in 1990 and won two Golden Thimble awards (Autumn-Winter 1990, Spring-Summer 1992).

Lanvin was sold to the Chinese businesswoman Wang Xiaolan. Alber Elbaz became the House's art director. The first show, showcasing the Autumn-Winter 2002 collection, was highly acclaimed in the media and by professionals.

Today, Lanvin has launched more that 65 specialty shops around the world. It still holds fast to the development and extension of multiple categories but takes fashion as the principal, continuous and unified.

inspiration [ˌinspəˈreiʃən] *n.* 灵感

renowned [ri'naund] adj. 著名的；有声望的

at the helm of 掌握着

浪凡是法国历史最悠久的高级时装品牌。其创始人珍妮·浪凡是"一战"和"二战"期间十分活跃的名师之一，她开创的优雅精致的风格，为时尚界带来一股积淀着深厚文化底蕴的思潮。

1867年1月1日，珍妮·浪凡出生。

1889年，珍妮·浪凡在Boissy d' Anglas 街和Faubourg St Honore街拐角开了一家衣帽店，这个地方后来就成为她自己的设计工作室。

1897年8月31日，她的女儿玛格丽特·玛丽白出生，女儿成为她重要的灵感源泉，她的缪斯。

1908年，童装部开张。1909年，少女和女装部开张，珍妮·浪凡加入时装集团，进入时装界。

1920～1921期间，珍妮·浪凡与著名装饰师Armand- Albert Rateau在 St Honore街15号开创了浪凡装饰。1923年，在 St Honore街15号创立了浪凡运动系列。

1926年，在 St Honore街15号创立浪凡西服衬衫。还创立了皮草与浪凡内衣。珍妮·浪凡被授予"荣誉骑士勋章"。

1946年7月6日，珍妮·浪凡去世。她的女儿接手掌管浪凡公司和浪凡香水（Lanvin Parfums S.A），12年后去世。

1964～1984年间，Jules-Francois Crahay设计高级定制系列，曾三次荣获金顶针奖（AH1977，PE1981，AH1984）。

1990年Claude Montana展示五个高级定制系列（Haute Couture）并两次获得金顶针奖（AH1990，PE1992）。

浪凡出售给华人实业家王效兰女士。Alber Elbaz成为设计室的艺术总监。2002年秋冬第一场发布会受到媒体和业界的一致好评。

如今，浪凡在世界各地的专卖店已超过了65家，它依然紧紧把握以时装为主的多元品类的开发和延伸，持续而统一。

5.（瑞典）海恩斯莫里斯 H&M

品牌名片

品　　类：服装、配饰、化妆品

标志风格：时尚、雅致

创 始 人：厄尔林·佩尔松（Erling Persson）

诞 生 地：瑞典

诞生时间：1947年

H&M，一个时尚、品质和低价完美糅合的时尚品牌，经营服装、化妆品，全球拥有3000多家专卖店。

品牌阅读

Timeline

The first store opened in Västerås , Sweden in 1947, selling women's clothing. The store was called Hennes.

In 1952, Hennes opened in Stockholm.

In 1964, the first store outside Sweden opens in Norway.

In 1968, Founder Erling Persson bought Mauritz Widforss, a hunting and fishing equipment store. Sales of men's and children's clothing began. The name was changed to Hennes & Mauritz.

In 1974, H&M was listed on the Stockholm **Stock Exchange**.

In 1976, the first store outside Scandinavia opened in London.

In 1977, impuls stores, focused on teenagers, were launched. Sales of cosmetics began.

During 1980s, stores opened in Germany and the Netherlands. H&M acquired the mail order company Rowells.

During 1990s, Progress continued in Europe with the opening of the first store in France in 1998. Newspaper and magazine advertising was complemented by outdoor advertising featuring famous models. In 1998, H&M online shopping began.

In 2000, the first US store opened on Fifth Avenue in New York. The same year stores opened in Spain. In subsequent years H&M opened in more European markets.

In 2004, H&M initiated designer collaborations starting with Karl Lagerfeld. More collaborations followed with Stella McCartney, Viktor & Rolf, Madonna, Roberto Cavalli, Comme des Garçons, Matthew Williamson, Jimmy Choo, Sonia Rykiel, Lanvin, Versace, Marni, and David Beckham.

In 2006, a major expansion of online and catalogue sales began with the Netherlands as the first market outside the Nordic region. The first stores in the Middle East opened via franchise.

In 2007, the first Asian stores opened in Hong Kong and Shanghai. In the same year, the new concept store COS was launched. The expansion of online and catalogue saled continued with the inclusion of Germany and Austria.

In 2008, H&M opened its first Japanese store in Tokyo and acquires fashion firm FaBric Scandinavien AB, which comprised the brands Weekday, Monki and Cheap Monday.

In 2009, the first H&M stores in Russia opened. Beijing also got its first H&M and Lebanon became a new **franchise** market. H&M Home was launched. Weekday and Monki opened in Germany.

In 2010, the first H&M stores in South Korea and Turkey open. Israel became a new franchise market. Online shopping started in the UK. The first H&M Home stores opened outside Sweden. Monki moved into Asia with a store in Hong Kong.

In 2011, H&M opened in Romania, Croatia and Singapore, as well as via franchise in Morocco and Jordan. COS opened in Sweden, and Monki and Cheap Monday in the UK. The H&M Incentive Program – a reward and recognition programme for all employees -started. COS and Monki launched online shopping in 18 markets.

In 2012, H&M opened in Bulgaria, Latvia, Malaysia and Mexico, and via franchise in Thailand. COS opened in Finland, Italy, Poland, Hong Kong and Austria, and opened via franchise in Kuwait. The Monki brand grew in China and Weekday opened in the Netherlands.

In 2013, the first H&M store in the **southern hemisphere** opened in Chile. H&M also opened in Estonia, Lithuania and Serbia. Indonesia became a new franchise market. H&M introduced online shopping in the US. The & Other Stories brand was launched in several European countries. COS, Monki, Weekday and Cheap Monday also opened in new markets and Weekday launched online shopping. A global clothing collecting initiative started in selected stores.

Stock Exchange 证券交易所
collaboration [kə,læbə'reiʃən] n. 合作；协作
franchise ['fræntʃaiz] n. 经销权；特许经营
southern hemisphere 南半球

时间轴

1947年，首家专卖店在瑞典Västerås成立，主营女装。店名为Hennes。

1952年，Hennes在斯德哥尔摩开业。

1964年，瑞典境外的首家专卖店在挪威开业。

1968年，创始人Erling Persson收购狩猎及垂钓用品店Mauritz

Widforss,开始销售男装和童装。店名改为Hennes & Mauritz。

1974年，H&M在斯德哥尔摩证券交易所上市。

1976年，北欧地区以外的首家专卖店在英国伦敦开业。

1977年，Impuls专卖店启动，开始销售化妆品。

20世纪80年代，德国与荷兰的专卖店开业。H&M收购邮购公司Rowells。

20世纪90年代，欧洲业务进一步扩展，1998年成立法国首家专卖店。报纸和杂志广告开始启用名模拍摄户外广告。同年涉足线上商店。

2000年，美国首家专卖店在纽约第五大道开业。H&M同时来到西班牙。随后几年，H&M又进驻多个欧洲市场。

2004年，H&M开始与Karl Lagerfeld开展设计师合作。随后的设计师合作系列包括Stella McCartney、Viktor & Rolf、Madonna、Roberto Cavalli、Comme des Garçons、Matthew Williamson、Jimmy Choo、Sonia Rykiel、Lanvin、Versace、Marni和David Beckham。

2006年，网购和邮购销售开始大举拓展，荷兰成为北欧地区以外的第一个市场。中东第一批加盟店开业。

2007年，亚洲首批专卖店分别在香港和上海开业。同年推出新概念店COS。网购与邮购业务扩展至德国和奥地利。

2008年，日本首家H&M专卖店进驻东京。H&M通过收购时装公司FaBric Scandinavien AB获得Weekday、Monki 和Cheap Monday。

2009年，俄罗斯首家H&M专卖店开业。北京第一家H&M专卖店成立，黎巴嫩成为新加盟市场。H&M Home问世。Weekday和Monki在德国开业。

2010年，韩国和土耳其首批H&M专卖店开业。以色列成为新的加盟市场。开始在英国涉足电子商务。瑞典境外首批H&M Home专卖店开业。Monki进入亚洲，在香港成立分店。

2011年，H&M在罗马尼亚、克罗地亚、新加坡、摩洛哥和约旦开业，其中摩洛哥和约旦为加盟店。COS在瑞典开业，Monki和

Cheap Monday登陆英国。面向所有员工推出的激励计划——H&M Incentive Program启动。COS和Monki在18个国家推出线上商店。

2012年，H&M在保加利亚、拉脱维亚、马来西亚、墨西哥及泰国开店，其中泰国为加盟店。COS已进入中国香港、意大利、芬兰、波兰、奥地利和科威特，其中科威特为加盟店。Monki同时也在中国扩展，Weekday也在荷兰开店。

2013年，H&M南半球的第一家专卖店在智利开业。公司也在爱沙尼亚，立陶宛和塞尔维亚开启新店。印尼也成为公司一个新的市场。公司计划在美国推出网上购物。“The & Other Stories”品牌在几个欧洲国家推出。COS, Monki，Weekday和Cheap Monday也在新城市开启新店，Weekday推出网上商城。全球服装收集倡议也在指定门店发起。

读书笔记

6.（英国）达克斯 DAKS

品牌名片

品　　类：时装、配饰

标志风格：时尚、英伦格调

创 始 人：西蒙·辛普森（Simeon Simpson）

诞 生 地：英国

诞生时间：1894年

达克斯的品牌标志是由英文字DAD（父亲）及SLACKS（西裤）的缩写构成的。

品牌阅读

The DAKS name has always been synonymous with British heritage, style and elegance.It was originally founded in 1894 by Simeon Simpson, who provided a bespoke tailoring service in Middlesex Street in the City of London and soon earned a reputation as Simpson's Suits.

In 1934, Alexander Simpson, the second son of Simeon Simpson, invented a completely revolutionary garment, a milestone in fashion, introducing a style of trouser that featured an adjustable waistband that eliminated the need for belts and braces that were restrictive yet necessary for British Gentleman up until this point.

Today the brand is one of the UK's most **quintessentially** British luxury labels, specializing in fine tailoring and accessories for both Men and Women. The brand's unique House Check, which is recognized worldwide, was introduced in 1976 and has become an international symbol for the brand, featuring heavily throughout the

clothing and accessories ranges.

Worldwide, DAKS is exported to 30 countries and sold in over 2,000 spccialty shops, major stores and concessions. With a strong reputation in the Far East markets, DAKS has been sold under license in Japan for over 30 years and in Korea is the number one non-domestic brand.

The flagship store in London's Old Bond Street underwent a major refurbishment programme and reopened in 2007. The new store gave DAKS the opportunity to **rejuvenate** its rich past.

DAKS, as one of Britain's major fashion companies, continues to uphold the values of quality, reliability and innovation first established by Simeon Simpson over 100 years ago. These values remain unchanged and **paramount** to the brand's identity, as does the pursuit to create much loved British classics.

quintessentially [ˌkwintiˈsenʃəli] adv. 典型地；标准地

scrutinize [ˈskruːtinaiz] v. 详细检查；审查

rejuvenate [riˈdʒuːvineit] v. 使更新；使复原

paramount [ˈpærəmaunt] adj. 最重要的，主要的

达克斯的名字一直被视为不列颠遗产，正统而优雅。品牌由西蒙·辛普森创建于1894年，他在伦敦市Middlesex Street提供量身定制服务，很快就赢得了Simpson's Suits的赞誉。

1934年，西蒙·辛普森的第二个儿子亚历山大·辛普森设计了一款完全具有变革性的服装，成为了时装界的一个里程碑。推出的裤子风格，以可调节束腰带为特色，消除了腰带和背带限制，而在这之前腰带和背带是英国绅士所必须的。

如今，该品牌成为英国最典型的奢侈品牌，专门为男性和女性

提供精细剪裁服装和配饰。1976年，公司推出其招牌格子套用于衣服及配饰上，成为DAKS的国际标记。

达克斯出口到全世界30多个国家并在2000多个专卖店、大商场进行销售。由于在远东市场有很高的名气，达克斯已经在日本许可销售长达30年，并且在韩国是头号进口品牌。

在伦敦Old Bond Street开设的旗舰店经过了大规模的整修并在2007年重新开业。新店给达克斯带来了重拾往日辉煌的机会。

作为英国主要的时装公司，达克斯始终坚持100多年前西蒙·辛普森建立起来的品质、信誉度和创新第一的价值观。这些信念始终保持不变并且像品牌身份一样重要，那就是不断追求创造更多人们喜爱的英伦经典。

读书笔记

7.（法国）皮尔卡丹 Pierre Cardin

品牌名片

品　　类：服装、皮具

标志风格：大胆、时尚

创 始 人：皮尔·卡丹（Pierre Cardin）

诞 生 地：法国

诞生时间：1950年

源于法国的皮尔·卡丹，推崇高贵、典雅、简洁、大方的产品风格，是身份地位的象征。

品牌阅读

Pierre Cardin's story has the makings of a legend. He rose from **humble** beginnings to reach the top of the fashion world, not forgetting that along the way he is accredited with breaking open the exclusivity of the haute couture milieu and bringing fashion to the masses. For many people, Pierre Cardin's legendary status comes from his dual success as an haute couture designer and the magnate of a huge fashion empire straddling the globe. Over the last few years he can ascribe his successes to his social actions: he has been able to achieve a considerable amount of work where official diplomatic efforts have failed. In this way he has contributed to the promotion of mutual understanding and harmony among peoples. He is considered a long standing friend by the Chinese people. For 30 years, his characteristic passion and strength have helped to build a bridge between the two great continents of Europe and Asia. Let us now look back together over the legendary life of Pierre Cardin.

Mr. Cardin was born on July 2nd, 1922 in Venice, Italy. Could the romanticism of southern Europe or his birth in the city of water have fostered his artistic talents? At the age of two, he moved with his family to Vichy in France. On leaving school he went to work in a company as an accountant and this financial grounding would stand him in good stead in his business dealings throughout his career. His family was forced to move out of Paris when Second World War bombings reached his family's courtyard. At the age of 22, nurturing great ambitions for his future but with little capital, he moved to Paris-the heart of Europe. If you have talent Paris can be your launch pad: a great capital with a rich history of heroes, politicians, officers, business men and artists. Paris can also be harsh city though, its doors can open to let in the successful but many others are kept outside. It is not difficult therefore, to imagine how difficult it would be for a young entrepreneur to go about setting up his own business.

Pierre Cardin's first job involved making the costumes and masks for the film "Beauty and the Beast". The glittering fashion world in the **haute** couture capital rapidly seduced him and his ambition to make a name for himself in this milieu was born.Soon he got work as an apprentice in the newly created Christian Dior fashion house. He started as a tailor and gained experience working his way around each department before mastering the necessary design skills. In 1950 he finally sets up his own **eponymous** fashion house. He presented his first collection in 1953, the date which marked the official start of his career as a designer. Twenty years of hard work followed and Pierre Cardin fulfilled his entrepreneurial dream: he became a world famous designer. His success was marked by the French Haute Couture world when he was awarded three times the "Dé d'Or". One nomination for

the award is the haute couturier's dream, but to receive it three times is unheard of and remains to this day unsurpassed. In 1992, Pierre Cardin confirmed his position at the top of the haute couture world by taking his place among the elite of the Académie Française. Nowadays the Pierre Cardin label is well known; but what is also remarkable is the designer's success as a business man. In the French fashion world, and to a certain extent, the western fashion world, there are three categories. At the top of this golden triangle is the Haute Couture world. Each year in Paris, Milan and New York the collections from the best couturiers are presented to the world, each more luxurious and extravagant than the next. The shows and their designers are the darlings of the media, who come from all other the world to cover the events. However, these clothes carry exorbitant price tags and are certainly not within the reach of ordinary people who mostly wear off the peg clothes. Mass production may have eased the price but the design value also suffers. Pierre Cardin set a new precedent by bringing haute couture off its sacred pedal stool, becoming the first fashion designer to "mass produce" haute couture. The repercussions are huge: firstly it made haute couture more accessible, moving it out of the exclusive domain of the upper classes. It brought the latest techniques of the fashion world within reach of the middle classes or even ordinary people. Secondly it launched the prêt-à-porter industry opening up a vast market. With hindsight this move seems quite logical, but at the time it was considered sacrilegious and was very badly received by the haute couture world. It even led to Pierre Cardin being expelled by the Chambre Syndicale, the monitoring body of haute couture in Paris. However, several decades later most of the major design brands have followed suit and now produce a prêt-à-porter line, proving that his decision at the time was a sound one. The head start that Pierre Cardin gained with this courageous step had, in the meantime, allowed his brand to secure huge market share all over the world. According to statistics "Pierre Cardin" is one of the highest selling brands in the world. Being the first on a market gives a company a commercial edge and this is precisely what Pierre Cardin proved again by this pioneering move, not to mention securing handsome profits for his company. Today, the Pierre Cardin fashion empire comprises 400 brand franchise contracts throughout the world, manufacturing and sales centers in more than 130 countries and a staff numbering 200,000. What must be noted is that these accomplishments result from Pierre Cardin's personal decisions, carried out under his supervision. He is the owner of this vast commercial machine. The portfolio of companies and brands that make up the group are firmly under the control of Pierre Cardin, which coupled with his design talents, makc him an unusual figure in today's business world.

Success in his profession and in the business world have never been enough for Pierre Cardin, and he has always striven to promote cultural relations through numerous social actions, to cnhancc cross cultural exchange and to help people work and live together without strife. With this in mind, in 1957, he undertook a trip to Japan, a country at that time just emerging from the war. This would be the first of over 30 visits to Japan where he was held in respectful admiration. From the 80s onwards, Mr. Cardin travelled to the ex USSR and even organized a fashion show on Red Square in Moscow. He has also travelled to Vietnam, Cuba and Libya, countries still closed to the world, to carry out diplomatic missions that could not be carried out by those in official positions. This led to Pierre Cardin being

named as an Honorary Ambassador to UNESCO in February 1992, responsible for the Chernobyl nuclear accident in the ex USSR and for the promotion of tolerance. The notion of tolerance can be defined as people from different backgrounds not discriminating based on race, wealth, education, gender, culture or religion, but living together in mutual respect and equality with a common agenda. Pierre Cardin designed the 6 colored tolerance flag which was hoisted in regions such as the Middle East, to inspire tolerance in people's hearts. For warring nations any sign of peace is extremely precious. Pierre Cardin has also been a patron of the arts. In 1970 he opened the Cardin Cultural Centre, just a short walk from the Élysée Palace, to create a platform to help launch young promising artists. To date such artists as the great Russian ballerina Maya Plisetskaya, the Canadian singer Céline Dion, the Vietnamese painter Daniel Jègoû or even the Chinese painter Deng Lin have all benefited from Pierre Cardin's support. At the end of 2000, a season of Chinese culture was presented through paintings. Pierre Cardin has also held the position of Secretary General of Mediterranean States Committee; has raised funds through auction to restore the Great Wall in China and to preserve Venice from rising waters; he has just recently created an international federation to oversee the restoration of the Alexandria lighthouse in Egypt. In short, although Pierre Cardin expends a huge amount of energy in his **philanthropic** work, he finds it enormously rewarding.

humble ['hʌmbl] adj.（级别或地位）低下的

haute [əut] adj. 高级的，豪华的

eponymous [ɪ'pɒnɪməs] adj. 以本名命名的

philanthropic [,filən'θrɔpik] adj. 博爱的；仁慈的

皮尔·卡丹先生绝对是一个传奇人物。他的传奇首先在于他的奋斗历程——从赤手空拳几乎一无所有到世界顶级服装设计大师；他的传奇还在于让高档时装走下高贵的T型台，让服装艺术直接服务于老百姓；集服装设计大师与商业巨头于 一身，卡丹的商业帝国遍布世界各地；他近年来的成就在于他的社会活动，他完成了许多职业外交家所无法完成的功绩，为世界各国人民的相互了解和和解做出了巨大的贡献；最后，对于中国人民来说，他又是一个久经考验的老朋友，三十多年来他以非凡的热情和充沛的精力在欧亚大陆之间架起了友谊的桥梁。让我们再来回顾一下卡丹先生的传奇一生吧。

卡丹先生于1922年7月2日出生于意大利的威尼斯，也许是南欧国家的浪漫和水城的风情为卡丹先生奠定了艺术家的基础。在他2岁的时候，他就随着家庭迁居到法国的维希市。从学校毕业后，就到一家公司任会计，在此期间掌握的知识使卡丹先生至今仍然受益。第二次世界大战的战火炸毁了卡丹先生的家园，一家人奔走他乡。年仅22岁的卡丹两手空空，但怀着干成一番大事业的雄心壮志，独自一个人来到了欧洲的中心——巴黎。巴黎这个具有悠久历史的大都市是友善的：她曾造就了无数的英雄，从政治家、军事家到商人和艺术家，只要你有才华，她就会给你施展的舞台。巴黎又是冷漠的，在为成功者开启大门的同时，又把平庸之辈拒之门外。一个初出茅庐的年轻人创业的艰难是可想而知的。

卡丹先生最早的工作是为电影“美女和野兽”制作布景和服装。他一下子就被服装之都的华美服装所吸引，立志要在服装行业有所作为。后来在刚刚开业的迪奥公司当学徒，从裁缝开始，掌握了服装设计、制作全过程的各项技术。1950年，卡丹先生终于创建了以自己的名字命名的服装公司，1953年他推出了第一台时装秀，正式开始了服装设计师的生涯。经过近20年的不懈努力，卡丹先生终于实现了自己创业的梦想：当一个世界级的服装设计师。他的成就得到了公认：卡丹先生曾三次获得法国服装设计的最高奖赏——

金顶针奖。这个奖项能得到一次提名已是设计师的最高成就，三次获得的更是凤毛麟角，直到今天，还没有人能超过卡丹先生。1992年，卡丹先生作为唯一的服装设计师入选精英荟萃的法兰西学院，从而奠定了卡丹先生作为世界顶级服装设计大师的地位。现在卡丹先生的服装设计已经广为人知，其实同样可贵的是他的商业成就。法国的时装，或者从广义上说西方的时装分为三个档次。在金字塔顶端的高档定制时装（La Haute Couture）。每年在巴黎、米兰和纽约展出顶级设计师的作品，豪华之至，代表了世界最高水平，因而是世界各国媒体争相报道的对象。美中不足的是这些服装开出的都是天价，绝对不是一般人能够享受的。而普通人穿的一般是成衣，即由工厂大批量生产的系列服装，成本虽然降下来了，但是艺术性却难以得到保证。卡丹先生开创先河，让高档时装走下神圣的T型台，成为第一个批量生产高档时装的设计师。此举具有非常重大的意义：一方面，它把从来只属于上流社会的高档时装“大众化”了，使中产阶级甚至平民百姓也可以享受时装的最新技术；另一方面，它给成衣制造业注入了巨大的活力，开阔了广大的市场。这个具有划时代意义的革命性创意在今天看来是理所当然的，而在当时，却被视为异端邪说，为当时的高档时装界所不容。卡丹先生因此还被开除出法国男装协会。可是时间和实践是最好的评判。数十年后，世界各大时装品牌几乎都走上了卡丹先生开创的道路：批量生产成衣。所不同的是，卡丹先生已经利用他的勇敢得到了“先机”，带有“皮尔·卡丹”商标的产品占领了世界市场。根据统计，“皮尔·卡丹”是世界上销售最多的商标之一。在商场上，“先机”往往意味着“商机”。卡丹先生以他的远见卓识再一次证实了这一点，他也从中得到了巨大的经济回报。今天，皮尔卡丹的商业帝国在全世界拥有400多个商标特许合同，在130多个国家生产和销售，直接从业人员达到20万人。特别需要指出的是，所有这些成就都是在卡丹先生的直接策划和指挥下取得的，他是这部巨大商业机器唯一的老板。在当今世界上，卡丹先生是集服装设计师和品牌、公司的百分之百所有权于一身的人，可以说是绝无仅有。

卡丹先生不满足于他在专业和商业领域所取得的成就，一直致力于通过各种社会活动增进各国人民的文化交流、建立友谊，从而减少战争，达到各国人民、各种文化和平共处、互相借鉴、共同发展的目的。为此，卡丹先生从1957年开始，就连续造访刚刚走出战争阴影的日本，至今他已访问过日本三十多次，深深受到日本人民的爱戴。卡丹先生自80年代以来多次访问苏联，并在莫斯科红场上举行卡丹服装表演。他还到访过越南、古巴、利比亚等尚未完全对外的国家，作为民间外交家，发挥了职业外交家无法企及的作用。因此，联合国教科文组织在1992年2月聘任卡丹先生为名誉大使，负责苏联切尔诺贝利核电站事故和促进相互包容。所谓包容是指各国人民不分种族、财富、教育、性别、文化、宗教等差异，互相容忍，平等相处，共同发展。卡丹先生亲自设计了六色包容旗帜，并在中东等地升起，以呼吁人民具有包容精神。对于处在战火中的人民，任何和平的信息都是十分宝贵的。卡丹先生还非常热衷于赞助艺术，1970年他在法国总统府隔壁开办了卡丹文化中心，为年轻有为的艺术家提供登台的场所。例如俄罗斯芭蕾舞艺术大师玛亚·普丽谢采斯卡亚、加拿大籍歌星席琳·迪翁、越南画家丹尼尔·尤、中国画家邓林等，都得到卡丹先生的帮助。2000年底，中国文化季系列活动也在那里举办了画展。卡丹先生还兼任了环地中海国家理事会秘书长的职务，并发起了拯救威尼斯和长城的拍卖活动，另外他组织国际力量重修了埃及亚历山大灯塔。总之，各种社会活动占去了卡丹先生的很大一部分精力，他亦乐此不疲。

Part 4 珠宝首饰

1.（法国）宝诗龙 Boucheron

品牌名片

品　　类：珠宝、腕表、香水

标志风格：尊贵、雅致

创 始 人：费德列克・宝诗龙（Frederic Boucheron）

诞 生 地：法国

诞生时间：1858年

宝诗龙是法国著名珠宝品牌。产品包括珠宝首饰、腕表和香水，是大胆奢华的现代珠宝首饰的代名词。

品牌阅读

With the Maison Boucheron's 150 years of history and heritage comes the duty to promote its legacy and respect its **savoir-faire** in order to pass them on to new generations. The Maison is a frontrunner of style, inventing a number of techniques such as the mirror setting or mosaic setting and holds many jewelry patents, like the invisible clasp system. For Bouchcron, it is fundamental to welcome its clients in a warm and personalized atmosphere. By keeping its development on a human scale and carefully selecting its number of boutiques, the Maison gives priority to a high level of service and never compromises on the quality of its creations.

Boucheron is first and foremost a signature style and aesthetic which is immediately recognizable. The Boucheron family is renowned for having anticipated the neo-gothic style of the end of the 19th century, enhanced the naturalistic style and created some of the Art Deco period's masterpieces. Today, more than ever, creativity is

essential to the Maison and triumphs over a paradox by combining 150 years of history and savoir-faire with ultra-contemporary creations.

In 1858, Frederic Boucheron opened his first boutique in the Galerie de Valois under the arcades of the Palais Royal which at that time was the center of the Parisian luxury trade.

In 1866, the Maison Boucheron created its workshop. In 1867, Frederic Boucheron is awarded the gold medal for the innovative spirit of his jewelry at the Universal Exhibition in Paris.

In 1887, the diamonds of the French crown were auctioned off. Frederic Boucheron was the only French buyer. This sale would give rise to the creation of numerous jewels inspired by the crown jewels. On the occasion of the Universal Exhibition in Paris in 1889, Boucheron presented its first point d'interrogation necklace. This style of necklace has remained a key element within the Maison Boucheron ever since.

In 1893, the Maison Boucheron opened its doors at 26 Place Vendôme and installed its workshop. Frederic Boucheron was the first jeweler to settle on the square. He shared the premises with the Countess of Castiglione who lived on the **mezzanine**.

In 1900, at the Universal Exhibition in Paris, The Maison Boucheron received the gold medal and was established as one of the forerunners of the Art Nouveau movement. In 1921, the Maison Boucheron created an exceptional diadem that would become one of the Queen Mother Elizabeth's favorites.

Launch of the first Reflet watch was in 1947.

In 1988, the Maison Boucheron celebrated its 130th anniversary with a major retrospective at the Jacquemard André Museum and launched its first fragrance.

The Ava collection in homage of the **eternal** grace of Ava Gardner was launched in 2003.

In 2012, it participated in the Biennale des Antiquaires at the Grand Palais in Paris.

The Maison Boucheron gives its clients the certainty of acquiring the most beautiful gemstones, of the best quality, cut and origin. In order to secure the exclusivity of the rarest and most desirable stones, the Maison has always nurtured close ties with the most exceptional mines. The ability to find the most **extraordinary** stones is at the heart of the Maison's identity.

A Maison Boucheron creation is the result of such savoir-faire and quest for perfection that it takes on a life on its own. In this way, when a woman chooses a creation of the Maison, she sets the spark for a link with that creation which is strong and unique. It is the beginning of a story to be written over the years and for generations to come, thanks to the moments of emotion and happiness which these exceptional pieces will witness. A Boucheron creation tells a story, that of the Maison and your own.

savoir-faire [sɑː'vwɑː'fɛə] n. 机智，机敏；处世的手段

mezzanine ['mezəniːn] n. 中层楼；夹楼

eternal [i'təːnəl] adj. 永恒的；不朽的

extraordinary [ik'strɔːdənəri] adj. 非凡的；特别的

拥有超过150年历史的宝诗龙品牌致力于保护传统工艺，将宝贵技艺世代传承并发扬光大。作为业内风格之先驱，宝诗龙发明了镜面镶嵌和马赛克镶嵌等多项技术，并提交了隐藏式表扣等多项专利。对于宝诗龙来说，在一个温馨而友好的氛围中接待顾客至关重要。宝诗龙注重维持工作人员数量，并对专卖店的开设数量进行适当限制，以

此向顾客提供优质服务，并在质量上严格要求，永不妥协。

宝诗龙，首先是一种风格，一种令人过目不忘的美学体现。工坊因参与19世纪末的哥特复兴风潮、倡导自然主义格调并创造精美绝伦的装饰艺术杰作而备受赞誉。宝诗龙如今更加明确，创造力乃是品牌之根本，正是这种卓越的创造力带领品牌走出了困惑，将宝诗龙150余年的历史、工艺与极具现代风范的作品完美结合，不断创造辉煌。

1858年，费德里克·宝诗龙在当时巴黎奢华时尚的中心——巴黎皇宫（Palais Royal）的法洛廊（Galerie de Valois）开设了第一家精品店。

1866年，宝诗龙开设品牌工坊。1867年，费德里克·宝诗龙凭借其珠宝制作的创新精神在巴黎世博会获得金质奖章。

1887年，法国王冠上的钻石拍卖。费德里克·宝诗龙是唯一拍得钻石的法国买家，之后以这些王冠瑰宝为灵感源泉创作出众多珠宝作品。1889年，在巴黎世博会上，宝诗龙展出了第一款“问号”项链。这种造型的项链从此成为品牌的经典设计。

1893年，宝诗龙入驻旺多姆广场26号，并将工坊也迁至此地。费德里克·宝诗龙成为在此投资的第一位珠宝商，与租下中二楼的卡斯蒂丽欧（Castiglione）伯爵夫人比邻而居。

1900年，在巴黎世博会上，宝诗龙品牌荣获金质奖章并成为新艺术的重要一员。1921年宝诗龙制作了一顶精美冠冕，后成为伊丽莎白皇太后（Elizabeth）的珍爱之物。

1947年，推出首款Reflet腕表。

1988年，宝诗龙于130周年庆典之际在雅克马尔·安德烈博物馆举办大型回顾展，并推出首款香水。

2003年，推出Ava系列作品，向不朽的优雅女神艾娃·加德纳（Ava Gardner）致敬。

2012年，参加在巴黎大皇宫举行的第二十六届古董双年展。

宝诗龙为顾客提供华美珍贵宝石、高品质切割和来源上的保障。为了确保得到最珍贵、最令人渴求的宝石专营权，品牌一贯与优质矿场建立持久的关系。品牌的核心竞争力正是拥有找寻最出众宝石的能力。

宝诗龙品牌的杰作是精湛工艺与追求极致的结晶，它如同拥有自己的生命。因而，当一位女性购买了一件宝诗龙珠宝，便与它产生了一种特殊的关联。从此，每一个生活的片段和幸福的时刻将与这些珍贵的珠宝一起，代代相传，书写一段不断充盈的历史。宝诗龙的作品是历史的诉说者，讲述着品牌与顾客的故事。

读书笔记

2.（意大利）宝格丽 Bvlgari

品牌名片

品　　类：珠宝、腕表、皮具、香水

标志风格：大胆独特、尊贵古典

创 始 人：索蒂里欧·宝格丽（Sotirio Bulgari）

诞 生 地：意大利

诞生时间：1884年

意大利宝格丽是继法国卡地亚和美国蒂芙尼之后的世界第三大珠宝品牌。以色彩为设计精髓，独创性地运用不同颜色的宝石进行搭配组合。

品牌阅读

Based in Rome, since 1884 Bulgari has been creating renowned fine jewellery. Today it is a global and diversified luxury brand with a product and services portfolio of jewels, watches, accessories, fragrances, skincare, hotels and resorts featuring exceptional quality, an innovative style and impeccable service.

Sotirio Bulgari, founder of the firm, was a skilled Greek silversmith originally from Epirus, region in the north west of Greece. After his arrival in Rome in 1881, he opened a number of silver and antique shops in just a few years. Only after 1910 did he begin, with his sons Giorgio and Costantino, to devote himself to jewels with precious stones, proving to be a successful jeweler whose production, however, would be influenced for many years by the Parisian style. His sons took over the management of the firm in 1932.

The silver artefacts created by Sotirio or by his father Georgis during the last quarter of the 19th century were in "Neo-Hellenic" style in their shapes and materials. Some of the older objects were produced in Epirus.

The jewels of the early 20s, inspired by the Art Deco style whose geometric design or stylized naturalistic motifs they adopted, are characterized by platinum mounts, a material that had only recently come into use in jewellery. There are no known examples of the previous production inasmuch as it was not **customary** to sign creations at that time and the lack of written documentation and of an original style makes any attribution difficult.

The jewels of the 30s are distinctive for their more imposing dimensions and marked geometric motifs in diamonds of different cuts or diamonds combined with a colored gemstone, such as a sapphire or ruby. Also fashionable during these years was the convertible jewel: necklaces may be divided, making it possible to wear the different elements separately as bracelets, clips, or brooches.

During the 40s, a radical change took place in the creation of jewellery: no longer in platinum encrusted with diamonds, but in gold with a parsimonious use of precious gemstones. These factors were determined above all by the restrictions caused by the Second World War. The rigid geometric design became softer and more naturalistic.

The post-war economic boom led to a return to jewels mounted in precious white metal and profusely covered with precious gemstones, in particular diamonds which, as in the 30s, reigned supreme as the most fashionable stones. High jewellery was still of a Parisian stamp, but with more sinuous motifs and softer lines than those of the pre-war period. The fifties, the years of Cinectta, *Roman Holiday* and *La Dolce vita*, of illustrated magazines, television

and **paparazzi**, were also years in which the Via Condotti 10 shop enjoyed great success, as can be seen from the numerous photographs of celebrities going into or coming out of Bvlgari. Famous stars like Gina Lollobrigida, Sophia Loren or Ingrid Bergman appeared at many public events sparkling with their Bvlgari jewels. At the end of the 50s, Bvlgari's preference for smooth outlines rather than the spiky ones that were fashionable in that period became clear, as well as its more insistent use of important cabochon cut gemstones (polished but not facetted), both distinguishing features of the nascent Bvlgari Style.

At the end of 50s, Bulgari design began to differentiate from that of Paris, as it created its own distinctive style. There was a departure not only from flowery asymmetrical motifs towards more structured, symmetrical and compact shapes that were almost always in yellow gold, but also from the conventional triad of colors composed of emeralds, rubies and sapphires that were combined exclusively with diamonds. In the following decades, Bvlgari developed a highly personal aesthetic of color as it opened up to unusual new combinations. At first, these were "simple" using **sapphires** in particular, but it later became much bolder as all kinds of gemstones came to be employed.

The third Bulgari generation took over the running of the firm in the 70s and the young input was soon evident in the creative exuberance of that period. Those were years of experimentation, provocation and hope, and in some way this is to be found in the great variety of motifs in the Bvlgari designs. These range from the elegant ones inspired by fireworks to those of oriental inspiration or even of optical or pop art, then arrive at the Stars and Stripes jewels.

One already notes a predilection for yellow gold in the creations of these years independently of the value of the **gemstones** employed. In so doing, Bvlgari allowed every jewel, even the richest, to be born in a more informal manner; traditionally, yellow gold was destined for daytime jewels while **platinum** and white gold were meant for the more important jewels of the evening. During the 70s, shops were opened in New York, Geneva, Montecarlo and Paris.

In serial production, an aspiration of the goldsmiths of antiquity as different objects of the Hellenistic age demonstrate, Bvlgari achieved extraordinary success with Parentesi (1982). During the 80s, the first modular line of high jewellery became an icon whose design continued to be amongst those that were most imitated.

“You can’t simply live on past glories: that’s foolish. To be a success, you have to combine the worlds of the past, present and the future. That is the challenge, and there are many horizons.” Nicola Bulgari stated in 1995.

customary ['kʌstə,məri] adj. 习惯的；通常的
paparazzi [,pɑ:pə'rɑ:tsi:] n. 狗仔队
sapphire ['sæfaiə] n. 蓝宝石
gemstone ['dʒemstəʊn] n. （经雕琢的）宝石
platinum ['plætinəm] n. 铂金

宝格丽创立于 1884 年，总部设在意大利首都罗马。100 多年来，它创造了无数名闻遐迩的顶级珠宝。时至今日已成为全球知名的奢侈品品牌。产品与服务包括珠宝、腕表、配饰、香水、护肤品、酒店和度假村，品牌以卓越的品质、新颖的造型和优质的服务著称。

宝格丽公司创始人索蒂里欧·宝格丽出生于希腊西北部伊庇鲁

斯地区的一个银匠世家。1881年，索蒂里欧移居意大利罗马。几年的时间内，他开创了许多银器和古董店。直到1910年后，他才开始和两个儿子柯斯坦提诺与乔吉奥共同制作镶嵌珍贵宝石的珠宝首饰，并且在很长时间内深受法国学院派风格影响。1932年，他的儿子完全接管了家族事业。

19世纪晚期，索蒂里欧或其父亲乔吉斯制作的银质工艺品无论在外形上，还是在材质上，都带有明显的新希腊风格。一些早期的工艺品是在伊庇鲁斯制作的。

20世纪20年代早期，装饰艺术盛行，几何设计或别具一格的自然图案备受推崇。受此影响，珠宝制作开始采用当时刚刚兴起的铂金材质。没有此类珍贵作品的实例，因为当时还未盛行在珠宝上留下印记。由于没有书面记载或原物，因此无从探究先前的制作经历。

20世纪30年代，珠宝首饰的尺寸和选材都有了更高的要求。以色彩为设计精髓，独创性地运用多种不同颜色的宝石进行搭配组合，如蓝宝石或红宝石。当时比较时尚的是可拆分珠宝，比如项链可以拆分成单独的手镯、夹子或胸针。

20世纪40年代，珠宝的制作发生了根本的改变。镶嵌钻石的铂金被镶嵌五彩宝石的黄金所取代。这些因素受到了“二战”的影响。几何设计变得更加流畅、自然。

战后经济复苏，珠宝再度盛行，珍贵的白金及珍贵宝石广泛运用于珠宝设计中，尤其是30年代占据统治地位的最时尚的宝石——钻石。顶级珠宝仍带有法国学院派风格，但与战前相比，图案更鲜明，线条也更柔软。50年代，电影《罗马假日》和《甜蜜生活》，画刊、电视、狗仔队风靡世界。与此同时Via Condotti 10号店取得了巨大的成功，这从无数名人进出店铺的照片中便可以看出。诸多明星，像Gina Lollobrigida, Sophia Loren 或Ingrid Bergman，都曾佩戴宝格丽珠宝出席各大公共活动。50年代末，宝格丽更加追求浑圆柔和的线条，开始研究蛋面切割法以代替多刻面切割宝石，树立了独特的宝格丽初期风格。

50年代末，宝格丽设计开始摆脱巴黎式风格，创建自己的独特风格。从过去的非对称花式图案转变为强调紧凑对称外形，但是同样以黄金材质为主；从传统的绿宝石、红宝石和蓝宝石（三色系）与珍贵的钻石搭配。在接下来的数十年里，宝格丽选用极具品牌个性的颜色搭配，带给人们全新的视觉体验。起初，主要使用蓝宝石，后来由于各种宝石的灵活应用而变得更加醒目。

20世纪70年代，宝格丽家族第三代传人接管了公司业务，为宝格丽品牌注入了创新活力。他们将宝格丽家族的制造传统与新的技术和理念完美结合，这从宝格丽的大量设计图案便可看出。有些优雅设计是受到了烟花的灵感激发，有些则是从东方元素中寻找灵感，还有些灵感源自光学艺术或流行艺术，星条旗图案珠宝便是代表之一。然而无论搭配何种价值的宝石，黄金仍然是贯穿始终的主题。通过黄金的运用，宝格丽的任何一件珠宝，即便是价格昂贵的珠宝，都可以在非正式场合佩戴；传统观念中，黄金适合白天佩戴，而铂金和白金则适合晚上佩戴。70年代，宝格丽陆续在纽约、日内瓦、蒙地卡罗和巴黎开设了分店。

在接下来的设计中，宝格丽深受罗马金匠学派和希腊主义的影响，并于1982年成功地推出了Parentesi系列。80年代，第一个模块化顶级珠宝系列诞生并成为时代标志，其设计一直被广泛模仿。

“你不能总沉浸在过去的荣耀中，这是很不明智的行为。要想获得成功，你必须反思过去、立足现在、展望未来。这不仅是一个严峻挑战，更是对所有人能力的重大考验。”这是Nicola Bulgari于1995年说过的一段话。

3.（法国）尚美 Chaumet

品牌名片

品　　类：珠宝、腕表

标志风格：自然、精致

创 始 人：马里 · 艾蒂安 · 尼托（Marie Etienne Nitot）

诞 生 地：法国

诞生时间：1780年

尚美是法国LVMH集团旗下品牌，跨越两个世纪依然展现璀璨光芒。

品牌阅读

The history of Chaumet dates back to 1780 and is closely interwoven with the history of France. Over five centuries, Paris has been celebrated for the magnificence of its jewelers. It was in this tradition that the founder of Chaumet, Marie Etienne Nitot, distinguished himself in the late 18th century.

The wedding of Napoleon and Josephine de Beauharnais, and later with the Archiduchesse Marie-Louise de Habsbourg-Lorraine, niece of Queen Marie-Antoinette, brought Chaumet numerous sumptuous orders. Nitot became the most famous jeweler in Europe and built up a loyal and prestigious clientele.

After the fall of the Empire, Nitot's successors devoted themselves to Romantic jewelry inspired by the decorative arts of the Italian Renaissance and of 17th century France. All the appeal and expertise of the firm also attracted a clientele composed of painters, sculptors, writers and theater actors.

By 1853, Paris had regained its place as the center of the world for luxury and fashion. A propitious atmosphere reigned for the creation of jewelry to be worn **by day and by night** with sumptuous evening dresses.

With steamships offering a faster mode of travel, Indian princes developed a taste for the pleasures of Europe. They were great collectors of jewelry and brought their pieces set with gemstones to the Place Vendome to have them re-set in light, supple platinum settings. The most magnificent stones were primarily reserved for men, as indicated in the famous pair of pear-cut diamonds Chaumet purchased in 1911 for the **maharaja** of Indore.

Chaumet created simplified designs contained within rigid geometric outlines compatible with the boyish looks of the 1920s and the more feminine silhouette of the 1930s. This style called Art Deco from the Exposition des Arts Decoratifs held in Paris in 1925, is characterized by strong contrasts of materials, colors and the cuts of the precious and semi-precious stones used.

After the 30s, responding to the continuous social, economic and artistic changes, Chaumet has maintained its legendary reputation. Design is determined by the good taste of the contemporary Parisienne always in search of something new, different and gorgeous. Easy to wear, gold jewelry appears in a concept store.

This knowledge has continuously been passed down since two centuries, through every “chef d'atelier”. The Chaumet workshop located 12, place Vendome, bears witness to this expertise.

In 2013, French actresses decided to wear Chaumet jewellery and illuminated the 66th edition of Cannes International Film Festival, adorned with parures from the house: Audrey Tautou, host of the

Opening & Closing Ceremony; Bérénice Bejo, awarded with the title of Best Actress for Le Passé (The Past), directed by Asghar Farhadi; Ludivine Sagnier, member of the Jury for *Un Certain Regard*; Laetitia Casta, while she handed over the Best Actor award; Alma Jodorowsky, actress from the Palme d'Or movie La Vie d'Adèle, directed by Abdellatif Kechiche.

by day and by night 日日夜夜

maharaja [ˌmɑː(h)əˈrɑːdʒə] *n.*（印度的）王公

尚美，创始于1780年，与法国的历史密不可分。5个世纪以来，巴黎始终以手工珠宝杰作而闻名。创始人马里·艾蒂安·尼托于18世纪末开始崭露头角。

拿破仑一世及其两任皇后：约瑟芬·德博阿尔内与玛莉安东尼皇后的侄女玛莉露易丝·阿斯部洛林，为 Chaumet 带来了可观的珠宝订单。从此，尼托（Nitot）成为了全欧洲最知名的珠宝商，也同时赢得了许多忠实的顶级珠宝客户的青睐。

帝国结束后，尼托的继承者延续其灵感来源于意大利文艺复兴运动和法国 17 世纪装饰艺术的浪漫主义珠宝风格。尚美作品独有的文化和精湛的工艺吸引了大批文艺界的忠实顾客：画家、雕塑家、作家和明星。

从 1853 年起，巴黎重新变成五彩不夜城，成为国际奢侈品和时尚的高地。当时的环境十分有利于珠宝的创作，为美丽的舞裙锦上添花。

蒸汽轮船加速旅行的进程，印度王子漂洋过海来到欧洲游玩。他们是珠宝收藏大家，把自家的宝石带到芳登广场，让珠宝师们在上面添加铂金框架。最美丽的宝石通常是由男人带走的——比如 1911 年，尚美就为印度王子特制了一对梨形钻石。

20世纪20年代的尚美作品，设计充满了简约的造型，以符合当时的“中性风”，直到30年代才再次转化为比较女性化的风格。这种风格称为装饰艺术，于1925年巴黎世界博览会上达到了顶峰，其凸显材质色彩及宝石和半宝石切割工艺的强烈对比。

30年代后，尚美在延续其传统风格之余，为作品再添现代化的一笔，充满巴黎高雅情趣，且一直持续寻找新鲜创意。尚美最新推出黄金系列珠宝，容易搭配，与时俱进。

位于芳登广场 12 号的尚美高级珠宝工作坊，自1780 年开始便不断将独家技艺代代相传，守卫着尚美的百年历史传承。

2013年，多位法国女演员均佩戴尚美的珠宝出席第66届戛纳国际电影节。柯德莉塔图（Audrey Tautou）担任电影节的开幕及闭幕礼主持。Bérénice Bejo 凭*Le Passé* 荣获本年度康城最佳女主角大奖。Ludivine Sagnier 担任电影《一种关注》（*Un Certain Regard*）的评审团成员之一。Laetitia Casta 担任最佳男主角的颁奖嘉宾。Alma Jodorowsky 为Abdellatif Kechiche 执导的金棕榈电影La Vie d'Adèle 担任女主角。

读书笔记

4.（英国）杰拉德 Garrard

品牌名片

品　　类：珠宝、腕表

标志风格：尊贵、大气

创 始 人：罗伯特·杰拉德（Robert Garrard）

诞 生 地：英国

诞生时间：1735年

杰拉德品牌标志由王冠及其名称组成，体现了杰拉德与王室贵族的密切联系及其举足轻重的地位。

品牌阅读

Gerrard was born in 1735 and has been given the good reputation "Crown Jeweller " by queen Victoria. It has ever designed coronation crowns for the royal family for many times, which shows its importance. In recent years, Gerrard has successfully marched into the youth market.

The 19th century continued with a succession of famous commissions for Royalty and the aristocracy, with designs of splendor, opulence and craftsmanship. Many commissions can be found in museums, national institutions and important private collections around the world. Since 1843, when Queen Victoria bestowed the honour of Crown Jeweller on the company, Garrard has served six successive monarchs. One of the most enduring images of Queen Victoria is of her wearing a small diamond crown made by Garrard in 1870.

Ceremony and pageantry has always been a key element in the

company's heritage as well as the association with great sporting events. Spectacular trophies and centrepieces display excellent examples of superb silver craftsmanship. Robert Garrard's hallmark of 1848 is found on the well-known America's Cup. For modern day sports enthusiasts, other presentation trophies include: the Dubai World Cup, the Cricket World Cup and the Premier League Trophy.

In recent years, Jade Jagger takes up the post of creative director in Garrard, successfully into the youth market. At the same time, it opens up many other markets, such as clock silverware, furniture and accessories which makes the products more diversified.

杰拉德珠宝品牌成立于1735年，曾被维多利亚女王颁赐Crown Jeweller（王冠珠宝商）的美誉，而且多次为王室人员设计加冕王冠，地位举足轻重。近年来，杰拉德珠宝成功打入年轻人市场。

19世纪时仍延续着王室和贵族委托制作的风格，设计美艳、奢华，技艺精湛。其中很多作品都能够在世界各地的博物馆、国家机构及个人珍藏中找到。自1843年维多利亚女王授予公司王冠珠宝商的荣誉开始，杰拉德已连续为六代君主效力。其中维多利亚女王佩戴时间最长的小钻石王冠就是1870年杰拉德为她制作的。

仪式和盛典一直是公司历史上的重要元素，也包括盛大的体育赛事。精美的奖杯与中心装饰是展示其精湛银工艺的绝好例子。1848年，罗伯特·杰拉德最好的证明就在著名的美洲杯上。对于现代体育爱好者来说，其他展示还包括Dubai World Cup, the Cricket World Cup, the Premier League Trophy。

近年来，杰拉德请来设计师Jade Jagger出任创作总监，成功打入年轻人市场。同时开拓了钟表、银器、家具及配饰等市场，令产品更加多元化。

5.（意大利）玳美雅 Damiani

品牌名片

品　　类：珠宝、腕表

标志风格：华丽、优雅

创 始 人：恩里科·格拉西·达米阿尼（Enrico Grassi Damiani）

诞 生 地：意大利

诞生时间：1924年

玳美雅珠宝所表现的传统代表了一种独一无二的遗产，由激情和对细节关注所筑成，引以为豪并子孙相传。这是共识的一种哲学，也是珠宝的生命源泉：至今所有产品还是意大利手工制作。

品牌阅读

Design of the highest level, taste and masterly techniques create unmistakably unique jewelry, examples of aesthetic perfection, beauty and harmony. Some are true masterpieces of master goldsmith expertise at the highest level: the Damiani Masterpieces have attained numerous awards and acknowledgements over the years, in particular, the Diamonds International Awards, the World Jewelry Oscars, rewarding the best design and best diamond jewelry creations. Damiani is the only International brand to have won 18, an unequalled record.

Valenza, homeland of the best Italian jewelry tradition: this is where the story of a leading brand of top end Italian made jewelry begins. It was 1924 when Enrico Grassi, founder of the family of jewelers, began designing and creating jewels with diamonds; small masterpieces destined for the noble families of the time, for which he soon became the trusted jeweler. For all the following years, Damiani was acclaimed in the Italian jewelry sector as the highest expression of classicism, balance and preciousness.

Damiano, Enrico's son, continued the family tradition, driven by great creativity and a strong entrepreneurial spirit: he created jewels with an unmistakable style that has remained unaltered over time, made significant investments in research and for the creation of new solutions. Through a perfect combination of tradition and innovation, Damiani products acquired increasing fame in Italy and across the world.

Starting in the 1980s, pioneer in the jewelry sector, the company innovated its communication style introducing highly prestigious testimonials, photographed by the world's greatest photographers.

Faithful to its heritage, the third generation also followed in the family steps with passion, creativity and commitment, expanding the development process that has enabled the shift from family business to organized corporation through the opening over the years of international subsidiaries and boutiques in the world's most famous and prestigious locations.

In 2007, the Group went public and was listed in the Italian stock exchange; today the Damiani brand is leader of the Italian jewelry market sector and is acknowledged worldwide as a synonym of top-end Italian style tradition.

Celebrities like Isabella Rossellini, Brad Pitt, Nastassja Kinski, Chiara Mastroianni, Milla Jovovich, Jennifer Aniston, Gwyneth Paltrow, Sophia Loren and Sharon Stone have collaborated with Damiani, which can claim princesses and prime ministers among its

clients.

Damiani jewelry features the excellent quality acknowledged worldwide and distinguishable for the sublime shapes, the quality of gems, the excellence of craftsmanship and the timeless elegance that it bestows on those wearing these pieces. Each jewel comes to life through the commendable craftsmanship ability and the endless passion of master goldsmiths, enclosing within all the artistic value of the best Italian jewelry tradition.

Over the years the Damiani Group received many prestigious Italian and International acknowledgements and is still the unmatched record holder of 18 Diamonds International Awards, in addition to the four attained with the Calderoni brand, acquired by the Group in 2006. The first Diamonds International Award attributed to a Damiani creation was in 1976, the year in which the award was assigned for the design of the jewel "Bocca di Squalo - Shark Mouth": a bracelet of **inestimable** value in platinum and yellow gold entirely brightened by a pavè of white and jonquille diamonds, designed by Gabriella Damiani.

From 1976, 18 Damiani creations have been awarded for the very high quality and refined craftsmanship and incomparable finish: collier, bracelets, rings and earrings by Damiani with a unique design, stemmed from the passion and high-end jewelry tradition of which Damiani represents one of the highest expressions.

Damiani Jewelry Necklaces

From diamond and gold necklaces to pearl necklaces: prestigious handcrafting and goldsmith excellence

Necklaces are probably the most ancient piece of jewelry:

originally, like all ornaments, they were used during magic rituals and considered capable of keeping malicious influxes at bay. Throughout history necklaces for men and women have acquired increasingly refined shapes, through goldsmith's techniques that varied according to the tastes of every single age. Only after the Renaissance necklaces became an exclusively feminine object, less bulky to better highlight the natural beauty of gems. Therefore, throughout history the good fortune of this jewel has been closely connected with fashion trends, while today necklaces for women and men are particularly cherished ornaments.

Damiani jewelry necklaces for women and men are elegant, modern and precious in the various interpretations and styles,and they are a fundamental piece of the jewelry house's collections. Prestigious craftsmanship, excellent quality materials and exclusive design characterize Damiani jewelry necklaces, made entirely by hand with the utmost attention to detail. And in some cases great masterpieces of goldsmith's art are made through a skillful combination of gold, diamonds, gems and pearls in the incomparable Damiani style. Traditional white, yellow, pink, black, brown and white gold necklaces; luxurious gold and diamonds necklaces; unequalled silver and diamonds necklaces for women; elegant and sophisticated pearl necklaces; refined pendant necklaces; precious gemstone necklaces, luminous spotlight diamond necklaces, modern gold and silver necklaces for men: all Damiani jewelry necklaces, **impeccable** creations of goldsmith mastery, can provide unforgettable emotions and express the personal style of whoever wears them at best.

Damiani Jewelry Rings

From rings with precious gems to solitaire rings: traditional and modern versions of the elegance and excellence of luxury.

In the past rings for men and women had a variety of functions in addition to being purely decorative: they were religious, authority and love symbols. The round shape shows the ring is a symbol of eternity, continuity of life and perfection: this is why the ring has always been seen as the symbolism of everlasting love in the past and today. It seems that even in ancient Rome engagement and wedding rings were used as an auspice of stability.

Damiani jewelry rings for women are fundamental jewelry accessories, with all the variations available in various collections: precious creations and expressions of master craftsmanship, refined elegance, modernity and luxurious excellence. Easily wearable, all Damiani jewelry rings are the result of continuous research focused on combining new styles with perfect accuracy through the highest levels of goldsmith techniques and the gemology expertise of Casa Damiani, acquired in nearly a century of history. Entirely handmade with painstaking care for detail, Damiani rings for women are masterpieces of the goldsmith's art, expressed through a skillful combination of gold, diamonds, precious gems and pearls, with the unmistakably unique style of the Italian jewelry Maison. Traditional rings in white, yellow, pink, black and brown gold; sparkling rings for women with precious gems; everlasting and romantic rings with diamonds; eternal wedding rings; extremely elegant pearl rings; Damiani jewelry rings are a special way of valuing the importance and eternity of an occasion to celebrate, able to fulfill wonderful dreams and give unforgettable emotions.

Damiani Jewelry Bracelets

From classic gold bracelets to the historic tennis bracelet: the preciousness of a world full of jewelry with wonderful surprises.

The root of the word "bracelet" is "brachile" (Latin meaning "braccio", or arm) and in French "barcel". The use of bracelets for men and women goes back to ancient times: for the Romans, a simple round gold bracelet was worn on the left wrist as a sign of military valour. From the Roman empire to the Renaissance the bracelet continues to be a popular jewel for both men and women, an element distinguishing the role and power for the former, simply as an ornament for the latter, increasingly richer with new shapes and new materials based on the tastes and styles of each age. In history, the success of this jewel is closely connected to fashion, but in our day and age jewelry bracelets for both women and men are favourite ornaments, known to be the source of new fashion trends.

Damiani jewelry bracelets for men and women are a fundamental jewelry accessory, a precious world to be explored with all its most elegant, modern and luxurious variations. Exclusive design, extremely high quality materials and excellent craftsmanship are the features of every jewelry creation of the Maison, one of the highest expressions of Italian craftsmanship across the globe. Damiani jewelry bracelets, in their many editions and interpretations, are part of most of the company's jewelry collections, created with skilful expertise by master artisans and goldsmiths, capable of highlighting the light and colour of gold, diamonds and gemstones. Traditional yellow, white and pink gold bracelets, more original ones in black and brown gold; spectacular bracelets in gold and diamonds; modern bracelets for women in silver and gems; very topical silver and stainless steel bracelets for men;

elegant and sophisticated pearl bracelets; the forever fashionable and luxurious tennis bracelet: Damiani jewelry bracelet offer responds to everyone's taste and way of making the most wonderful wishes come true.

Damiani Jewelry Earrings

From pearl earrings to diamond stud earrings: elegant varieties of luxury.

The first archaeological findings of earrings date to the third millennium BC, when men wore them as symbols of virility and military audacity. Constantly present as a detail of attire, all earrings, even for women, disappeared during the middle Ages but were once again fashionable during the Renaissance period, when there was a return especially of pearl earrings. In the 17th century pearl earrings fashion gave way to diamond stud earrings, with the rapidly increasing predominance of this gem in every ornament.

In general, earrings add light to the face; highlight expressions and the intensity of both smile and glance. Because of this, jewelry earrings for women are an irreplaceable element of the Italian Maison's jewelry collections, often proposed in elegant parures: earrings - ring and earrings - bracelet, or in more traditional parures: **pendant** necklace - earrings, precious and enriched with gems for more formal occasions, with pearls, diamonds or discrete decorations for everyday life.

Like all Damiani creations, jewelry earrings for women also have an exclusive design, very high quality materials and excellent craftsmanship, available in the various collections with different interpretations and use of materials and gems. Traditional yellow, white and pink gold earrings; original black and brown gold earrings; always current pearl earrings; unforgettable diamond stud earrings; modern earrings for women with precious coloured gems; essential and very elegant spotlight diamond earrings: with all the skillful combinations of materials and gems in the stud and pendant versions, jewelry earrings enhance the face of their owner and have the power to express the style of every woman at best.

Men's Jewelry by Damiani

Talking about men's jewelry is a little bit like going back to the debut of jewelry art: it was created to honour authority, military ability, courage and power. Women learnt the value and pleasure of wearing precious ornaments from men.

Until the 18th century, there wasn't a clear distinction between men's jewelry and women's jewelry; all ornaments were worn indifferently by men or women, feeding the vanity of men and women with the ostentation of precious creations.

Every age and culture has ascribed great importance to men's jewelry: from the Humanistic period and the Renaissance to 18th century Russia and the Czars and English Lords in the 19th century, history is full of men who celebrated the luxury of their clothing and jewelry with pearls, gems and diamonds.

Today, never as before has men's jewelry experienced a period of absolute glory. A jewel bought to celebrate a professional achievement, or simply to affirm one's personality through exclusive design and precious materials: men's jewelry proposes precious and elegant objects to respond to men's distinct tastes.

Damiani men's jewelry portfolio includes remarkable and

valuable jewelry creations with a strong **masculine** character, perfect for a variety of situations: precious men's cufflinks for the most elegant man; modern men's bracelets for a man who cares about fashion trends; various men's necklaces for both classic and modern men; practical men's key-chains for a very dynamic man; useful men's money clips for the more traditional man.

There are two Damiani men's jewelry collections:

Justman: collection of all men's silver jewelry, with an austere style, a distinctive and innovative design and the light effects of the silver and semi-precious gemstones;

Prestige: a men's jewelry collection with a minimalist and elegant design, in gold, enamel and diamonds, for precious and refined creations.

Damiani's men's jewelry is today more than ever the perfect **long lasting** gift that underlines a relationship and recalls important moments experienced together or special occasions of a man's life.

Today the Damiani Group can proudly claim ownership of a prestigious portfolio of perfectly complementary brands: Damiani, Salvini, Alfieri & St. John, Bliss, Calderoni and Rocca, the jewelry and high level watches chain.

inestimable [in'estiməbl] adj. 无价的；难以估计的
impeccable [im'pekəbl] adj. 无瑕疵的；没有缺点的
pendant ['pendənt] n. 坠饰；吊坠
masculine ['mæskjulin] adj. 男性的；阳性的；男子气概的
long lasting 持久的，耐用的

高水准的设计、品位以及熟练的工艺创造出独一无二的珠宝作品，是美与和谐的完美体现。其中一些是运用高端专业技能的真正

的大师之作：多年来玳美雅“大师杰作”已经取得了无数的奖项和认可，尤其是钻石国际大奖、世界珠宝奥斯卡，以表彰最好的设计与最好的钻石珠宝作品。玳美雅是唯一一个取得18个钻石国际大奖的国际品牌。

瓦伦萨，最好的意大利珠宝传统之乡：是高端意大利珠宝领导品牌的传奇开始的地方。1924年，这个珠宝世家的创始人Enrico Grassi开始采用钻石设计和制作珠宝饰品。精巧的杰作被送往当时的贵族家庭，因此不久之后他便在业界取得了良好的声誉。从此之后，玳美雅一直因其对古典、平衡和考究的高品质演绎而受到意大利珠宝界的赞誉。

Damiano, Enrico的儿子，在伟大的创造力和强烈的创业精神的驱动下，继续着家族传统，他为旗下的珠宝产品确定了延续至今的鲜明风格，在新技术的研发上大量投入。通过对传统和创新的完美结合，玳美雅的产品在意大利乃至全世界都赢得了更高的成就。

从20世纪80年代开始，该公司对其宣传推广风格也做出了改革，成为了珠宝界的先锋，在客户中声望卓著，邀请世界上最好的摄影师拍摄产品。

忠于传统，家族第三代领导者同样以满腔的热情、创造力和承诺沿袭着先辈之路，扩大发展进程，多年来在世界上最为著名的地方开设国际子公司和专卖店，将一个家族企业转变成集团公司。

2007年，集团在意大利证券交易所上市。如今玳美雅已经是意大利珠宝市场的领导者，并且成为世界上公认的高端意大利传统风格的代名词。

明星名人们，诸如伊莎贝拉·罗西里尼、布拉德·皮特、娜塔莎·金斯基、齐雅拉·马斯楚安尼、米拉·乔沃维奇、珍妮弗·安妮斯顿、格温妮丝·帕洛特、索菲娅·罗兰还有莎朗·斯通均与玳美雅有过合作，连王妃和首相们都是它的客户。

Damiani珠宝以世界认可的卓越品质而著称：鲜明的形式、精选

的珠宝材质、精湛的工艺以及为佩戴它的人们带来永恒的优雅。每一件珠宝都因手工技艺和珠宝制作大师无尽的热情而变得生动，蕴含最好的意大利珠宝传统的艺术价值。

多年以来，Damiani得到了意大利和世界的认可，并且迄今仍是他人难以望其项背的18个钻石国际大奖的获得者，还包括与Calderoni品牌在2006年的4个合作获奖作品。Damiani产品第一次获得钻石国际大奖是在1976年，当时奖项被颁给了珠宝作品“Bocca di Squalo（鲨鱼嘴）”—— 一款无价的铂金和黄金制成的手镯，密密镶满了白色和浅黄色钻石，由Gabriella Damiani设计。

自1976年以来，18件Damiani作品以其高品质、精致工艺以及无与伦比的完成品而获得奖项：Damiani出品的项链、手镯、指环还有耳环都拥有独特的设计、充沛的激情以及Damiani所代表的高端珠宝传统。

Damiani珠宝项链

从钻石项链到金项链以及珍珠项链：声望卓著的卓越工艺

项链或许是最古老的珠宝，在最开始，如同其他所有的装饰品一样，它们被应用在宗教仪式上，被认为可以禁锢住邪恶的力量。纵观历史，不同时期、不同审美品位，珠宝制作技术也有所不同，男士和女士项链有了越来越精致的外形。而在文艺复兴时期之后，项链成为了女性专用的饰品，少了笨重之感，愈加突出宝石的自然之美。从历史上看来，这一饰品的前景与时尚趋势有着非常直接的联系，今天的男士、女士项链仍旧是珍贵的饰品。

不同阐释和风格的Damiani男士、女士珠宝项链，或高雅、或现代、或贵重，都是该珠宝品牌系列产品中的基础款式。极富声望的工艺、顶级的材质还有独特的设计是Damiani珠宝项链的特色所在，全手工制作，照顾到每一个细节。有的更称得上是珠宝制作艺术的杰作，巧妙地将黄金、钻石、宝石还有珍珠用无可比拟的Damiani风格结合在一起。传统的白金、黄金、粉金、黑金，还有棕金项链；奢华的黄金镶钻石项链，无可比拟的银质镶钻石女士项链；优雅而精美的珍珠项链；精致的吊坠项链，珍贵的宝石项链，闪耀的钻石项链，现代感十足的男士金银项链，所有的这些Damiani珠宝项链，都是无瑕的珠宝制作工艺精品，蕴含难忘情感，彰显佩戴者个性风格。

Damiani珠宝指环

从宝石戒指到钻戒：典雅与奢华的传统与现代演绎

在过去，无论是男人还是女人的指环，除了纯粹的装饰作用外，还有着许多不同功能，比如象征宗教、体现权威，以及表达爱情。指环的圆形被视为永恒的象征，生命的延续，以及至全至美，这也是为什么指环从古到今都比其他饰品更能代表永恒之爱的缘由。甚至在古罗马，订婚戒指和结婚戒指也被当作象征稳定的吉祥物。

Damiani女士珠宝指环是最基本的珠宝配饰之一，在不同的系列中有着不同的演绎：珍贵的创造，专业工艺的体现，精致的优雅，现代感以及奢华卓越。可佩戴性高，在近一个世纪以来，所有的Damiani珠宝指环都是精确应用新风格的结晶，通过Damiani工坊高水准的珠宝制作工艺和专业的珠宝学知识使一切变得可能。注重细节的全手工制作，Damiani女士指环都是珠宝制造艺术的杰作，巧妙地将黄金、钻石、珍贵的宝石还有珍珠结合在一起，体现着该意大利珠宝品牌独有的风格。传统的白金、黄金、粉金、黑金还有棕金指环；镶有珍贵宝石的女士闪耀指环；永恒浪漫的钻石指环；永恒的婚戒；极为优雅的珍珠指环，Damiani珠宝指环以一种特别的方式表现了那个值得纪念的场合的重要价值和永恒，让你美梦成真，永生难忘。

Damiani珠宝手镯

从经典的金手镯到历史悠久的钻石手镯：充满奇妙惊喜的珠宝世界

“bracelet”（手镯）一词来源于“brachile”（拉丁文“胳臂”之意），而在法语则为“barcel”。男士、女士手镯的历史可以追溯到古代，古罗马人将一个简单的圆形金手镯戴在左腕上，是英勇战士的象征。从古罗马帝国到文艺复兴时期，手镯都是深受男女喜爱的饰品，在古罗马，它代表着与众不同与力量，而在文艺复兴时期，它只是单纯的饰品，而随着时代风格和品位的变化，又衍生出更为丰富的新形式和新材料应用。在历史上，这一饰品的成功与时尚进程有着直接的联系，到了今天，男士和女士珠宝手镯，作为深受喜爱的饰品，已经成为了新的时尚潮流之源。

Damiani珠宝手镯是珠宝配饰中的基本款式，组成了一个优雅、现代和奢华丰富的珍贵世界。独特的设计、顶级的材质和精湛的工艺是该品牌每一件珠宝作品的特色所在，是展现世界级意大利工艺的巅峰之作。各种不同款式的Damiani珠宝手镯，是该品牌旗下大部分珠宝系列的必备款式，在专业珠宝制作师精妙的工艺制作下，展现出金、钻石还有宝石的色泽之美。传统的黄金、白金还有粉金手镯，还有更为别致的黑金和棕金材质；华丽的金镶钻石手镯；现代感十足的女士宝石银手镯；流行的男士银与不锈钢手镯；优雅精致的珍珠手镯；时髦与奢华的钻石手镯，Damiani的珠宝手镯适合不同人士的品位，让最美好的愿望成真。

Damiani珠宝耳环

从珍珠耳环到钻石耳钉：各式考究的奢华

关于第一对耳环的考古学发现可以追溯到公元前3000年，当时男人们佩戴着这种饰品，以增强男子气概和彰显军事能力。作为服饰细节的一部分的耳环，甚至是女性的耳环，在中世纪消失了，但在文艺复兴时期又开始重新成为流行，尤其是珍珠耳环的复兴。从17世纪起，随着钻石在各种饰品中逐渐广泛的应用，珍珠耳环一统天下的地位渐渐被钻石耳钉取代。

总的来说，耳环为容颜增添光彩，让你的一颦一笑都别具风情。 正因为如此，女士珠宝耳环便成为这个意大利珠宝品牌系列中不可或缺的元素，常常出现在全套饰品中：耳环—指环和耳环—手镯。或者是更为传统的配搭：吊坠项链—耳环，添加上珍贵的宝石以适应更正式的场合，配以珍珠、钻石或者一些装饰单品也可以适合日常佩戴。

和所有的Damiani产品一样，女士珠宝耳环同样拥有独特的设计、一流的原料和精湛的做工，适应各种选材与主题不同的系列。

传统的黄金、白金、粉金耳环；别致的黑金和棕金耳环；长盛不衰的珍珠耳环；让人一眼难忘的钻石耳钉；采用各种珍贵有色宝石的现代女士耳环；经典优雅的闪耀钻石耳环，金属材料和宝石的巧妙结合，既有耳钉款式又有吊坠款式，这些珠宝耳环为佩戴它们的女士们面部增添光彩，让她们表现出自己最好的一面。

Damiani男士珠宝

谈到男士珠宝，有点像是要回到珠宝艺术的最初阶段：事实上它们的确是为了彰显权威、军事才能、勇气还有力量而创作。女人们从男人那里了解到了佩戴珍贵饰品的价值与乐趣。

一直到18世纪，男士珠宝和女士珠宝之间都没有明显的划分，所有的饰品都是不分男女地混戴，贵重的饰品激发着男人和女人们的虚荣心。

过去的每个时代和每种文化都对男士珠宝起到了重要的影响：从人文主义和文艺复兴时期到18世纪的俄国与沙皇，到19世纪的英国贵族，历史是男士们服饰还有镶有珍珠、宝石和钻石的珠宝的奢华的见证。

而今天的男士珠宝，则正在经历一个绝对荣耀的时期。人们购买珠宝饰品，是为了庆贺事业成功，亦或只是简单地通过独特的设计和贵重的材质彰显个性，男士珠宝旨在创作符合男士品位的珍贵和高雅的作品。

Damiani的男士珠宝饰品包括价值非凡的珠宝系列，且有着强烈的阳刚之气，完美地适应各种时刻：为最为优雅的男士设计的珍贵男士袖扣；为关注流行趋势的男士设计的现代男士手镯；各种各样的男士项链，适合无论是古典还是现代的男士；为充满活力的男士设计的实用钥匙扣；为更为传统的男士设计的实用男士钱夹。

Damiani男士珠宝系列包括以下两种：

Justman: 男士全银珠宝系列，特点是风格质朴，设计创新独特，闪耀着银与次宝石的光芒。

Prestige: 一款有着极简而优雅设计的男士珠宝系列，采用金、珐琅还有钻石制成，是珍贵而精致的作品。

Damiani男士珠宝如今愈发成为完美、长久的礼物，留住人生重要时刻珍贵回忆的重要角色。

如今的Damiani可以骄傲地宣称自己对一系列声名赫赫的名牌的所有权：Damiani、Salvini、Alfieri & St. John、 Bliss、Calderoni和Rocca，珠宝和高端表链。

读书笔记

6.（美国）蒂芙尼 Tiffany&Co.

品牌名片

品　　类：珠宝、腕表、配饰

标志风格：典雅、知性

创 始 人：查尔斯·路易斯·蒂芙尼（Charles Lewis Tiffany）

诞 生 地：美国

诞生时间：1837年

蒂芙尼以珠宝为经营重点，其制定的宝石、铂金标准被美国政府采纳为官方标准。其蓝色礼盒是经典标志。

品牌阅读

Since 1837, the masterpieces of Tiffany&Co. have defined style and celebrated the world's great love stories.

In 1845, Tiffany published the first mail-order catalogue in the U.S.

In 1851, Tiffany was the first American company to institute the 925/1000 silver standard which was later adopted by the United Stated. This precious metal comprises Tiffany's hollowware and gleams today in chic jewelry designs.

In 1878, Charles Lewis Tiffany purchased a 287-carat fancy yellow diamond. It was cut to 128.54 carats and named the Tiffany Diamond.

Charles Lewis Tiffany introduced the Tiffany Setting diamond engagement ring in 1886, and it has played a part in the world's greatest love stories ever since.

Louis Comfort Tiffany, son of Charles Lewis Tiffany, became the

company's first official design director in 1902.

In 1926, the United States adopted Tiffany's standard of purity (95%) as the country's official standard for platinum.

Legendary designer Jean Schlumberger joined Tiffany in 1956.

In 1960s, Audrey Hepburn embraced Tiffany's New York style in "Breakfast at Tiffany's".

In 2012, Tiffany&Co. celebrated 175 years of legendary style. The Tiffany Diamond was reset in honor of the 175th anniversary.

Tiffany designs embody sophistication, energy and intellect. The innovative iconic collections are famous worldwide and sought by style-setters for their stunning originality and enduring beauty.

自1837年以来，蒂芙尼传奇杰作引领风格，见证着世间无数至臻至美的爱情故事。

1845年，蒂芙尼出版了全美第一本可邮购的产品目录。

1851年，蒂芙尼成为第一家制定92.5%纯银标准的美国公司，该标准后来通行全美。蒂芙尼采用这种贵金属打造出各种餐具器皿。时至今日，纯银材质依然在各款时尚珠宝设计中闪耀着动人光彩。

1878年，查尔斯·路易斯·蒂芙尼购买了一颗287克拉的黄钻。它被切割至128.54克拉，并命名为Tiffany Diamond。

1886年，查尔斯·路易斯·蒂芙尼推出了著名的Tiffany Setting订婚钻戒，该款钻戒至今仍是山盟海誓与真挚爱情的不朽象征。

1902年，查尔斯·路易斯·蒂芙尼之子路易斯·康福特·蒂芙尼成为公司第一任设计总监。

1926年，美国决定采用蒂芙尼的铂金纯度标准（95%）作为通行全国的官方标准。

著名设计师让·史隆伯杰（Jean Schlumberger）于1956年加盟蒂芙尼。

20世纪60年代，奥黛丽·赫本在影片《蒂芙尼的早餐》中淋漓尽致地展现了蒂芙尼的纽约风情。

2012年，为纪念蒂芙尼175周年，Tiffany Diamond以崭新的项链设计隆重呈现于世。

蒂芙尼的设计体现了典雅、活力与知性。款式独特的经典产品以其新颖卓绝的创意和恒久不竭的魅力征服了全世界，成为了各界名流竞相追捧的时尚名品。

读书笔记

7.（法国）梵克雅宝 Van Cleef&Arpels

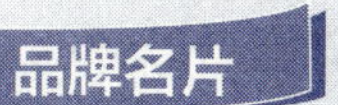

品牌名片

品　　类：珠宝

标志风格：新颖、别致

创 始 人：梵克雅宝（Van Cleef&Arpels）

诞 生 地：法国

诞生时间：1906年

具有百年历史的珠宝品牌，以独树一帜的设计理念和精湛的工艺赢得赞誉。坚持采用上乘宝石和材质，加以精湛镶嵌技艺，成就了不朽的传奇。

品牌阅读

Understated elegance, refinement, grace and a taste for innovation, renewal and **asymmetrical** design… Together, these define the Maison's Spirit of Beauty. The Maison Van Cleef & Arpels was created in 1906 and opened at 22 Place Vendôme.

Innovation:

The Minaudière precious case

With its combination of grace and ingenuity, the Minaudière precious case bag pays homage to the essence of femininity. In the Roaring Twenties, ladies began carrying their beauty accessories with them in a vanity case. While visiting his socialite friend Florence Jay Gould, Charles Arpels was surprised to see her tossing her lipstick, powder case, cigarettes and lighter into a Lucky Strike cigarette tin. From this encounter the idea for the Minaudière precious case was born.

The Zip necklace

Invented in late 19th century America as a fastening for boots, the humble zipper seems far removed from the realm of sophistication. Yet despite its humble origins, it has inspired one of Van Cleef & Arpels' most iconic pieces. The Zip necklace blends humor and refinement by reappropriating an everyday object into a radically different context.

This astonishing feat in jewelry-making can be credited to the Duchess of Windsor. Circa 1938, she suggested to Renée Puissant - the Maison's artistic director and daughter of Alfred Van Cleef - that she should create a piece based on the zip fastener. Crafted in round and **baguette-cut diamonds** mounted in platinum, the necklace was not produced until 1951. An outstanding technical achievement, it soon achieved iconic status.

Extraordinary Dials

The Extraordinary Dials truly **epitomize** the Poetry of Time that inspires Van Cleef & Arpels' watch-making philosophy. Hidden behind these amazing works of arts is a story exploring a new facet of the legacy and universe of the Maison.

For Van Cleef & Arpels, a timepiece is not just a utilitarian object. It is composed of emotions conveyed through the delicacy of its design and the extraordinary craftsmanship involved in its creation. The mechanism of a timepiece is its heart. But its dial is its soul and, as such, should be gifted with life.

Dials at Van Cleef & Arpels are more than still images. They should evolve over time and change with it. More than anything, they should tell a story in perpetual motion to their owners. These are

Extraordinary Dials.

Van Cleef & Arpels has applied all its savoir-faire in the fields of inlaying, stone selection, cutting and setting, lacquering, hand engraving and enameling to the creation of exquisitely precious dreamlike dials.

Limits are expanded, new crafts are mastered. They all contribute to the aura and fascination that surrounds a single concept: the Extraordinary.

asymmetrical [,æsi'metrikəl] *adj.* 非对称的；不均匀的

baguette-cut diamond 狭长方形钻石

epitomize [i'pitəmaiz] *v.* 成为……的缩影

低调的优雅、精致、创新与革新，以及不对称设计……构成梵克雅宝的美之魂。1906年，百年珠宝世家梵克雅宝创立，并在芳登广场22号开设专卖店。

创新之作：

Minaudière百宝匣

Minaudière百宝匣集优雅与精巧于一身，体现了女性魅力的精髓。在“咆哮的20世纪20年代”，女士们开始将美妆用品都装在一只化妆盒里。有一次，查尔斯·雅宝（Charles Arpels）在拜访社交名媛佛罗伦斯·杰·古尔德（Florence Jay Gould）时，惊讶地发现她把口红、粉盒、香烟和打火机一股脑儿塞进一只好彩香烟盒里。创作Minaudière百宝匣的灵感便由此诞生。

Zip拉链项链

拉链本是19世纪末期美国人为了扣紧靴子而发明的，不起眼的拉链似乎跟优雅没有丝毫关联。然而，尽管出身卑微，它却是梵克

雅宝最具代表性作品的灵感之源。Zip拉链项链将日常用品放置于全新情境下，融幽默与精巧于一体。

最初提出这项珠宝制作惊人创意的是温莎公爵夫人。1939年，她建议梵克雅宝的艺术总监阿尔弗莱德·梵克之女Renée Puissant以拉链为原型创作一款珠宝。1951年，以铂金为底镶嵌圆形和长方形切割钻石的Zip拉链项链诞生了。因其杰出的技术突破，Zip拉链项链也很快在高级珠宝领域中取得了标志性的地位。

Extraordinary Dials非凡表盘系列

Extraordinary Dials非凡表盘系列是时间的诗篇的缩影，而后者激发了梵克雅宝的制表哲学。这些令人惊叹不已的艺术作品背后蕴藏着一个探索梵克雅宝百年传承和创新的传奇故事。

对于梵克雅宝而言，钟表并不只是一个功能性的物件，它更承载着深厚情感，来自创作过程中的精巧设计与非凡工艺。机械是钟表的心脏，表盘是它的灵魂，因此表盘应该是有生命的。

梵克雅宝的表盘不只是静止的图像，它们会随着时光流转而变化。更重要的是，它们会在永恒的运行中向主人诉说着故事。这就是Extraordinary Dials非凡表盘系列。

梵克雅宝将其所有精湛工艺运用在这些如梦似幻的珍贵表盘上，包括镶嵌、宝石挑选、切割和镶嵌、漆艺、手工雕刻和珐琅工艺。

梵克雅宝不断冲破限制，掌握和运用创新工艺。这一切努力所展现的灵气与魅力都围绕着一个概念：非凡。

8.（英国）格拉夫 Graff

品牌名片

品　　类：珠宝

标志风格：高雅、精巧

创 始 人：劳伦斯·格拉夫（Laurence Graff）

诞 生 地：英国

诞生时间：1960年

格拉夫意味着世界上最难以置信的宝石、钻石的品质，其设计、工艺均是最顶级的。

品牌阅读

The founding of Graff Diamonds in 1960 by Laurence Graff marked the start of an extraordinary journey spanning over five decades, which continues to this day.

Throughout its rich history, Graff is said to have handled more diamonds of notable rarity and beauty than any other jeweler, and to this day continues to inspire and excite the world's most discerning clientele with its jeweler.

Graff is more than just a name - it is Laurence Graff's lasting legacy, whose passion and distinctive style has now been passed down to a new generation of designers and craftsmen, who continue to collaborate each day to make the world's incomparable jewelry.

In 2009, Graff's client magazine Graffiti launched, distributed globally to Graff's VIP clients in English and Simplified Chinese.

2010 witnesses a year of record breaking diamonds. The Graff Constellation at 102.79 cts - the largest ever round brilliant cut, D colour internally flawless diamond. The Delaire Sunrise at 118.08 cts - the largest ever square emerald cut, fancy vivid yellow diamond and the extremely rare Graff Pink at 23.88 cts.

Graff Unveils the Icon Collection

Graff Diamonds is proud to unveil its latest collection: the Graff Icon.The Graff Icon has an enthralling history, having appeared in a number of different forms, the world over, during Graff's **illustrious** history.

The delicate lines and flowing curves that form the Graff Icon draw inspiration from a renowned 1 million Hair and Jewel **coiffure**, made by Mr. Graff in 1970.

This piece created an aura of myth and excitement around the jewels crafted by Graff Diamonds, which continues to this day.

A highly ornate creation of diamonds and gems, it was influenced by the royal hair fashion of 18th century Versailles, which possessed a graceful femininity and qualities, reflected in the delicate design of the Graff Icon.Nevertheless, this is the first time this timeless motif has been incorporated into a jeweler collection.

Each mesmerizing piece begins its journey at the hands of Graff's Master Craftsmen at its London workshop, where every diamond is meticulously set to perfectly showcase its natural beauty.

illustrious [ɪ'lʌstrɪəs] adj. 辉煌的

coiffure [kwɑ:'fjuə] n. 头饰

劳伦斯·格拉夫在1960年成立了格拉夫珠宝，为之后50多年的辉煌传奇拉开序幕。

纵观其璀璨的历史，格拉夫出品的珍贵华美钻石比其他珠宝商

都要多，至今仍然不断呈献让人惊艳的瑰宝，令世界各地的客户为之惊叹。

格拉夫品牌代表了创办人劳伦斯·格拉夫的辉煌成就。新一代设计师和工匠团队现在仍然秉持他对钻石的热诚和出类拔萃的风格，联手打造世界上最无与伦比的珠宝。

2009年，格拉夫为其客户推出杂志Graffiti，以英语和简体中文编制，分发全球的格拉夫珠宝贵宾客户。

格拉夫在2010年创下多项钻石纪录，包括打造出重达102.79克拉的世界上最大D色无瑕明亮形切割圆钻“格拉夫星座之石”，重118.08克拉的世界上最大正方形祖母绿切割艳彩黄钻“德拉里日出之石”以及重23.88克拉、极为罕见的粉红钻“格拉夫粉红钻”。

格拉夫推出Icon系列

格拉夫珠宝隆重推出最新的格拉夫Icon系列。

新系列却有炫人的历史，曾以不同的形式出现在格拉夫辉煌的过去。

格拉夫Icon系列的线条优美，婉约流丽，创作灵感源自劳伦斯·格拉夫于1970年创作、价值高达100万美元的经典“发式与珠宝”发饰。

这件传奇发饰奠定了格拉夫珠宝设计令人眼前一亮的醉人魅力，至今仍然叫人赞叹不已。

华贵不凡的发饰镶满钻石和宝石，取材自18世纪凡尔赛皇室的发饰造型，散发绰约柔美的魅力。这份高雅气息与格拉夫Icon的设计一脉相承。而且，这是首次将超越时间限制的设计用于珠宝系列。

每一件扣人心弦的非凡珠宝均由格拉夫伦敦工作室的大师级工匠精雕细琢而成，一丝不苟地镶嵌每一颗钻石，尽显美钻的天然妍姿。

9.（奥地利）施华洛世奇 Swarovski

品　　类：珠宝

标志风格：圣洁、高雅

创 始 人：丹尼尔·施华洛世奇（Daniel Swarovski）

诞 生 地：奥地利

诞生时间：1895年

施华洛世奇的品牌标志中有一只天鹅，天鹅象征着纯洁，而SWAROVSKI的前音与天鹅相同。

品牌阅读

In 1892, Daniel Swarovski invented a revolutionary machine that allowed crystals to be cut more precisely than with existing manual methods.

In 1895, Daniel Swarovski founded the company in Wattens, Tyrol, with the vision of bringing joy to people through crystal. His guiding principle is still followed by the company today: "To constantly improve that is good."

Sew-on-crystal-studded ribbons were launched in 1931, providing fashion and accessory manufactures with new design possibilities.

In 1949, SWAROVSKI OPTIK was founded, and went on to become a leading manufacturer of precision optical instruments for hunting and nature observation (binoculars, telescopes, rifle scopes, range finders, and night vision and optronic devices).

In 1965, the first Swarovski crystals for chandeliers and lighting were launched, and in 1977 were registered under the STRASS

Swarovski Crystal name. Today they adorn classical chandeliers, such as those in the Palace of Versailles and the Metropolitan Opera, New York, as well as more modern lights. Swarovski starts to manufacture precision-cut gemstones.

In 1976, the first decorative crystal figurines won the hearts of consumers. Swarovski began machine-cutting cubic zirconia.

As a tribute to the company founder, the Daniel Swarovski couture line was launched in1989.

In 2003, Swarovski developed Crystal Fabric: countless tiny crystals create a delicate shimmer over a variety of materials.

1892年，丹尼尔·施华洛世奇发明了革命性的仿水晶切割机器，切割准确度远胜当时的手工切割技术。

1895年，丹尼尔·施华洛世奇在泰利来华登斯市创立了公司，愿景是借着仿水晶为人们带来喜悦。施华洛世奇公司至今仍严谨遵循他所定下的原则：不断精益求精。

1931年推出手缝水晶石配饰带，为时装及配饰制造商开创设计新领域。

1949年，SWAROVSKI OPTIK成立，提供精密光学仪器（双筒望远镜、望远镜、步枪瞄准镜、测距仪、夜视仪器与光电仪器）作狩猎与自然观察用途，现已发展成为领导市场的光学仪器制造商。

1965年，用于仿水晶吊灯及灯饰的施华洛世奇仿水晶首度面世，并于1977年以STRASS Swarovski Crystal的名字注册商标。目前，这些仿水晶配件可见于凡尔赛宫和纽约大都会歌剧院等文化场所的古典吊灯及不少现代灯饰上。施华洛世奇开始制作精密切割宝石。

1976年，首度推出装饰仿水晶塑像，深得消费者喜爱。施华洛世奇开始切割合成立方氧化锆。

1989年，为向公司创始人献上诚挚敬意，施华洛世奇推出丹尼尔·施华洛世奇高级定制系列。

2003年，施华洛世奇研发出仿水晶布：数之不尽的小巧仿水晶，为各种物料营造微妙的璀璨质感。

读书笔记

Part 5 皮具

1.（意大利）菲拉格慕 Salvatore Ferragamo

品牌名片

品　　类：鞋子、饰品、香水

标志风格：华贵典雅、实用性和款式并重

创 始 人：萨尔瓦托勒·菲拉格慕（Salvatore Ferragamo）

诞 生 地：意大利

诞生时间：1911年

菲拉格慕是意大利的女鞋王国，因为异常关注质量和细节，有“明星御用皮鞋匠”的称号。产品包括皮鞋、皮革制品、配件、服装和香氛。

品牌阅读

Salvatore Ferragamo is one of the most **prominent** shoemaking families in Italia. Salvatore Ferragamo dedicated his life to the search for a secret: the shoe that fits well. When he began studying human anatomy in the United States, he found his first cluc to the problem in the distribution of the body's weight over the joints of the foot. He wrote "I discovered that the weight of our bodies, when we are standing erect, drops straight down on the arch of the foot. I constructed my revolutionary lasts, which support the arch, make the foot act like an inverted pendulum".

Salvatore ferragamo was born in Italia in 1898. When he was 13 years old, he set a shop in Bonito and made the first pair of tailored women's shoes.

In 1923, Salvatore Ferragamo opened up the Hollywood Boot

Shop in Las Palmas, Hollywood, which became a place the movie actresses always came to.

During the war, Salvatore Ferragamo experimented with humble materials such as raffia and cork to create the cork wedge.

In 1947, Salvatore Ferragamo won the "Neiman Marcus Award", fashion's Oscar equivalent, with the "Invisible sandal".

In 1948, the first Ferragamo store in New York opened on Park Avenue (now on Fifth Avenue).

The Company created a velvet ankle boot for the actress Brigitte Bardot in 1966.

The Ferragamo store in the Mandarin Hotel, Hong Kong, marked the start of expansion into the Far East in 1989.

In 1994, Ferragamo opened its first shop in Shanghai.

In 2001, Ferragamo Parfums was established.

Salvatore Ferragamo is now in its third generation. Shoes remain Ferragamo's core business and the creative engine of its entire production. High quality is ensured by the attention given to model construction and the strong manual component that characterizes the production.

The Golden Rules for Shoe Care

1. A new pair of shoes should never be worn for many consecutive hours. Once your feet are completely accustomed to the shoes, you can begin to wear them all day.

2. Never wear the same pair of shoes two days in a row. Let them rest for at least a day before wearing them again.

3. Always use a shoehorn when putting on your shoes.

4. Before removing a **lace-up** shoe, loosen the laces completely

so the shoe slips off more easily.

5. Once shoes are taken off, insert the made-to-measure shoetrees.

6. Shoetrees should also be used when shoes are wet from rain or snow: left to dry for an entire day.

7. Each time you wear a pair of shoes they should be cleaned and polished.

8. When you don't wear your shoes, wax and put them in a drawstring, and keep down in a box.

prominent ['prɔminənt] adj. 杰出的；卓越的

lace-up ['leisʌp] adj. 系带的

菲拉格慕是意大利最显赫的制鞋家族之一。萨尔瓦托勒·菲拉格慕先生致力于研究发现让鞋子穿着更为舒适的秘密。当他在美国学习人体工程学的时候，他有了最初的发现，那就是：鞋子是否合脚的关键是在于人体重量的分布。他在自传中写道："当人站立时，重量落在延伸下来到足弓部分的直线上。由此我设计出一种能够支撑足弓的新型鞋，让脚像倒挂的钟摆。"

萨尔瓦托勒·菲拉格慕于1898年出生于意大利。当他13岁时，在Bonito开设店铺，并制作出第一双量身定做的女式皮鞋。

1923年，萨尔瓦托勒·菲拉格慕在好莱坞Las Palmas大道开办好莱坞鞋店（Hollywood Boot Shop），成为电影女明星经常光顾的地方。

在战争期间，菲拉格慕用拉菲亚树叶纤维和软木等简陋材质演绎其创意。

1947年，"隐形"凉鞋为菲拉格慕赢得了"Neiman Marcus"奖——时尚界的奥斯卡奖。

1948年，纽约的首家菲拉格慕专卖店在林荫大道（现第五大道）开业。

1966年，菲拉格慕为女明星碧姬·巴铎（Brigitte Bardot）设计了一双天鹅绒及踝短靴。

1989年，菲拉格慕专卖店入驻香港文华酒店（Mandarin Hotel），标志着菲拉格慕向东方拓展的开端。

菲拉格慕上海美美百货（Shanghai Maison Mode）店于1994年开业。

2001年，菲拉格慕旗下的香水公司成立。

如今，萨尔瓦托勒·菲拉格慕公司现已步入第三代。鞋业仍旧是菲拉格慕公司的核心业务及整套产品的创新引擎。菲拉格慕在产品制造过程中，高度重视鞋款模型结构和牢固的手工制作等重要环节，这是其产品卓越品质的保证。

皮鞋保养黄金法则

1. 请勿连续数小时穿着一双新鞋。一旦您的双脚完全适应了新鞋，您便可以开始长时间穿着。

2. 请勿连续两天穿同一双鞋。再次穿之前至少让鞋休息一天。

3. 穿鞋时请务必使用鞋拔。

4. 脱下系带鞋之前，请将鞋带完全解开，这样可以更加轻松地将鞋脱下。

5. 一旦将鞋脱下，请放入量脚定制的鞋楦。

6. 鞋履在雨雪天气中潮湿后也请使用鞋楦，并晾干一整天。

7. 即使鞋履看上去仍很光亮，每次穿着时也请擦拭并上光。

8. 如果一段时间不穿鞋品，请涂上一薄层鞋油，放入随鞋赠送的布袋，并将其鞋底朝下放入盒中。

2.（瑞士）巴利 Bally

品牌名片

品　　类：皮具、时装

标志风格：精巧、摩登、时尚

创 始 人：卡尔·兰斯·巴利（Carl Franz Bally）

诞 生 地：瑞士

诞生时间：1851年

创立伊始，巴利就成为世界上第一家真正的全球奢华产品公司，代表品位、价值和品质。螺旋边烤花皮鞋、靴子上的铜扣、鲜红的边线都是巴利的招牌风格。

品牌阅读

Bally Switzerland: Modern craftsmanship since 1851

The Bally hallmark is thc crafting of exquisite leather. Since 1851, Bally has been globally recognized for its Swiss Made quality and its contemporary style.

Bally: Swiss Roots, Global Perspective

The visionary founder, Carl Franz Bally, whom employees used to call Papa Bally, set the global brand phenomenon in motion. His vision: to create exquisitely crafted footwear in the finest materials that are divine to look at, whilst **simultaneously** functional and enduring.

Bally: Pioneer of Luxury

Production had reached a staggering 3.9 million pairs of shoes a year. Bally was committed to pushing the envelope in terms of

elegance and luxury.

Bally not only pioneered the realm of shoe making, but also the worlds of retailing and advertising. The first retail store opened in 1881 on London's prestigious New Bond Street.

BALLY Today: Responsibility and passion

The Bally name became synonymous with highly functional, quality shoes and famously graced the soles of dancers, soldiers, pioneers, sportsmen and even **astronauts**' footwear.

Sir Edmund Hillary relied on Bally hiking boots for his first ever Mount Everest climb in 1953. Even NASA collaborated with Bally for the creation of the sole that took the famous "giant leap for mankind" in the boots of Neil Armstrong during the historic first moonwalk in 1969.

Bally heralds its 160th year anniversary with a celebratory range of shoes and bags for men and women. These **eye-catching** creations speak of the heritage and craftsmanship of Bally, with a hint of contemporary wit.

simultaneously [saiməl'teiniəsli] adv. 同时地
astronaut ['æstrənɔ:t] n. 宇航员，航天员
eye-catching ['ai,kætʃiŋ] adj. 引人注目的；显著的

瑞士巴利：源自1851年的现代工艺

从1851年起，Bally已经将精湛的瑞士传统制作工艺运用于其丰富的奢华皮革产品中，Bally始终凭借“瑞士制造”的卓越品质和时尚优雅的独特风格而得到全球的广泛认可。

巴利：源于瑞士，着眼全球

不断创造全球奇迹的Bally创始人Carl Franz Bally，曾被员工亲切地称做“Bally 爸爸”。他的理念是：将优质精湛的瑞士传统手工艺应用于品种丰富的奢华皮件系列中，打造时尚耐穿、功能实用的产品。

巴利：奢侈品领域的先锋

巴利创造了年均390万双鞋的销售纪录，这一惊人的数字也同时激励着Bally始终将优雅奢华的设计概念融于产品中。

巴利不仅是制鞋方面的先锋，更是世界零售及广告领域的领先者，巴利于1881年开设第一家精品店，就位于伦敦著名的新邦德街。

巴利之今日：责任与热情

巴利鞋履已成为了功能实用、质量上乘、极具优雅的代名词，深受舞者、士兵、时尚爱好者、体育运动员和宇航员的喜爱。

1953年，Edmund Hillary穿着Bally Hiking登山靴首次征服了珠峰。甚至美国宇航局（NASA）也于1969年同Bally合作开发了特殊材料鞋底，运用于阿姆斯特朗首次登月的太空漫步靴，完成人类历史上的巨大跨越。

在Bally160周年庆典上，发布了涵盖男士和女士鞋履和箱包的周年纪念系列，以诠释巴利的时尚设计理念。这些引人注目的作品是巴利传统手工制作在当代的传承。

读书笔记

3.（意大利）铁狮东尼 A.Testoni

品牌名片

品　　类：鞋、皮具

标志风格：优良制作、风格独特

创 始 人：阿米迪奥·铁狮东尼（Amedeo Testoni）

诞 生 地：意大利

诞生时间：1929年

铁狮东尼坚持以最精美的设计创造超值品质，以卓尔不凡的独特风格深受欧洲广大成功男士的青睐。

品牌阅读

The young Amedeo opened his first workshop in 1929, after having learnt the secrets of the most important Bolognese craftsmen. In the 50's he improved the Bolognese production to fulfill his dream of creating the most beautiful shoes in the world. To make the dream come true, he has carried the real essence of Italian craftsmanship to luxury markets throughout the world.

A.Testoni' secret construction

The shoe is made, kept in the shape and then deconstructed. The upper is firstly taken apart and then put together and sewed to the sole using a revolutionary process, entirely hand-made, patented by A.Testoni. The result is a shoe as light as a feather that guarantees at the same time a perfect foot isolation from hot, cold and humid weather conditions.

The Materials-In Search of Absolute Quality

The great variety of leathers used that ranges from **calfskin** to **ostrich**, **iguana** and **crocodile**, constitutes a continuous challenge and commitment. It is necessary to select the best leathers, test their resistance and find experts capable of hand-sewing complex materials that even the most sophisticated machines are unable to cut.

The Bolognese Construction

The Bolognese construction is the feature which best defines the handicrafts values of an A.Testoni's shoe. A special lining of very soft goatskin - hand sewn to the upper - fits the foot like a glove and gives remarkable elasticity to the front part of the shoe, whereas the rear part presents a harder structure in order to support the heel correctly.

The Norwegian Construction

The peculiar braided stitching, also called "the chain", that contrasts the upper is entirely hand-made with rough linen twine. This ancient process derives from typical mountain boots conceived to face the most adverse weather conditions.

The Spiral

Originally, the spiral was used to hide the twine utilized for the sewing of the shoe bottom. In this ancient technique, a thin ribbon of leather was wound around the twine after each sewing point. A detail, applied to the sole hem, is today a sort of trademark of production in A.Testoni's shoes.

From the wheeling and stamping of the soles to the trimming of the edges, from the delicate procedures of antique and shaded

polishing to the final brushing: hemming, assemblage and finishing can involve at least 200 manual operations in an A.Testoni's shoe.

Old **methodologies**, unique competences, very rigorous materials selection, research for quality without compromises, technical and esthetical tension towards new and original solutions: this is the philosophy of a company that has in itself and in its history; the requisites for a continuous innovative development and for the international recognition of its products and Italian style.

calfskin ['kɑ:fskin] n. 小牛皮
ostrich ['ɔ:stritʃ] n. 鸵鸟
iguana [i'gwɑ:nə] n. [动] 鬣蜥蜴
crocodile ['krɔkə,dail] n. 鳄鱼
methodology [,meθə'dɔlədʒi] n. 方法学，方法论

1929年，年轻的阿米迪奥在掌握了博洛尼亚最重要制鞋匠的精髓后，开设了他的第一家店铺。50年代，在“创造世界上最美的鞋子”这一梦想的推动下，阿米迪奥在实践过程中改良了博洛尼亚式制鞋工艺，并且在这一过程中将意大利手工工艺理念带入世界奢侈消费品市场。

A.Testoni的制鞋秘诀

先将鞋子制作成型，然后分解开来，拆下的鞋面使用一种革新工序重新固定并缝合到鞋底上。该工序全部使用手工，如今已成为A.Testoni的专利。通过这一方法制作出的鞋子如同羽毛一般轻巧，同时又将脚部与外部的炎热、寒冷和潮湿隔离。

材料——追求完美品质

使用种类繁多的皮革是一种持续的挑战，需要不断投入精力：从小牛皮到鸵鸟皮，到巨蜥皮，再到鳄鱼皮。所有工序包括选择最好的皮革，研究出它的用途，寻找有能力对复杂材料进行手工加工的能工巧匠，因为即使最精密的机器也无法裁剪那些复杂的材料。

手套式缝法

A.Testoni制鞋工艺之特色在于使用博洛尼亚制鞋工艺。鞋帮里手工缝制了极为柔软的山羊皮衬里，如同手套一般包裹双脚并使鞋的前部拥有非常高的弹性。而鞋后帮的结构则较坚实以正确承托脚跟。

挪威式缝法

使用未加工亚麻线纯手工缝制而成的特殊辫形或“链形”缝线与鞋面形成反差。这种古老的工艺起源于典型的登山鞋，用于应对各种恶劣的气候条件。

螺旋式缝法

原本是用于隐藏鞋底的缝线。在这个古老工艺中，一条极细的皮条交织于每一针针脚周围。这一细节应用到鞋底边缘之后，在一定意义上就变成了A.Testoni制鞋的“商标”。

从鞋底的滚压和模压到其边缘的设定，从精妙的皮革古法花式上光到最终的刷拭：A.Testoni制鞋中，锁边、缝合和整饰这些工艺可包含两百道不同的工序。

古老的方法，一脉相传的卓越技艺，严苛的材料选择，对质量的执着追求，为了获得与众不同的款式而在技术和美学上的不懈坚持：正是基于这一传统文化，铁狮东尼的品牌得以持续不断地创新其产品和意大利风格，以确保其国际知名度。

4.（法国）伯尔鲁帝 Berluti

品牌名片

品　　类：鞋、皮具、成衣

标志风格：高贵、优雅

创 始 人：阿里桑罗德·伯尔鲁帝（Alessandro Berluti）

诞 生 地：法国

诞生时间：1895年

伯尔鲁帝在制鞋过程中沿袭了在足底弓部采用小块锤打而成的皮革这一传统，奠定了其高贵而艺术品的品牌形象。

品牌阅读

Since 1895, each generation of Berluti has cultivated exceptional knowhow in the mastery of last-making and a deep understanding of footwear. The result has consistently been shoes of incomparable comfort and elegance.

Alessandro Berluti was born in Senigallia, a tiny Italian port town in Le Marche on the Adriatic coast, on October 20th, 1865. It was here that he began carving out his future as an apprentice, constructing carriages from wood, seats and reins in leather. Years of hard work laid solid foundation for Alessandro in shoe industry in the future: skilled wood carving to ensure the **upmost** accuracy of the last, due attention to the leather to ensure the quality of the shoe, and the necessity of perfection to please the client. In 1882, with a strong desire to explore the world, Young Alessandro began his two years of journey and adventure which eventually led him to Paris, the city of light and joie de vivre.

A hard-working perfectionist, Alessandro rapidly found work with orders from a number of fellow-countrymen and experienced shoemakers with their own establishments.

Everywhere between the Opéra and the Tuileries the newly established grand hotels of Paris welcomed an international clientele in search of novelty and Parisian elegance. And here Alessandro set up his own bootmaking workshop to craft shoes for these wealthy men who were not only connoisseurs but also extremely exacting clients.

During the search for a poetic aesthetic, Alessandro was fine-tuning his own style, and in 1895 he created an extraordinary lace-up shoe for men, in an unusual design using a single piece of leather with no visible stitching, smooth and supple as a leather glove.

By 1922,Torello plunged himself enthusiastically into the bootmaker's craft that his father had taught him to love. His approach was very advanced from the start: he thought in terms of volume while others were still thinking simply in sizes. Hc was particularly focused on the beauty of the finished shoe.

Echoing the Art Deco style of the period, he preferred simple and clean lines, introducing the "lace-panel Oxfords"and comfortable "Sans Gêne" elasticated boots. In 1928, to satisfy the flood of orders and receive his clients in comfort and style, Torello bought the lease of a shop at 9 rue du Mont Thabor. From there his fame spread, to such a point that wealthy international clients from the nearby grand hotels had their names put down on his waiting list for the privilege of wearing shoes made by Berluti.

With typical visionary enthusiasm and **audacity**, Talbinio (the son of Torello) introduced ready-to-wear de luxe shoes in 1959, a selection of entirely hand-made models in the great bootmaking

tradition, but immediately available. This idea, at the dawn of a new era, opened the door to a very specific and younger clientele.

For the boutique, he designed a modern functional decor, where new customers could mingle with established clients to discover both ready-to-wear and **made-to-measure** shoes. Even fervent advocates of bespoke footwear, such as Edie Constantine, Truffaut, Godard, or Chabrol found immediate satisfaction in the new ready-to-wear models offered at rue Marbeuf. Cultivated, charming and attractive, by introducing remarkable changes, Talbinio had written, with grace and some success, a new page in the history of the House. Subsequently, Talbinio was joined by his young cousin Olga, who injected yet another burst of creative energy into the family business.

During 70s, Olga brought a touch of spice to luxury, perfecting Berluti's Venezia leather and introducing a hand-finished patina in a palette of exclusive shades. The House's very individual shoes and the soul Olga discovered for them made the magic that to this day remains the romantic signature of Berluti.

Perfected during the 1980's, the famous Berluti patinas revolutionized the world of male footwear by introducing colour at a time when the majority of men's shoes were either black or brown.

upmost ['ʌpməʊst] adj. 最高的；最重要的

audacity [ɔ:'dæsəti] n. 大胆

made-to-measure ['meidtə'meʒə] adj. 定做；特制

自1895年起，伯尔鲁帝家族每一代都不断钻研鞋楦制作的工艺，提高对鞋履工艺的理解，最终成就了无可比拟的优雅舒适的鞋履。

1865年10月20日，Alessandro Berluti出生于意大利Adriatic海岸旁的小村庄Sinegallia。青年时期的Alessandro潜心研习木刻工艺，用木头制造马车，皮革制座椅和缰绳。多年的勤奋工作为Alessandro日后投身制鞋业奠下坚实的基础，丰富木刻技艺令他精确掌控制鞋工艺中每个细节，而对皮革的严苛挑选亦确保所制鞋履的质量，为每位顾客带来极致完美的体验。1882年，年轻的Alessandro带着探索世界的强烈渴望，开始了历时两年的游历与冒险，最终，他抵达了充满阳光与欢乐的大都会巴黎。

Alessandro是一名勤奋的完美主义者，很快，他从自己的同乡们和已颇有建树的制鞋工匠们那里得到了许多订单。

在巴黎歌剧院和杜乐丽花园之间的区域不断兴建起奢华的酒店，聚集了大批来自世界各地的宾客们，他们兴致勃勃地在这座时尚之都寻找巴黎式的优雅与时髦。Alessandro在这个充满生机的区域建立了自己的工作坊，为这些富有的顾客设计鞋履，他们不仅深谙时尚之道而且也是最挑剔的客人。

在对诗意美学的追寻过程中，Alessandro逐渐定位了自己的风格。1895年，他史无前例地推出一双绑带男式皮鞋，显示出不同寻常的设计才华。这双皮鞋采用一整张皮切割制作而成，通身看不到明显的缝线，宛如皮手套一样光滑柔软，赋予双足前所未有的舒适感。这双奠定了伯尔鲁帝品牌风格的绑带男式皮鞋堪称一个传奇，在往后的岁月中亦渐渐成为人们口中传颂的神话。

到1922年，在父亲的影响下，Torello充满热情地投入到制鞋工艺中。他的追求在当时已十分超前：当其他的鞋匠还在简单地考虑尺码时，Torello则在思考如何设计并表现鞋子的轮廓（体量），他尤其注意完成品美的展示。Torello特别钟爱简单清晰的线条，他推出了“绑带牛津鞋”（lace-panel Oxfords）和具有弹性的Sans Gêne便鞋，呼应着当时风行的装饰艺术风格（Art Deco）。与此同时，Berluti的生意蒸蒸日上，顾客与订单不断增多。1928年，Torello买下了Mont Thabor街9号的店铺开设精品店。他个人亦盛名远播，以至于那些下榻于附近奢华酒店的豪客们慕名而来，想定制一双Berluti皮

鞋，也不得不先将名字列入预约单上排队等候。

1959年，充满热情与勇气的Talbinio（Torello的儿子）富于远见地推出奢华成衣鞋履系列：完全采用传统精湛手工艺制作，顾客去店内即可购买，无需等待。这个系列立刻在年轻顾客群体中大受欢迎。

Talbinio设计的精品店十分摩登且具有功能性，新老顾客在这里自在交谈，分享他们对成衣鞋履和定制鞋履的经验。甚至那些像Edie Constantine、Truffaut、Godard、Chabrol这样热衷于定制鞋履的老顾客，在Marbeuf街的Berluti店里试穿新推出的成衣鞋履时也感到很满意。风度翩翩、知识渊博的Talbinio成功地在Berluti品牌历史上书写了优雅的新篇章，为这个高级鞋履品牌带来革命性的发展。很快，Tolbinio的堂妹Olga也加入了家族生意，为Berluti注入全新的活力与创意。

20世纪70年代，Olga在Berluti经典的奢华风格中融入几分趣味，使其专有的Venezia皮革更加完美，通过手工Patina技术赋予皮革独一无二的明暗色调。Olga从Berluti那些深具风格的鞋履设计中提炼出灵魂之光，使之在今天仍焕发出魔力光彩，继续谱写着Berluti那充满浪漫风格的经典篇章。

经过持续的探索，伯尔鲁帝的patina工艺在80年代臻于完美，不同色彩的皮鞋，革命性地颠覆了男鞋世界。而当时，大部分男鞋都是黑色或棕色的。

读书笔记

5.（意大利）芬迪 Fendi

品牌名片

品　　类：皮具、时装、香水

标志风格：高贵、典雅

创 始 人：阿戴勒·芬迪（Adele Fendi）

　　　　　爱德华多·芬迪（Edoardo Fendi）

诞 生 地：意大利

诞生时间：1925年

"双F标志"出自卡尔·拉格菲尔德手笔。常常不经意地出现在芬迪服装、配件的扣子细节上，后来甚至成为布料上的图案。

品牌阅读

It was launched in 1925 by Edoardo Fendi and Adele Fendi, as a fur and leather shop in Via del Plebiscito, Rome; but today is a **multinational** luxury goods brand owned by LVMH. Karl Lagerfeld is the creative director.

The signal coloration of Fendi, yellow, was born in 1933. The yellow Fendi shopping bag at that time, made of **parchment**, is still the brand logo, clear at a glance .

During 1980s, Fendi developed from many other aspects and launched jeans, ties, glasses and perfume, which made it more famous.

Perfume

Fendi launched its first perfume, Fendi for Women, in 1985. The line has been expanded to Theorema Uomo and Fendi Uomo (for men) and Celebration, Asja and Fantasia (for women). The latest, "Fan di

Fendi", was released in August 2010.

Eyewear

Fendi's eyewear line is licensed to Marchon Eyewear and includes prescription eyeglasses and sunglasses in addition to non-prescription sunglasses.

After the world war II, Edoardo and Adele's five daughters, Paola, Anna, Franca, Carla and Alda, worked into the **family business**. In postwar Italy, working women were still rare. The join of the five sisters, injected new vitality into brand collections by their innovative style and **far-sight**.

In 2007, FENDI held an amazing fashion show on top of the Great Wall of China. At last, the great double F logo was projected to the surrounding mountains. This is the first fashion brand holding a fashion show on the Great Wall in the history.

multinational [ˌmʌlti'næʃənəl] adj. 跨国公司的

parchment ['pɑ:tʃmənt] n. 羊皮纸

family business 家族企业

far-sight ['fɑ:sait] n. 远见

1925年，Edoardo Fendi 和 Adele Casagrande 在罗马的Via del Plebiscito开设了一家皮草专卖店；现今成为LVMH旗下的跨国际奢侈品品牌。Karl Lagerfeld担任创意总监。

象征 Fendi 品牌的黄色标志色在 1933 年诞生，在当时以羊皮纸制成黄色 FENDI 购物纸袋，此标志至今仍是大众一目了然的品牌标志。

20世纪80年代，芬迪的发展更多元化，推出牛仔裤、领带、眼镜及香水，使品牌形象更深入民心。

香水

芬迪在1985年开始销售品牌香水“Fendi for Women”。现今已拥有男性使用的“Theorema Uomo and Fendi Uomo”与女性使用的“Celebration, Asja and Fantasia”。最新的“Fan di Fendi”，在2010年8月上市。

眼镜

芬迪眼镜许可授权Marchon Eyewear，芬迪的眼镜包括了一般有度数的眼镜以及太阳眼镜，和没有度数的太阳眼镜。

“二战”结束，Edoardo 和 Adele 的五个女儿 Paola、Anna、Franca、Carla，以及 Alda 进入到家族事业工作，在战后的意大利，女性工作尚属凤毛麟角。五姐妹的加入，以创新的风格和远见为品牌系列注入新的生命力。

2007年，FENDI 在中国长城之巅举办了一场令人惊艳的时尚秀，最后巨大的双 F 标志投射到周围环绕的群山之上。这是历史上第一家在长城举办时装展的时装品牌。

读书笔记

6.（德国）MCM

品牌名片

品　　类：皮具、饰品

标志风格：高贵、优雅

创 始 人：迈克尔·克罗默（Michael Cromer）

诞 生 地：德国

诞生时间：1976年

MCM的桂冠图案体现了其浓郁的历史气息。图案饰有带缎带的月桂叶子，以示尊重路德维格一世的豪情壮志，代表了新古典主义风格，象征着胜利、成就与荣誉。

品牌阅读

Founded in 1976, German brand MCM (Mode Creation Munich) crafts luxury leather goods, apparel and footwear for the world's most seasoned travelers.

Through innovation and timeless design, MCM combines iconic German-engineered functionality with traditional craftsmanship, offering a heritage of elegance.

MCM establishes itself as a global luxury brand through European artisanship with a refined mastery of skills, handcrafting elegant products with flawless quality materials.

A long-time favorite of royalty and celebrities, MCM boasts architect-designed boutiques in chic cities such as Berlin, Dusseldorf, London, New York, Athens, Beijing, Shanghai and Seoul, and is sold by prestigious retailers all over the world.

First Lady

Handcrafted with original cow hide body & trim, the iconic First Lady Collection boasts a minimalist aesthetic refined by **exuberant** tones, deep hues and vibrant shades. Boasting a voluminous natural canvas interior with gilded brass hardwares, the structured shapes are designed as daytime handbags for convenient and practical use. The classy First Lady Collection befits virtually any attire, affording style versatility for style mavens and tastemakers alike.

URBAN STYLER

The smart & urbane Urban Styler collection sports a refined minimalist multifunctional appeal. With an emphasis on practicality, this collection was designed for **dexterous** and versatile use, handcrafted with original cowhide. With a bevy of pockets & compartments, this clever collection is built for the urban businessman **on-the-go**.

exuberant [ig'zju:bərənt] adj. 繁茂的；充溢的

dexterous ['dekst(ə)rəs] adj. 灵巧的；敏捷的

on-the-go adj. 忙个不停的；活跃的

成立于1976年的德国正统名牌Mode Creation Munich（MCM）针对极其睿智的顾客——全世界旅行爱好者而制作生产高级皮质物品、服装和鞋类产品。

以革新和超越时空设计而闻名的MCM，结合德国设计的卓越功能性和传统手工匠人精神，展现出MCM传统高贵优雅的气质。

MCM凭借上等材质配以精致而细腻的欧洲传统制作技术，制造出优雅而高贵的产品，从而成为国际化奢侈品品牌。

皇室和名人对于MCM的长期喜爱，使MCM在柏林、杜塞尔多

夫、伦敦、纽约、雅典、北京、上海、首尔等世界有名的时尚城市拥有着彰显建筑美的卖场，并在世界有名的百货店和购物商城均有出售。

First Lady 系列

经典的 First Lady 系列采用牛皮手工制作，融汇了丰富色彩、深邃色调和鲜明的明暗对比，呈现出精致亮丽的抽象派风格。该系列采用大量的天然帆布衬里和镀金黄铜配件，结构化外形设计，作为日间手提包方便实用。First Lady 系列可与任何服饰搭配，可以满足时尚达人或时尚先锋人士的需求。

URBAN STYLER精品系列

精致都会感十足的URBAN STYLER精品系列呈现出洗练的极简主义。款式设计注重品质、高效及实用性，采用上乘牛皮手工加工而成。这一系列为日常工作和休闲提供可观的储物空间，专为都市精英打造。

读书笔记

7.（意大利）皮尔袋鼠 Pierre Kangaroo

品牌名片

品　　类：皮具

标志风格：典雅、浪漫

创 始 人：皮尔（Pierre）

诞 生 地：意大利

诞生时间：1952年

皮尔袋鼠是一家专业从事都市高品位皮具经营的设计公司。品牌寓意沉稳、经典的同时，像袋鼠一样富有朝气。

品牌阅读

Founded in the late 1950s by Mr. PIERRE, Italian PIERRE KANGAROO showed itself in front of the world as a stylish leather products designer facing high end customers. Mr. PIERRE, the father of PIERRE KANGAROO brand, was an art lover since his childhood. When he grew up, he joined the army and became an excellent pilot. Not long after he took off his uniform, he became a successful fashion designer until one day he was captivated by leather design. In 1952, he resigned from his fashion designer job, created the PIERRE brand (named after his own name), and started a leather company in Turin, Italy.

PIERRE once said, his military life taught him a lot: seriously treat life, carefully treat every detail, follow the classical tradition, and honor every promise…all that Mr. PIERRE tried to **implant into** his design concepts and his expectation and requirements for young

generations. From the very beginning, he focused on young men as his major customer group and centerd his design on military style. In 1960s, the PIERRE leather quickly gained favor of Italian customers. Soon, over a dozen of PIERRE franchises were established in Italian. In 1970s, PIERRE's son took over his father's business. Inspired by his trip in Australia, he redesigned PIERRE's operation strategies, trying to add energetic and lively elements into the original calm and classical style, just like the Kangaroo. Later on, he changed the brand name to PIERRE KANGAROO.

Brand in Europe&America

Entering the 21st century, PIERRE KANGAROO began implementing global brand strategy. After a few years, it has successfully opened PIERRE KANGAROO franchises in many large and middle cities in Netherland, Finland, Czech Republic, Bulgaria, German and the U.S.A., and laid a good foundation for his globalization efforts. Now, there are over 180 PIERRE KANGAROO franchises operating in the world market.

Brand in Asia

Asia market has always been an important component in PIERRE KANGAROO's global brand strategy. PIERRE KANGAROO has already started its franchises in Tokyo, Osaka, Seoul, Singapore, Manila, New Deli and many other major Asian cities. In 2009 Hong Kong Fashion Week, the full spectrum **debut** of PIERRE KANGAROO stormed the entire global leather industry. This is just PIERRE KANGAROO's first handshake with Asia market.

Brand in China

In January 2010, Italian PIERRE KANGAROO (Hong Kong) was incorporated and began to lead its operation and development in China. According to its market development plan, by the end of 2015, there was going to be 80~100 PIERRE KANGAROO Franchises operating in mainland China.

In December 2010, in view of the quick development of emerging markets in Asia, especially, In Chinese market, Italian PIERRE KANGAROO sponsored Chinese Painting and Calligraphy Exhibition at the 16th Guangzhou Asian Games as the only sponsor representing leather industry. Italian PIERRE KANGAROO has the greatest confidence in China, the largest emerging market in the world, and is preparing to bring into China the latest Italian.

Brand's Target Customer

Urban men that respect traditional culture have stylish tastes and attach importance to high quality. They are serious toward their life and details, honor every promise being made. They pay attention to the world and **courageously** face every challenge. Usually, they are the elites in different professions who are keen on everything new that embodying the latest trend in the world and urban lives. They see PIERRE KANGAROO as brand that is actively changing its long-existing conservative and traditional image.

implant into 植入
debut ['deibju:] n. 初次登台
courageously [kə'reidʒəsli] adv. 勇敢地

意大利PIERRE KANGAROO皮具品牌公司创办于20世纪50

年代末，是一家专业从事都市高品位皮具经营的设计公司，由PIERRE先生创立。作为该品牌的创始人，PIERRE先生从小喜爱美术。其早年是位优秀的飞行员，退役后成为一位成功的服装设计师，在工作期间又对皮具设计深深着迷。1952年，他辞去了服装设计师的工作，在意大利都灵市创办了以自己名字命名的皮具品牌PIERRE皮具公司。

PIERRE说：军旅生活对他的影响很深，对生活态度的严谨，对细节的认真，对经典的沿承，对承诺的恪守，这些都被PIERRE植入他的设计理念和对年轻一代的期许中。所以PIERRE一开始锁定青年男士作为设计目标，产品以军旅文化为题材。20世纪60年代迅速受到意大利消费者的青睐，并陆续在意大利环境内开出10多家店铺。20世纪70年代，PIERRE的儿子继承了父业，一次澳洲旅行让他转变了PIERRE品牌的经营策略，他希望PIERRE皮具在沉稳、经典的同时，应该像澳洲的袋鼠一样更加活跃富有朝气，随后公司也随之更名为PIERRE KANGAROO皮具品牌公司。

品牌在欧美

进入21世纪后，PIERRE KANGAROO开始实施品牌全球化战略，近几年先后在意大利以外的荷兰、芬兰、捷克、保加利亚、德国、美国等国家、地区的大中型城市设品牌专卖店，为其品牌的全球化做了良好的铺垫工作。目前全球共设有180余家品牌专卖店。

品牌与亚洲

亚洲市场是PIERRE KANGAROO品牌全球化的重要部分，在东京、大阪、首尔、新加坡、马尼拉、新德里等地均开设有PIERRE KANGAROO品牌皮具专营店。在2009年的香港时装周上，PIERRE KANGAROO的亚洲完整闪亮登场引起皮具界的轰动，这是PIERRE KANGAROO首次和亚洲市场的亲密接触。

品牌与中国

2010年1月，意大利皮尔袋鼠国际集团（香港）有限公司成立，具体负责中国市场的经营与拓展，公司计划到2015年在中国内地发展80~100家PIERRE KANGAROO品牌皮具专营店。

2010年12月，由于对亚洲及新兴的中国市场的憧憬，意大利皮尔袋鼠公司赞助了第16届广州亚运会中国书画展，并成为亚运会书画展唯一的皮具赞助商。意大利皮尔袋鼠公司对全球最大的新兴市场——中国充满信心，大力的投入及全新的设计与策划，必将给中国皮具市场带来时尚的意大利皮具新理念。

品牌的目标顾客

尊重传统文化并向往和拥有高品质生活的中青年，他们对于生活的态度是严谨的，对待细节是认真的，对待承诺是恪守的。他们关注世界动向，勇于接受挑战，是各个专业领域的精英，热衷于尝试新事物，体验世界和城市生活中的最新潮流。他们视PIERRE KANGAROO品牌为存在已久的传统及保守的形象的积极转变。

读书笔记

Part 6 豪车系列

1.（意大利）法拉利 Ferrari

品牌名片

品　　类：车

标志风格：一级方程式赛车、赛车及高性能跑车

创 始 人：恩佐·法拉利（Enzo Ferrari）

诞 生 地：意大利

诞生时间：1929年

法拉利（Ferrari）的跃马徽标最初出现在车手制服上，后来它成为每一辆法拉利Gran Turismo 跑车和赛车最骄傲的象征。

品牌阅读

Ferrari is an Italian automobile manufacturer, founded by Enzo Ferrari in 1929. It mainly manufactures Formula One Car, car racing and high-performance sports car.

Headquartered in Modena, Italy (Modena), its most cars are manufactured by hand, with an annual output about 4,300. Early Ferrari sponsored racer and produced racing. It independently produced automobile in 1947, thereafter into today's scale. Now Fiat Company owns 50% equity of Ferrari but Ferrari can operate independently.

A total of 7,318 cars were delivered to the **dealership** network in 2012 (up 4.5 per cent on 2011), while revenues of 2.433 billion euro (up 8 per cent) were recorded. Trading profit jumped by 12.1 per cent to 350 million euro, with net profits coming in at just under 244 million euro (+17.8 per cent) and ROS (Return on Sales) of 14.4 percent which is very much on a par with the top companies in the

luxury sector.

Ferrari's continued success is thanks to two men who have provided **unrivalled** strong leadership - Enzo Ferrari and Luca di Montezemolo - and its talented and dedicated team of employees. Many elements: passion, diligence, innovation, determination, research, motivation, excellence, investment, technology, talent, training, exclusivity, selection, style, merit, and team spirit go to make up Ferrari's DNA. The secret is in its people - behind exceptional cars there are equally exceptional men and women - and in the knowledge that goes into combining all the ingredients in every sector of the company's activities: from design to production, from road cars to race cars, from the sales network to the development of the brand, from training to services provided for the employees, from customer care from the order to final delivery, this is Formula Ferrari.

Ferrari: the world's most powerful brand

Ferrari is the world's most powerful brand. And not simply in the opinion of millions of Prancing Horse enthusiasts the world over, indeed, the clients that continue to buy the cars built at Maranello year after year, but according to the annual list compiled by leading brand valuation experts Brand Finance.

Ferrari took the number one spot of the top five most powerful brands in 2013 ahead of the likes of Google, Coca-Cola, PwC and Hermes on a list that included the 500 most famous companies in the world. Because of its size, the Maranello Company cannot compete with the large multinational brands in terms of overall revenues. However, its brand rating takes into account other financial metrics, such as net margins, average revenue per customer and advertising and marketing spend, as well as qualitative parameters, such as brand affection and loyalty.

"It is always a pleasure to top any list and still more so when the competition includes some of the world's most famous companies. This achievement proves that even in very tough economic times, Italy can still offer the world businesses of excellence." commented Ferrari chairman Luca di Montezemolo,"Behind this acknowledgement are exceptional products made by equally exceptional men and women. They made it possible and for that I thank them."

A new and complete range

There are five models in today's range, all of them delivering their own interpretation of Ferrari's unique DNA made up of performance, excitement and technological innovation.

The three 8-cylinder models (California 30, 458 Italia, 458 Spider) and the two V12s (F12berlinetta and FF) are a new generation of cars which fully meet the philosophy of "different Ferraris for different Ferraristi", with each model meeting a different set of criteria. The theme of the sporty 12-cylinder Gran Turismo is interpreted by the FF, the first four-seater, four-wheel-drive car produced by the Prancing Horse. Very high performance with the ability to deliver driving pleasure at lower speeds too is guaranteed with the multi-award winning F12berlinetta. Of the 8-cylinder machines, the California 30 is the convertible Gran Turismo which combines a sporty feel with usability, without making compromises. The pure sports car, the 458 Italia, and its open top sibling, the 458 Spider, are fitted with the same mid-rear mounted V8, which for two straight years – 2011 and 2012 – has won two categories in the International Engine of the Year award

and which continues the glorious tradition of Ferrari cars with this engine **configuration**.

Added to these cars is the special limited-edition La Ferrari, of which only 499 will be built and which represents the highest expression of the company's excellence. Its development has allowed for experimentation that could be applied to the range in the future.

Leadership in technological innovation

Every new Ferrari features a high level of technological innovation, with ground-breaking solutions that usually then find their way onto cars from other manufacturers.

Among the many innovations introduced by the Maranello marque in the past, one only has to think of the steering wheel-mounted gear change, which went from F1 to road cars and then soon became the standard for any sports-oriented car. It's not by chance that Ferrari registered no less than 150 patents in the decade from 2003 to 2012, some of them revolutionary, such as the 4WD system that allows all-wheel traction in the FF only when it is required, ensuring light weight, efficiency and a sporty handling that was simply not possible with traditional 4WD technology.

Main innovations from Ferrari over the past 20 years

1997: F355 - first car with F1 electronically-actuated gear change with steering wheel mounted paddles

1999: 360 Modena - first car with a chassis and bodywork made entirely from **aluminium**

2002: Enzo Ferrari - first road car with Carbon Ceramic Brakes and active aerodynamics

2004: F430 - first car with electronic differential (E-Diff)

2006: 599 GTB Fiorano - first car with traction control (F1-Trac)

2008: Ferrari California - first car with F1 dual-clutch gear change with steering wheel mounted paddles

2011: FF - first car with 4RM (4WD) system

2013: LaFerrari – first car with HY-KERS **hybrid** technology

dealership ['di:ləʃip] n. 代理权；代理商

unrivalled [ʌn'raɪv(ə)ld] adj. 无与伦比的；无敌的

configuration [kən,figju'reiʃən] n. 配置

aluminium [,ælju'minjəm] n. 铝

hybrid ['haibrid] adj. 混合的

法拉利是一家意大利汽车制造厂，1929年由恩佐·法拉利创办，主要制造一级方程式赛车、赛车及高性能跑车。

法拉利总部位于意大利摩德纳，其生产的汽车大部分采用手工制造，年产量大约4300台。早期的法拉利赞助赛车手及生产赛车，1947年独立生产汽车，其后变成今日的规模。现在菲亚特公司拥有法拉利50%股权，但法拉利却能独立于菲亚特公司运营。

2012年，共有7318辆公路版跑车交付经销商（同比增加4.5%），营业收入为24.33亿欧元（增加8%）。营业利润上涨了12.1个百分点，达3.5亿欧元，净利润近2.44亿欧元（增加17.8%），销售利润上涨了14.4%，该业绩在奢侈品行业的顶尖企业中非常出色。

法拉利的持续辉煌来自于两位拥有非凡领导力的传奇人物——恩佐·法拉利（Enzo Ferrari）和卢卡·迪·蒙特泽莫罗（Luca di Montezemolo），以及其具有才干和献身精神的员工团队。激情、勤奋、创新、坚定、专研、激励、卓越、投资、技术、才华、培训、独特、精粹、风格、荣誉以及团队精神，诸多品质和要素共同铸就法拉利品牌的精髓。秘诀在于人，将所有这些品质和要素在整

个公司的每个方面实现完美的有机结合：从设计到生产，从公路跑车到赛车，从经销商网络维护到品牌研发，从培训到为员工提供服务，从关爱客户到个性化定制，从接收订单到最终交付。这就是伟大法拉利的成功秘诀。

法拉利：全球最具影响力品牌

法拉利为全球最具影响力品牌。这不仅是全球跃马热衷者的心声，也是那些年复一年从马拉内罗工厂购买法拉利的客户们的观点，全球知名品牌价值评估专家、英国品牌顾问公司Brand Finance的评级。

2013年榜单涵盖了全球500家知名企业，如谷歌、可口可乐、普华永道和爱马仕等，法拉利排名首位。由于商业模式原因，法拉利公司在整体收入上与大型跨国品牌没有可比性。但该品牌评级考虑到了包括财务指标在内的其他诸多因素，如净利润、用户平均收入、广告和营销支出以及诸如品牌情感和忠诚等定性参数。

“在任何一项排名中能名列前茅总会令人倍感欢欣，尤其是评比对象囊括了一些世界最知名的品牌。这一成绩证明，即使是在非常艰难的经济时代，意大利仍然可以造就卓越的世界级企业。”法拉利主席卢卡·迪·蒙特泽莫罗（Luca di Montezemolo）表示，“这一卓越成就的背后是同样卓越的员工所创造的卓越的产品。是他们使这一切成为可能，为此，我对他们表示感谢。”

新款及完整车型

现今主要有五种车型，它们都完美地诠释了法拉利独一无二的品质精髓——性能激情和技术创新。

新一代车型配备三个8缸发动机（California 30，458 Italia，458 Spider）或两个V12（F12berlinetta和FF）发动机，充分体现了“特别的法拉利献给特别的你”的设计理念，每款车型都符合一个不同的标准。运动型12缸GT（Gran Turismo）跑车的主题在跃马家族首款四座四驱车型FF上得到了完美演绎。屡获殊荣的高性能F12berlinetta跑车，可以保证低速行驶时享受同样愉悦的驾驶乐趣。在8缸车型中，California 30是完美结合了运动感与实用性的敞篷GT跑车。458 Italia及敞篷版458 Spider，都是纯正的跑车，配有相同的中后置V8发动机，该发动机在2011年和2012年连续两年赢得年度国际发动机奖，延续了配置有该发动机的法拉利跑车的光荣传统。

在这些车型中，增加了特别限量版La Ferrari跑车，La Ferrari将只生产499辆，它代表了迄今法拉利最卓越的成就。该车型的研究与开发将为未来汽车领域的探索积累丰富的经验。

引领技术创新

每一款法拉利的新车型都以高水平的技术创新为特色，其他汽车生产商常常会模仿其独创的设计方案。

在品牌过去推出的众多创新中，唯一必须想到的就是安装在方向盘上的变速装置，从最初的F1到公路跑车，然后迅速发展成为所有运动车型的标配。这绝非偶然，从2003年至2012年的10年中，法拉利注册了不少于150项专利，其中一些是革命性的发明，例如FF车型配备的全新四轮驱动系统，能够实现必要时的四轮牵引，确保重量轻、效能高和操控便捷，而这是传统的四轮驱动技术根本不可能做到的。

法拉利在过去20年的主要创新

1997年：F355 —— 应用了F1电子驱动变速的第一款车型，方向盘上安装有拨片

1999年：360 Modena —— 底盘和车身完全为铝制成的第一款车型

2002年：Enzo Ferrari ——碳陶瓷刹车系统和主动式空气动力学

的第一款公路跑车

2004年：F430 —— 带有电子差速器（E-Diff）的第一款车型

2006年：599 GTB Fiorano ——带有牵引力控制系统（F1-Trac）的第一款车型

2008年：Ferrari California —— 应用了F1双离合变速的第一款车型，方向盘上安装有拨片

2011年：FF —— 带有4RM（四轮驱动）系统的第一款车型

2013年：LaFerrari —— 使用了HY-KERS混合动力技术的第一款车型

读书笔记

2.（德国）宝马 BMW

品　　类：车

标志风格：高质量、高性能

创 始 人：卡尔·斐德利希·拉普（Karl Friendrich Rapp）

诞 生 地：德国

诞生时间：1916年

BMW是巴伐利亚发动机制造厂的缩写，标志的色彩和组合来自巴伐利亚州的州旗。

品牌阅读

In March 1916, the engineer Karl Friendrich Rapp and a friend founded the Bayerische Flugzeugwerke in Munich, Germany.

On July 21st, 1917, Rapp-Motorenwerke was renamed Bayerische Motoren Werke GmbH. The ongoing war meant that the small company grew quickly. With expansion in mind, the firm built a spacious plant right next to the Oberwiesenfeld airfield in Munich and continued to build engines for army planes until 1918.

Developed on the drawing board in 1922, the first BMW R32 motorcycle caused a sensation when unveiled at the Berlin Exhibition in 1923. To improve air cooling, Chief Engineer Max Friz had positioned the flat motor crosswise in a double-tube frame and transmitted its power via a cardan shaft directly to the wheel - a construction principle that is still used in BMW motorcycles today.

The company made train brakes and retrofitting engines after the war: constructing aircraft engines was forbidden. In 1922 it sold its

engine production and the name BMW to Bayerische Flugzeugwerke ("Bavarian Aircraft Works") and moved into their factory. The aircraft-maker's founding date, March 7th, 1916, thus became the new founding date of Bayerische Motoren Werke AG.

In 1925, BMW began working on the car, which laid a foundation for entering into the automobile industry. Afterwards, BMW bought the Eisenach automobile plant, where the Austin Seven was successfully produced under the name "Dixi 3/15 PS". This vehicle was developed further, going on sale in 1929 as the BMW 3/15 PS DA 2 with **a range of** different **bodyshells**, a small car with a lot of appeal. Its popularity helped the company to survive the lean years of the Depression.

Air raids destroyed the Munich plant in 1944, but the Allach plant was virtually unharmed at the end of the war. In mid-1945 BMW received permission to start repairing US army automobiles in Allach. It could also make spare parts for farming machinery and bicycles. Motorcycles could also be made again, but BMW was initially not in a position to do so.

In the early Eighties BMW bought a former barracks in Munich's northern suburbs and set about turning it into a research and engineering centre (FIZ). It consisted of design, construction and test facilities, a prototype construction unit and pilot plant. The first teams started work in 1985. Officially opened in 1990, the FIZ continued to increase its range of activities.

BMW Motorsport

BMW group has long history and brilliant record in Motorsport, and remains to be a main competitive force in Formula One. Going one step further in the Formula One season 2006, BMW was competing independently in Formula One to continue the success in the top racing games.

BMW Golf sport

BMW has been involved in golfing for 20 years. Both golfing and BMW are well-known for **exclusiveness**, aesthetics and perfection. For BMW the global **prevalence** of the sport allows for worldwide media interest.

a range of 一系列

bodyshell ['bɔdiʃel] n. 车架；车身外壳

exclusiveness [ik'sklu:sivnis] n. 独特性，独有性

prevalence ['prevələns] n. 流行

1916年3月，工程师卡尔·斐德利希·拉普（Karl Friendrich Rapp）与另一位朋友在德国慕尼黑创建了巴依尔飞机公司。

1917年7月21日，Rapp更名为BMW GmbH。接连不断的战争使得BMW快速增长。为了BMW得到更快的增长，决策者们决定在慕尼黑的Oberwiesenfeld机场附近建立一个宽敞的厂房，在1918年前继续为军队生产军用飞机。

1922年在BMW开始研制摩托车发动机，第一辆BMW摩托车R 32终于在1923年的柏林展览会上面世。一经面世，该车就博得了大众欢欣。为了改进该车的冷却效果，首席设计师Max Friz将原来的扁平发动机放置在双管框架上，并直接通过一个Cardan shaft将动力传输到车轮。该项构造在BMW摩托车的制造中沿用至今。

战后，BMW一度从事火车刹车器和Retrofitting发动机的生产，最终飞机发动机的生产遭到禁止。1922年，将其所有发动机产品以及“BMW”商标品牌出售给当时的巴伐利亚飞机制造厂，并且迁入

了他们的工厂。因此，该飞机制造厂的创始时间（1916年3月7日）就成了巴伐利亚汽车制造厂（即BMW）的创始时间。

1925年宝马开始研制汽车，为以后进军汽车业打下了基础。之后，BMW成功收购了Eisenach汽车制造厂，也就是成功生产Austin Seven的“迪昔Dixi3/15 PS”汽车的制造厂。这款车经过改进，于1929年作为“BMW 3/15 PS DA 2”品牌出售。该品牌的汽车包括不同的外型。汽车虽小，魅力无穷。BMW汽车帮助BMW在经济大萧条时期渡过难关。

1944年的空袭摧毁了慕尼黑的厂房，但位于Allach的厂房直到战争结束基本保持完好。1945年中期，BMW获得许可，对美军的军用汽车在Allach进行维修。同时还可以生产部分农用机械部件和自行车。摩托车最终也被允许生产，但最开始BMW并没有被列入可以生产摩托车的名单之内。

80年代中期，BMW收购了位于慕尼黑北郊的废旧兵营，并着手将其改建成BMW研究工程中心（FIZ）。该中心具有设计以及测试装备，是BMW又一处生产中心的雏形和试点。1985年在这里开展了第一个团队合作项目。1990年该中心正式成立，并一直扩大其活动范畴。

BMW汽车运动

在汽车运动方面具有光辉传统的宝马集团是一级方程式赛车运动的重要力量。在F1 2006赛季中，BMW车队，首次以独立身份参与F1世界锦标赛的竞争，在这项世界顶级赛事中书写自己新的辉煌。

BMW高尔夫运动

BMW致力于高尔夫运动的历史长达二十年，高尔夫运动和BMW品牌均以其尊崇个性、独特的美学品位和精益求精的品质而闻名于世。对BMW而言，这种运动在全世界范围内的流行也使之成为全球媒体关注的焦点。

3.（意大利）兰博基尼 Lamborghini

品牌名片

品　　类：车

标志风格：彪悍、狂野

创 始 人：费鲁基欧·兰博基尼（Ferruccio Lamborghini）

诞 生 地：意大利

诞生时间：1963年

兰博基尼的标志是一头充满力量、正向对方攻击的斗牛，这与兰博基尼大马力高速跑车的特性相吻合，据说这一标志也体现了创始人兰博基尼斗牛般不甘示弱的脾性。

品牌阅读

The history of Lamborghini Automobili officially started in 1963. Its founder was Ferruccio Lamborghini. Born in 1916, this capable, impetuous, **strong-willed** Taurus was the leading character in the foundation of the company and the early phases of its extraordinary history.

1963-1964

By the time he decided to build a factory of luxury sports cars, Ferruccio was already a very wealthy man. In the period following World War II, he founded his tractor factory, which he launched with energy and determination, creating a major point of reference in this industry. Other businesses followed, and he amassed his fortune at the perfect time, before his fiftieth birthday. By the early Sixties, Lamborghini was a powerful and successful man who knew exactly

what he wanted, but when he said he would build a super sports car to compete with Ferrari, many people thought he was mad. Constructing that kind of car was viewed as an **unexplainable extravagance**, a **hazardous** leap in the dark, and something that would squander his fortune without ever turning a profit.

He started working on this project in late 1962, and by May 1963 he had already founded Automobili Ferruccio Lamborghini, buying a large plot of land in Sant'Agata Bolognese, about 25 kilometres from Bologna, to build a new large and ultramodern factory. Because of the experience he had gained with his other companies, he was in a position to set up the best facilities for his purpose: a very functional structure that, at the time, was unrivalled in its field. The enormous and well-let central building was adjacent to the office building, so that the management could constantly monitor the production situation. This was ideal for Lamborghini, who would often **roll up** his shirtsleeves and go to work on the cars personally when he saw something that wasn't done just the way he wanted.

1964 was an extraordinary year. The 350 GT was born. The immediate and almost inevitable offshoot of the 350 GT, of which 120 were built, was the 400 GT. Its engine was increased to a four-litre model and it featured the first gearbox designed in-house by Lamborghini. Based initially on the two-seater body, which was later developed into the 400 GT 2+2 with two occasional seats behind the two regular ones, the 400 GT reached the respectable overall production figure of 273 units.

1965-1966

By early 1965 the coupes from Sant'Agata were starting to be noticed. This was the first, great phase of the Lamborghini company, and one of its most prolific and creative periods. Between October 1965 and June 1966, the company presented an astonishing number of new models.

The year was 1967, and Lamborghini could now look towards the future far more optimistically. The flood of orders for the Miura pumped new cash into his company, but above all it generated unparalleled interest and publicity. At least in this, Lamborghini had been right on target: a model like this was destined to overwhelm the minds and souls of all car buffs. Lamborghini thus became a symbolic name in the auto world, the emblem of excess, of going "further"at all costs, of always doing more and better than any rival without preconceptions of conventional limitations. This configuration did not prevent numerous aficionados from buying and appreciating the 400 GT, a serious and mature model by this time, but the Miura gave the company unique prestige.

The changes that were taking place around Lamborghini, however, reflected the social situation around the world, particularly in Italy. Labour unions' unrest in that period created a difficult situation in all factories, particularly at engineering companies in northern Italy, in which the owner's control was openly contested and proper organisation became increasing difficult. For Lamborghini, long accustomed to the direct, sometimes rough, somewhat paternalistic but attentive control of his factories, this new situation became intolerable. In 1972 he sold his majority stake to the Swiss Georges-Henri Rossetti, and the following year he sold his remaining shares to a friend, René Leimer. Thus, the company founder - the man who had been the driving force behind its extraordinary, vital explosion during

the first eight years - left the scene for good.

1972-1980

The oil crisis sparked by the 1973 Arab-Israeli War created a climate of fear about petrol supplies. As a result, the big, fuel-guzzling super sports cars rapidly became passé. They were considered the expression of unjustifiable luxury, whose exploitation of too much of our planet's natural resources was no longer acceptable. These were extremist stances that were destined to pass, but at the time they created enormous difficulties for all the makers of this type of car. Given its market position at the top end of the super car segment, Lamborghini was dealt a particularly harsh blow and the company did its best to react. In an attempt to overcome these problems, two new Urraco models were presented. In effect, they were spin-offs of the P250 range: a two-litre model (P200), again with a single camshaft but this time with a lower engine displacement in deference to tax restrictions, and a more powerful and mature 3-litre model (P300), with double overhead camshaft timing system and the power raised to 250 hp.The gradually deteriorating social situation and the drop in sales made it necessary to streamline the production range.

1987-1994

On April23, 1987, Nuova Automobili Lamborghini SpA was taken over by the US Chrysler company.The American owners quickly settled in at Sant'Agata and a period of intense activity began, this time in close collaboration with a major automotive industry. The premises were good, although there were a few false steps at the beginning: the prototype of the Portofino. Production of the Quattrovalvole series stopped in 1988, with a total of 631 units. In the meantime, the company gained experience with composite materials and a special Countach, the Evoluzione, demonstrated the full potential of this project. Weight reduction permitted by these new materials, coupled with a more powerful engine achieved above all using new engine technologies management, offered extraordinary performance. Unfortunately, however, the Evoluzione never went into production.

1994-1998

Chrysler's subsequent sudden decision to sell the Bologna Company to a group of unknown Indonesian investors seems far more difficult to explain. This change of hands became official on January21, 1994, destabilizing the company management.

Lamborghini turned to several top-level carmakers, including Audi, to request their technical collaboration. The initial idea was to ask for the 8-cylinder engine of the A8 flagship to power the future baby Lamborghini, but Audi's technical staff went back to company headquarters in Germany with very positive reports on the status of the company, its newfound good management and the professional level of the development work being done on its cars.

The first letter of intents between Audi and Lamborghini was signed on June12 1998, and the contract for the complete and definitive transfer of all the shares from the last Indonesian shareholder to the German company was completed on July27 of the same year, just 50 days later.

1998-Nowadays

The first major innovation came in 2001 with the successor to the Diablo: the Murciélago. It is almost superfluous to point out that this new model was also named after a famous, fierce fighting bull. The

fact that this Spanish word actually means bat only serves to augment the dark, almost nocturnal magnetism of this magnificent new car. Its power has also been boosted to 580 hp, and this obviously increases its speed, muscle and acceleration. What has been augmented above all is the sensation of the overall quality of the car, with a level of finishing touches that is even better than the already excellent results of the last Diablos. Sales have immediately gone well, and Lamborghini can count on selling each one it makes, as these cars are reserved by customers well in advance.

On the occasion of the 2003 Motor Show in Frankfurt Lamborghini showed for the first time a race version of its highly acclaimed super sports car, the Lamborghini Murciélago. Named Murciélago R-GT, Lamborghini was developing the competition car jointly with race experts Reiter Engineering and mother company Audi's sports division, Audi Sport. The new Murciélago R-GT will offer Lamborghini clients a highly competitive car to participate in professional motorsport events on an international level. With the Lamborghini Murciélago R-GT clients can compete in national and international race events such as the European FIA GT Championship or the American LeMans Series in the United States.

In July 2005 it was presented the Special Edition of the Gallardo, the Gallardo SE which was limited to 250 units and was characterized by a two-tone body paint, an even more sporty interior and technical improvement.

2013 marked the 50th anniversary of Lamborghini. The company's history is one of challenges and uncontested records, set by the ambitious talent of its founder Ferruccio Lamborghini, who decided to create the world's most beautiful - and powerful - super sports cars at Sant'Agata Bolognese in Italy's Emilia Romagna region. 100 years of innovation in half the time: Lamborghini was born under the sign of the Bull, with a constant view to the future, a desire to achieve the impossible and to make innovative design and technology its signature. Cars like the 350 GT, the Miura, the Countach, the LM 002 and today's Gallardo and Aventador are the perfect embodiment of Lamborghini's future vision.

strong-willed ['strɔŋ'wild] *adj.* 意志坚强的

unexplainable [ʌnɪk'spleɪnəb(ə)l] *adj.* 费解的；无法说明的

extravagance [ik'strævəgəns] *n.* 奢侈

hazardous ['hæzədəs] *adj.* 有危险的；冒险的

兰博基尼汽车有限公司的历史正式开始于 1963 年，创始人是费鲁基欧·兰博基尼。费鲁基欧·兰博基尼出生于 1916 年，具有金牛座的一切特征：能干、果敢、意志坚强。他是公司成立和早期发展的灵魂人物。

1963～1964年

在决定成立豪华跑车制造厂时，费鲁基欧已经非常富有。“二战”结束后，他成立了自己的拖拉机厂，在他的努力下，这家工厂成为行业的主要参考标准。随后，他审时度势，陆续发展其他行业，在五十岁生日之前已经积聚了大量的财富。在他六十岁时，费鲁基欧已经成为拥有巨大影响力的成功人士，他清楚地知道自己想要什么。但是，当他宣布要生产最好的超级跑车时，许多人都觉得他疯了。在当时，生产这类车被视为是一种无法解释的奢侈，是在黑暗中进行危险的跳跃，人们认为他会耗尽他的巨额财富但却得不到回报。

他在 1962 年底开始该项目，到 1963 年 5 月，他已经成立了费鲁基欧·兰博基尼汽车股份有限公司，在距离博洛尼亚 25 公里的

圣亚加塔·波隆尼买了一大块地，用来建造大型超现代化工厂。凭借他在运营其他公司得到的经验，他能够根据自己的目标建立最好的设施：在该领域无与伦比的功能性结构。照明良好的巨型中心建筑邻近办公大楼，使管理层能够持续监控生产状况。这非常适合费鲁基欧，当他看到工作没有按照他的预期开展时，他经常会卷起袖子，亲自对汽车进行作业。

1964 年是非常特别的一年。350 GT 正式面世。350 GT（共生产了 120 辆）的直系及近乎必然的分支是 400 GT。它的发动机增大为4升，并具有兰博基尼内部设计的第一款变速箱。400 GT 最初基于双座椅车体构建，后来在原有的座椅后方增加了2个座位，推出 400 GT 2+2，该型号共生产了 273 辆。

1965～1966年

到 1965 年初，来自圣亚加塔的轿车已广受关注。这是兰博基尼公司的第一个里程碑，是它最具创意和多产的阶段之一。从 1965 年 10 月到 1966 年 6 月，公司陆续推出一系列新型号。

这一年是 1967 年，兰博基尼现在可以更乐观地展望未来了。汹涌而至的Miura订单为公司注入了新的资金，但最重要的是，它激发了无与伦比的兴趣和广告效应。至少在这方面，兰博基尼已经实现了目标：这个款式注定要占据汽车发烧友的思想与灵魂。因而，兰博基尼成为汽车世界的代名词，奢华、不惜代价“更进一步”、无视传统限制、始终比对手做得更多更好的标志。该配置并不能阻止无数的发烧友购买和欣赏 400 GT，这是当时非常成熟的主流款式，但 Miura 为公司带来了独特的声望。

然而，兰博基尼周围发生的改变反映了全世界（尤其是意大利）的社会状况。当时的工会罢工使所有工厂面临困境，尤其是意大利北部的工程公司，公司拥有者的管理行为被公开抵制，正常的组织管理日益困难。费鲁基欧一直习惯于对工厂进行直接（有时非常强硬）、略带家长式作风但细致的控制，因此他对这种新状况更难以忍受。1972 年，他将大部分股权卖给了瑞士人 Georges-Henri Rossetti，第二年，他将余下股权卖给了他的朋友 René Leimer。这样，公司的创始人——这个在公司前8年一直推动它做出非凡业绩和爆炸性发展的男人，永远地离开了这家公司。

1972～1980年

1973年阿以战争导致的石油危机引发关于汽油供应的恐慌。结果，大型耗油的超级跑车很快变得过时了。它们被视为无理挥霍的象征，耗费了我们星球太多的自然资源，人们已经无法接受了。这种极端主义的观点虽然会过去，但在当时给这类汽车的所有制造商都造成了极大的困难。由于其在超级跑车市场的领导地位，兰博基尼遭遇的打击尤其沉重，公司做出最大努力回应。为了尝试克服这些问题，公司推出两款新的 Urraco。实际上，它们是 P250 系列的分支：2 升型号（P200），配备单凸轮轴，但发动机排量减少，以应对税收限制；以及动力更强、更成熟的 3 升型号（P300），该型号配备双顶置凸轮轴计时系统，动力提升至 250 匹马力。由于社会环境逐渐恶化和销量下降，必须对生产系列进行精简。

1981～1987年

幸运的是，由于这些汽车极具魅力，其炫耀的名称在当时已经成为一个传奇，再加上 Countach 绝对无与伦比的光环，这都引起了外界对该公司的极大兴趣。公司一开始进行清算便有无数仰慕者争先恐后想要接管。法官将公司委托给了两兄弟，简・克劳德和帕特里克・米勒曼。他们非常富有，在塞内加尔拥有一个糖果帝国。自然，他们是跑车爱好者。两兄弟在其圣亚加塔全权代表埃米尔・诺瓦罗的支持下立即开始重建公司。因此，“诺伐兰博基尼汽车制造公司”于 1981 年元月成立，并从那时开始，所有工作又重新开始

了。公司最初的决策之一便是聘请工程师朱里奥·奥菲瑞来担任公司的技术总监，这是一个明智的技术决策。

1987～1994年

1987 年 4 月 23 日，“诺伐兰博基尼汽车制造公司”被美国克莱斯勒公司接管。

这位来自美国的所有者迅速在圣亚加塔安顿下来，并展开了一系列紧张的活动。这次，公司与一个主要汽车制造业开始密切协作。尽管在一开始走了几次弯路，开端依然非常好：Portofino 的原型车诞生了。Quattrovalvole 系列于 1988 年停止生产，总共生产了 631 辆。在此期间，公司获得了关于复合材料的丰富经验，特别版 Countach（即 Evoluzione）也显示出这个项目的巨大潜力。这些新材料使得整体重量得以减少，配合一台采用全新发动机管理技术、功率更强大的发动机，可提供非凡的性能。然而，不幸的是 Evoluzione 一直没有投入生产。

1994～1998年

克莱斯勒随后突然决定把这个博洛尼亚的公司卖给一个不知名的印度尼西亚投资者，这似乎非常难以解释。公司于 1994 年 1 月 21 日正式移交接管权，这动摇了公司的管理。

兰博基尼转而向包括奥迪在内的几位顶级汽车制造商寻求技术合作。兰博基尼最初的想法是请求使用 A8 旗舰车型的 8 缸发动机为“兰博基尼雏形”提供动力，但奥迪的技术人员回到公司德国总部后，对公司的状况、新近发现的良好管理水平和开发跑车的专业水平做出了非常积极的评价。

奥迪与兰博基尼于 1998 年 6 月 12 日签订了第一份意向书，50 天后，即同年 7 月 27 日，最后一位印尼股东同意将所持股份转让给该德国公司，宣告奥迪收购兰博基尼举措的成功完成。

1998 年至今

2001 年，兰博基尼推出被收购后的第一款创新车型，Diablo 的后继型号：Murciélago。无需赘述，该款新车型的名字同样源自一头著名的、英勇善战的公牛。Murciélago 在西班牙语是“蝙蝠”的意思，但这只能增强该豪华大气车型的神秘感和无限的诱惑力。其功率也增加到 580 匹马力，这无疑提高了速度、力量和加速度。最重要的是，跑车的整体质感得到极大的提升，其内饰之精致，甚至超过之前广受好评的 Diablo 系列。Murciélago 的销量大增，由于车辆都是客户提前预订的，兰博基尼可以安心制造，无需担心销售问题。

在 2003 年法兰克福车展上，兰博基尼超级跑车 Murciélago 首次亮相就一炮而红，大受欢迎。赛车 Murciélago R-GT 由兰博基尼与其母公司奥迪的跑车部门 Audi Sport 以及赛车专业公司 Reiter Engineering 三方共同开发而成。新款 Murciélago R-GT 可为兰博基尼客户提供强悍无比的性能，让他们在国际级别的专业赛车活动中尽情驰骋，一决胜负。客户可以驾驭 Murciélago R-GT 参加众多国内外赛事，如国际汽联欧洲锦标赛（European FIA GT Championship）和美国勒芒系列赛（LeMans Series）。

2005年7月，兰博基尼推出Gallardo特别版——Gallardo SE，全球限量发售250辆，其特色在丁车身采用双色油漆工艺，同时搭配更具动感地带内饰，技术方面也有较大改进。

2013 年标志着兰博基尼进入其第 50 个年头。该公司的历史是一部由充满雄心，立志打造全世界最美、最强劲的超级跑车的创始人费鲁基欧·兰博基尼在意大利艾米利亚·罗马涅地区的圣亚加塔·波隆尼谱写出的载满挑战与闪亮纪录的史诗。用 50 年的时间完成 100 年的创新：兰博基尼自诞生起即以公牛为标志，始终放眼于未来，力求实现以往不可能的挑战，并专注于其标志性的创新设计和技术。诸如 350 GT、Miura、Countach、LM 002 以及今天的 Gallardo 和 Aventador 等跑车是兰博基尼愿景的完美体现。

4.（意大利）玛莎拉蒂 Maserati

品牌名片

品　　类：车

标志风格：时尚、动感

创 始 人：玛莎拉蒂兄弟

诞 生 地：意大利

诞生时间：1914年

玛莎拉蒂的品牌标志是在树叶形的底座上放置的一支三叉戟，这是公司所在地意大利博洛尼亚市的市徽，相传于罗马神话中的海神纳普秋手中的武器，显示出海神巨大无比的威力。

品牌阅读

Officine Alfieri Maserati was founded on December 1, 1914 in Bologna, Italy. Since then, Maserati has played a consistently important role in the history of sports car culture and its development. More than a century of activity has brought with it glorious achievements both on the road and the track as well as more challenging times, which have helped forge the company's character and personality.

The Maserati Brothers

The seven Maserati brothers were born in Voghera to Rodolfo, a train driver and Carolina Losi.

Carlo, their first son, was born in 1881, Bindo in 1883 and Alfieri in 1885. At just a few months old, Alfieri sadly passed away and his parents decided to name their next son, born in 1887, after him. They were to have three more children: in 1890 Mario was born, followed by Ettore in 1894 and Ernesto in 1898.

All of the Maseratis were involved in the engineering, design and construction of cars, except for Mario, who was a painter and artist. However Mario's contribution to the Maserati company was just as important and lasting as his engineer brothers: he created the company trademark, the Trident, inspired by the statue of Neptune in the square of the same name in their home city of Bologna.

The first of the brothers to become involved with engines was Carlo, who worked in a bicycle factory in Affori, near Milan. He designed a single-cylinder engine for a velocipede, which was later manufactured by the Marquis Carcano di Anzano del Parco. Carlo Maserati also raced on Carcano bikes equipped with the engine he had designed, winning a few races and setting a speed record of 50 km/h (31 mph) in 1900.

Carlo moved to Fiat in 1901 when Carcano closed down and then, in 1903, to Isotta Fraschini, where he worked as a mechanic and test driver. Thanks to his influence, Isotta also employed his brother Alfieri, despite the fact that he was only 16 at the time. Carlo had a brilliant but ultimately short career, dying when he was just 29, by which time he had worked and raced for Bianchi, become General Manager of Junior, and started up his own workshop with his brother Ettore to manufacture both low and high **voltage** electrical transformers for cars.

Alfieri soon emerged as Carlo's spiritual heir, with the same extrovert personality and skills as a technician and driver. In 1908 Isotta entrusted a car to him which he brought home in 14th place in the Grand Prix for Voiturettes in Dieppe, despite his carburettor

breaking. In the meantime, Bindo and Ettore had also joined Isotta Fraschini, where Alfieri had started out as a mechanic and progressed to driving. In 1912, after having represented the company in Argentina, the USA and Great Britain with his brother Ettore, Alfieri was put in charge of Isotta's customer service structure in Bologna.

The wide-ranging experience he had built up during his career convinced Alfieri that he was ready to explore the possibility of going into business in his own right to exploit his talents and creativity to the fullest extent. In 1914 he rented office space in Via dé Pepoli, in Bologna's old town centre and this went on to become the first headquarters of the Società Anonima Officine Alfieri Maserati.

The beginning: from 1914 to 1937

After the First World War, the company moved from Via dé Pepoli to new offices in the suburbs of Bologna.

The Maserati brothers' main activity was still tuning Isotta Fraschini cars, but they also worked on other marques.

Alfieri began his career as a racing driver and soon proved his worth, winning on the Susa-Moncenisio, the Mugello Circuit and the Aosta-Great Saint Bernard. Diatto offered him a chance to design cars for the company and even to race with them. Unfortunately, in 1924, after having dominated the San Sebastiano GP, he was disqualified for five years, even though he had retired, for having replaced the 2-litre engine in his car with a 3-litre unit. The penalty was lifted a few months later.

Away from the racing world, Alfieri completely dedicated himself to the workshop and in 1926, after leaving Diatto, he produced the Tipo 26, the first all-Maserati car, and the first to sport the trident badge. The Tipo 26 won its class in its debut race, the Targa Florio, and was driven by Alfieri Maserati himself.

In 1927 Alfieri had a serious accident in the Messina Cup at the wheel of the Tipo 26B, after taking third place at the Targa Florio. But even with him sidelined, Maserati still won the Italian Constructors' Championship. In 1929 the V4 appeared, with a 16-cylinder engine, making its debut at the Italian Grand Prix and setting the world Class C speed record over 10 km at 246.069 km/h in Cremona, with Baconin Borzacchini.

The record set by the V4 helped to further enhance the company's image and guaranteed a considerable influx of funds, allowing both the company and its activities to expand. In 1930 the V4 driven by Borzacchini won Maserati's first outright Grand Prix victory in Tripoli.

In 1931 came the 4CTR and the **front-wheel-drive** 8C 2500, the last car to be designed by Alfieri Maserati, who died on March 3, 1932. An enormous crowd attended his funeral in Bologna, including workers from the plant, famous drivers and ordinary people, who all wanted to show their affection for the great man.

Alfieri's death did not discourage the Maserati brothers; Bindo left Isotta Fraschini and returned to Bologna to continue the great venture begun by Alfieri, alongside Ernesto and Ettore. Maserati's racing activities continued to be both intense and successful; an 8-cylinder, 3-litre engine also appeared.

In 1933 Tazio Nuvolari joined the team, making a significant technical contribution, particularly in fine tuning the chassis, adapting it to the characteristics of the new engine; Nuvolari won the Belgian Grand Prix, and those of Montenero and Nice. That was when Mercedes-Benz and Auto Union began a sustained assault on the

racing scene, making life difficult for Maserati in the more important races.

In spite of this, the company continued to notch up victories in more minor, national races, and this led the brothers to concentrate output in this area. In 1936 they found a patron in Gino Rovere who invested a great deal in the company and appointed Nino Farina, his protégé, as Chairman. The 6CM appeared, which gave Maserati the competitive edge in the voiturette class.

The golden years: from 1937 to 1967

In 1937 the Maserati brothers sold their shares in the company to the Orsi family from Modena.

The company relocated from Bologna to the now historic headquarters on Viale Ciro Menotti in Modena. Ernesto had already designed the 4CL and 8CL engines, which powered the cars of the same name in the late 1930s. The Maserati brothers stayed on in Modena as chief engineers until 1948.

The company dominated the racing scene again, despite strong competition from Mercedes. On 30 May, 1939 it scored an important victory in the Indianapolis 500 with Wilbur Shaw at the wheel of the 8CTF, a feat it repeated the following year. Maserati remains to this day the only Italian marque to have won the Indy 500.

During the Second World War Maserati adapted its production accordingly, turning out machine tools, electrical components, spark plugs and electric vehicles, but returned to its original activities after the war, with a new GT car, the A6 1500.

The recent years: from 1968 to nowadays

The big news came in 1968, when Citroën bought out the Orsi

family's shares, although Adolfo Orsi remained the company's Honorary Chairman.The Giugiaro-designed Bora, the first mass-produced mid-engined Maserati, was presented at the 1971 Geneva Motor Show; Maserati also built the occasional racing car engine, and that same year, a Citroën SM with a Maserati engine won the Morocco Rally.

With the launch of the Merak and Khamsin, Maserati's production continued apace. But in 1973 the Yom Kippur War sparked the Oil Crisis, making life increasingly uncertain for the company, although it still had enough vitality to introduce both the Quattroporte II prototype, bodied by Bertone, and the Merak SS.

The situation worsened, and on May23, Citroën announced that Maserati had gone into liquidation (the French car maker had signed an agreement with Peugeot but had lost interest in Maserati). Pressure from the industrialists' association and the local and provincial councils succeeded in persuading the government to intervene, and Maserati avoided closure by handing over control to GEPI (a government agency that financed companies in difficulty in order to save jobs).

The turning point for Maserati came in 1993, when the company's entire share capital was acquired by Fiat Auto. A year later the first new arrival under Fiat ownership appeared in the form of the Quattroporte. Designed by Marcello Gandini, it boasted all of the refinement, luxury and sportiness for which the marque was renowned. On July1, 1997 Fiat sold Maserati to Ferrari, and a new era began for the company. That year the historical plant in Viale Ciro Menotti, Modena closed temporarily while an ultra-modern **assembly line** was installed, to produce a new car, the 3200 GT.

In early 2005, ownership of Maserati was transferred from Ferrari to Fiat, which allowed the two marques to achieve important industrial and commercial synergies with Alfa Romeo. Close technical and commercial collaboration within the group has provided Maserati with the impetus to position itself as the leader in its sector. It has also broadened its presence throughout the international markets thanks to models including the GranSport, the GranSport Spyder and the MC Victory, developed to celebrate successes in the FIA GT series. In 2007, above all, Maserati's impressive performance was mainly thanks to the GranTurismo.

The GranTurismo is a car that can be used everyday. It has superb handling and a sporty captivating ride. At the same time, on board comfort is not ignored and the choice of materials, the attention to detail, and the generous interior space that comfortably seats four adults are all features that make it a true leader in its class. The international press deemed the car an immediate success and lavished it with praise as it made the covers of countless magazines.

voltage ['vəultidʒ] *n.* [电] 电压

front-wheel-drive 前轮驱动

prototype ['prəutətaip] *n.* 原型

assembly line 装配线

Officine Alfieri Maserati于1914年12月1日在意大利博洛尼亚成立。从此，玛莎拉蒂就一直在跑车文化及发展史中发挥着重要作用。在一个多世纪的拼搏中，玛莎拉蒂度过了一次又一次的困难时期，在公路和赛道方面都取得了辉煌的成就，并在此过程中历练出了鲜明的公司品质和个性。

玛莎拉蒂兄弟

玛莎拉蒂7兄弟出生于Voghera，父亲Rodolfo是火车司机，母亲是Carolina Losi。

大儿子卡洛出生于1881年，Bindo、阿尔菲力分别于1883年、1885年出生。几个月后，阿尔菲力不幸夭折，于是父母决定把1887年出生的儿子取名为阿尔菲力。玛莎拉蒂夫妇还有三个孩子：1890年出生的Mario、1894年出生的Ettore和1898年出生的埃内斯特。

除Mario外，玛莎拉蒂兄弟都从事汽车工程、设计和生产方面工作。Mario是画家，据推测，正是他创作了公司的三叉戟商标，其设计借鉴了博洛尼亚三叉戟广场的海神尼普顿雕像。

兄弟中第一个涉足发动机领域的是卡洛，他在米兰附近Affori的自行车厂工作。他为脚踏车设计了单缸发动机，后来Carcano di Anzano del Parco侯爵生产了这款脚踏车。卡洛为Carcano脚踏车配备了自己设计的发动机，并骑着它参加了赛车比赛，结果获胜几场，并在1900年创造了50公里/小时（31英里/小时）的速度纪录。

1901年Carcano倒闭，卡洛转投菲亚特；并于1903年来到Isotta Fraschini，担任机械和测试驾驶员。在他的帮助下，Isotta雇用了他弟弟阿尔菲力，尽管当时他只有16岁。卡洛在29岁时去世，其职业生涯短暂但不失辉煌：他为比安奇（Bianchi）工作、参赛，并成为了年轻的总经理；与兄弟Ettore开办了自己的工厂，生产车用低压、高压变压器。

阿尔菲力与卡洛一样个性外向，同样具备技术师和驾驶员的技术，因此很快继承了卡洛的事业。1908年，Isotta赠予阿尔菲力一辆赛车，他驾驶这辆车代表Voiturettes参加了Dieppe大奖赛，尽管化油器破损，还是取得了第14名的成绩。与此同时，Bindo和Ettore也加盟了Isotta Fraschini。在这里，阿尔菲力从机械工做起，并最终成为了一名驾驶员。和兄弟Ettore一起担任公司驻阿根廷、美国

和英国代表之后，阿尔菲力于1912年开始负责Isotta在博洛尼亚的客户服务构架。

职业生涯积累的丰富经验让阿尔菲力深信自己能够凭借一己之力在商界闯荡，并最大程度地发掘自己的聪明才智和创造潜能。1914年，他在博洛尼亚老城中心的Via dé Pepoli租得一处办公场所，随后这里成为了Società Anonima Officine Alfieri Maserati的第一个总部。

早期：1914～1937年

战后，公司从Via dé Pepoli迁到位于博洛尼亚郊区的新办公地点。

玛莎拉蒂兄弟的主要工作仍然是调试Isotta Fraschini车，但他们也从事其他和法拉利相关的工作。

阿尔菲力开始职业赛车生涯，并很快证明了自己的价值，赢得了Susa-Moncenisio、 Mugello Circuit和 Aosta-Great Saint Bernard大赛。Diatto向他提供了为公司设计汽车的机会，甚至让他驾驶公司的车辆参赛。不幸的是，在包揽圣塞瓦斯蒂安大奖赛后，因用3升发动机取代2升发动机，他被禁赛5年，即使当时他已退休。但数月之后，该处罚得以取消。

在比赛之外的闲暇时间，阿尔菲力就埋身于生产车间。离开Diatto之后，他在1926年制造出了Tipo 26，这是第一辆纯粹的玛莎拉蒂车，也是第一辆带有三叉戟标志的跑车。Tipo 26首次登场参加Targa Florio耐力赛就独领风骚，车手正是阿尔菲力·玛莎拉蒂本人。

获得Targa Florio大赛第三名后，阿尔菲力于1927年驾驶Tipo 26B参加Messina杯大赛时发生了严重事故。即使失去了这员大将，玛莎拉蒂仍然获得意大利制造商冠军。1929年，巴克宁·波尔扎奇尼驾驶搭载16汽缸发动机的V4跑车在克雷莫纳首次参加意大利Grand

Prix大赛就表现出色，以246.069公里的时速创造了世界C级时速纪录（行驶距离大于10公里）。

V4创造的纪录进一步提升了公司形象，保证了资金的大量涌入，让公司及各项活动得以拓展。1930年，波尔扎奇尼驾驶V4在黎波里为玛莎拉蒂首次赢得大奖赛冠军。

1931年，阿尔菲力·玛莎拉蒂的绝作4CTR和前轮驱动的8C2500问世，不久以后他即于1932年3月3日与世长辞。数以万计的人——包括工厂工人、著名驾驶员和普通民众都来到博洛尼亚，参加了他的盛大葬礼，向这位伟人表达缅怀之情。

玛莎拉蒂兄弟并没因阿尔菲力的去世而一蹶不振，Bindo离开Isotta Fraschini并回到博洛尼亚，与埃内斯特和Ettore一起接手阿尔菲力开创的企业。玛莎拉蒂的赛事激烈而成功，8缸3升发动机亦研制成功。

1933年，Tazio Nuvolari加盟，并在技术上，特别是底盘改良方面做出了突出贡献，从而让底盘能够适应新型发动机的特性。Nuvolari获得比利时大奖赛、Montenero大奖赛和Nicc大奖赛的胜利。此时，奔驰和汽车联盟在赛场开始了持续不断的激烈角逐，令玛莎拉蒂在这些重要赛事上举步维艰。

尽管如此，公司在国内小型赛事上却屡有斩获，这让玛莎拉蒂兄弟们开始将精力集中在这个领域。1936年，玛莎拉蒂兄弟在Gino Rovere结识的一位赞助商向公司投入了大笔资金，并任命自己的亲信尼诺·法里纳为公司董事长。6CM问世后，玛莎拉蒂在小型车领域获得了竞争优势。

黄金岁月：1937～1967年

1937年，玛莎拉蒂兄弟将公司股份出售给摩德纳的奥斯家族。公司从博洛尼亚迁回到了如今位于摩德纳Ciro Menotti大街历史悠久的总部。埃内斯特已经设计出了4CL和8CL发动机，它们在20世纪30

年代晚期的玛莎拉蒂跑车上得到了应用。1948年前，玛莎拉蒂兄弟一直在摩德纳担任首席工程师。

尽管与奔驰的竞争激烈，但玛莎拉蒂还是重新主宰了赛场。威尔伯·肖于1939年5月30日驾驶8CTF赛车夺得了印第安纳波利斯500英里大奖赛的桂冠，并在第二年再次夺魁。

“二战”期间，玛莎拉蒂对产品进行了相应调整，开始生产机床、电气配件、火花塞和电动汽车，但在战后很快回归了正轨，并推出了全新的GT车A6 1500。

1968年至今

1968年爆出了一则重大新闻，雪铁龙买断了奥斯家族的全部股份，尽管阿道夫·奥斯仍然担任公司的名誉董事长。Giugiaro设计的Bora首次亮相于1971年日内瓦车展，并成为了首批量产的中置发动机玛莎拉蒂汽车。玛莎拉蒂也偶尔生产赛车发动机，同年，搭载玛莎拉蒂发动机的雪铁龙SM获得了摩洛哥拉力赛冠军。

随着Merak和Khamsin的推出，玛莎拉蒂的产量继续保持快速增长。1973年第四次中东战争导致的石油危机给公司的前景蒙上了一层阴影，但公司依然引进了博通（Bertone）车身的Quattroporte II原型和Merak SS。

形势继续恶化，5月23日，雪铁龙宣布玛莎拉蒂进入清算（该法国汽车生产商已与标致签署协议，对玛莎拉蒂失去了兴趣）。行业协会、地方以及省理事会联合施压，成功说服政府介入，由GEPI（为保留工作职位向境况不佳的公司提供资金的政府机构）接管玛莎拉蒂，后者才逃过了倒闭厄运。

菲亚特汽车公司于1993年购买了玛莎拉蒂的全部股份，这堪称是公司的转折点。一年后，玛莎拉蒂在归入菲亚特后首次推出了新款汽车：Quattroporte总裁系列。这款车由马塞罗·甘迪尼（设计师）设计，完美传承了玛莎拉蒂品质精良、奢华动感的特色，品牌也因此而闻名。1997年7月1日，菲亚特将玛莎拉蒂售予了法拉利，从此公司迎来了新的纪元。那年，玛莎拉蒂临时关闭了位于摩德纳Ciro Menotti大街历史悠久的工厂，以安装生产新车3200GT所需的超现代化生产线。

2005年初，法拉利将玛莎拉蒂所有权转让给菲亚特，两大品牌由此获得了与阿尔法·罗密欧开展行业和商业协作的重要机会。集团内密切的技术和商业协作为玛莎拉蒂获得行业领先地位提供了巨大助力。同时，得益于GranSport、GranSport Spyder和MC Victory（为庆祝荣获世界超级跑车锦标赛冠军而开发）等多款车型的推出，玛莎拉蒂也扩大了自己的国际市场占有率。公司在2007年的非凡业绩表现主要归功于GranTruismo跑车再次带来的不菲利润。

GranTurismo跑车可以用于日常生活。它具有一流的操控性和动感迷人的驾乘感受，同时乘坐的舒适感亦可圈可点。另外，这款车的精良选材，对细节的关注以及可容纳4名成人的宽敞内部空间也令其在同档车型中脱颖而出。这款车迅速获得了巨大的成功，不仅成为各大国际媒体关注和褒奖的对象，还登上了无数杂志的封面。

读书笔记

5.（意大利）布加迪 Bugatti

品牌名片

品　　类：车

标志风格：新颖、流畅

创 始 人：艾托里·布加迪（Ettore Bugatti）

诞 生 地：意大利

诞生时间：1909年

布加迪品牌标志中的英文字母即布加迪，上部EB即为艾托里·布加迪英文拼音的缩写，周围一圈小圆点象征滚珠轴承，底色为红色。

品牌阅读

To fully appreciate the fascinating world of Bugatti, you need to look back in time. This automobile company has a one hundred year history with its founder, Ettore Bugatti, at its core.

At the time of Bugatti's birth, the era of the automobile had just begun. Hundreds of small companies were building their first motor vehicles, largely hand-made. Although they were already fitted with **combustion engines**, their forms were still strongly reminiscent of the horse-drawn carriage. And every drive was an adventure. The roads were often unsuitable and the local **pharmacy** was the only place you could buy petrol. This all changed in 1916 with the introduction of the assembly line. To meet growing international demand, Ford began the mass production of automobiles in the USA. The engineers of this transformational time were living legends. While many of them have long been forgotten, a few have become household names, among them Ettore Bugatti. The history of the automobile is inextricably linked with the lifetime achievements of these pioneers.

His talent was to take the greatest innovation of the early 20th century, the automobile, and infuse it with uncompromising artistic aspiration, beauty, luxury and technical performance. A myth was born whose magic has endured for a century, even though fewer than 8,000 automobiles in total have emerged from the Alsatian factory in Molsheim. That's because the fundamental values of the Bugatti name - elegance, power, exclusivity, quality and outstanding design - are as valid today as they were 100 years ago.

Bugatti has always been the epitome of exclusivity, luxury, elegance, style, extraordinary design and a great passion for automobiles.

Unique visions, the strong legacy of legendary sports cars, and high-precision engineering in development, construction and manufacture distinguish this outstanding automotive brand. The elegant, individual and independent character of Bugatti automobiles is reflected in the brand logo: the pearl-framed oval sporting 60 pearls, the stylized initials of the brand's founder Ettore Bugatti and the elegantly simple Bugatti word mark have adorned each Bugatti model since 1909. The logo embodies the official statement and the tradition-conscious promise that Bugatti offers its **discerning** customers.

combustion engine 内燃机
pharmacy ['fɑ:məsi] n. 药房
discerning [di'sə:niŋ] adj. 有辨识能力的；眼光敏锐的

想要体会布加迪的品牌魅力，就必须了解这家汽车企业数百年的历史。而其中的核心人物是企业创始人艾托里·布加迪。

艾托里·布加迪的降生恰逢汽车工业时代拉开序幕。当时有数

百家小型企业开始用手工生产的方式制造内燃机动车，但外观最初仍然模仿马车。驾驶汽车犹如探险：大多数道路并不适合汽车行驶，而汽油也只在药房才有销售。然而从1916年开始，由于全球汽车需求不断增加，美国的福特公司投入流水线开始大规模生产汽车。在这蓬勃发展的时代出现了众多传奇般的工程师，而他们的名字现在早已被人们所淡忘。相反，艾托里·布加迪这个名字如今却已是家喻户晓。汽车工业的历史正是与这些业界先驱们的毕生努力紧密相连的。

他成功地将艺术追求、精致外观、奢华品位以及顶尖技术完美地融汇在汽车这项20世纪最伟大的创造发明上。 他的工厂坐落在阿尔萨斯地区的莫尔塞姆小镇，出产的汽车总量虽然还不到8000辆，但其强烈的影响延续至今，撰写出汽车行业的一个神话故事。这些汽车优雅、强劲、奢华、品质卓越、设计精湛——100年来始终如一。

布加迪品牌自创办之日起就是个性独特、豪华高雅、造型优美、激情四射的代名词。

独一无二的设计思路、经典跑车的悠久历史以及在研制、设计和生产时普遍采用手工制作以确保精度，这些都是布加迪品牌的核心价值所在。布加迪汽车高雅、独特、不受拘束的个性在车标上体现得淋漓尽致：由60个小圆点、创始人艾托里·布加迪姓名开头字母“E”的异体字和线条鲜明的公司名称Bugatti组成，从1909年开始，每辆布加迪汽车都使用了这个车标。这代表了布加迪企业对其高级、有品位的客户们的庄严承诺。

6.（英国）劳斯莱斯 Rolls-Royce

品牌名片

品　　类：车
标志风格：怀旧、大气
创 始 人：查理·史蒂华特·劳斯（Charles Stewart Rolls）
　　　　　亨利·罗易斯（Henry Royee）
诞 生 地：英国
诞生时间：1906年

劳斯莱斯汽车的标志图案采用两个“R”重叠在一起，象征着你中有我，我中有你，体现了两人融洽及和谐的关系。

品牌阅读

The best cars in the world have always been surrounded by stories about legendary models, their renowned performance and their owners.

Every Rolls-Royce motor car is built by hand at the state-of-the-art head quarters and manufacturing facility at the Home of Rolls-Royce Motor Cars at Goodwood. Designed by architect Sir Nicholas Grimshaw, the building was designed to have minimal impact on the environment.

Since 1904 Rolls-Royce has created instantly recognisable motor cars that have made the marque an enduring icon all over the world.

Phantom redefined the **marque** for the 21st century - a fitting celebration of the principles of Sir Henry Royce. This continuing pursuit of innovation, realised in EX programme and the models it has produced, has created new benchmarks for the industry.

Ghost Family

Ghost's designers were inspired by this photograph of Don Carlos de Salamanca at the 1913 Spanish Grand Prix. His serene expression after winning the gruelling 190-mile race in his Rolls-Royce Silver Ghost suggested the simple and effortless driving experience they re-created for the 21st Century Ghost.

Ghost is the essence of Rolls-Royce in its simplest and purest form. Advanced engineering combined with a host of hidden technology creates a dynamic yet comfortable drive. The principle of delivering simplicity out of complexity runs throughout Ghost and Ghost Extended Wheelbase. Everything is designed, engineered and crafted to be so invitingly approachable, so simplc, it encourages you to regard either car as appropriate for any occasion. Inside it's like being cocooned in your own **convivial** private sanctuary that leaves you relaxed and **unruffled** after the longest journey.

Phantom Family

Every Phantom is hand-built at the Home of Rolls-Royce at Goodwood in England. From seamstresses to surface finish technicians and French polishers, it takes 60 pairs of hands to design, craft and construct a Rolls-Royce before it's ready for its owner.

Designed without compromise, the Phantom family is the result of complete creative and engineering freedom. Created with the desire to build the best car in the world, Phantom combines compelling charisma with design cues that are unmistakably Rolls-Royce.

marque [mɑ:k] n. 商品型号

convivial [kən'viviəl] adj. 欢乐的，愉快的

unruffle [ʌn'rʌf(ə)ld] v. 变得平静

作为世界上最经典的汽车，劳斯莱斯拥有许多关于其传奇车型、卓越性能及车主的故事。

每一辆劳斯莱斯汽车都出品自劳斯莱斯诞生地古德伍德。在现代化总部，运用先进生产设施，经手工打造而成。劳斯莱斯总部的建筑物由建筑师Nicholas Grimshaw爵士设计，处处体现尽可能环保的设计理念。

早在 1904 年，劳斯莱斯就制造出了一眼即可辨认的汽车，并将品牌打造成为享誉全球的不朽标志。

幻影是向亨利·莱斯爵士理念的致敬之作，更是重新定义了21世纪的劳斯莱斯汽车。这种对创新技术的不懈追求，在 EX计划以及其生产的车型中得以实践，并为汽车行业设立了全新基准。

古斯特系列

1913 年西班牙大奖赛中车手 Don Carlos de Salamanca 的一张照片，令古斯特的设计者大受启发。Don Carlos de Salamanca驾驶其劳斯莱斯银魂赢得190英里高强度比赛之后展现出的平静而从容的神态，触动了设计者们: 21 世纪的古斯特需要为驾驶者再次带来这种简单而又从容自如的驾驶体验。

古斯特以最简单、最纯正的方式体现了劳斯莱斯的精髓所在。先进的工程设计结合众多隐藏技术，带来动感十足而又舒适备至的驾驭体验。化繁为简的原则贯穿整个古斯特及古斯特加长版的设计。每个细节都经过精心设计及精工打造，从而造就出如此动人的简约身姿，成为适宜出席各种场合的心仪之选。置身车内，如同身处美妙无比的私人殿堂，漫漫旅途，尽享一路轻松怡然。

幻影系列

每一辆幻影都是在劳斯莱斯之家——英格兰的古德伍德手工打造而成。在向车主交付产品之前，从女裁缝师到表面抛光技师和法国打磨师，每一辆劳斯莱斯都需要 60 双手来设计、制作和打造。

幻影系列的设计无懈可击，它是全方位创意与工程技术充分结合并自由发挥的结晶。以“打造世界上最好的汽车”为宗旨，完美融合了引人瞩目的外观和设计元素，成为经典的劳斯莱斯汽车。

读书笔记

7.（英国）捷豹 Jaguar

品牌名片

品　类：车

标志风格：英伦风

创 始 人：威廉姆·里昂斯（William Lyons）

诞 生 地：英国

诞生时间：1935年

捷豹的品牌标志是一只正在跳跃前扑的“美洲豹”雕塑，矫健勇猛，形神兼备，具有时代感与视觉冲击力，它既代表了公司的名称，又表现出向前奔驰的力量与速度，象征该车如美洲豹一样驰骋于世界各地。

品牌阅读

After the glittering launch of the SS Jaguar 2.5 Litre Saloon in 1935, Jaguar quickly moved into sports car production and pioneering work on new engines.

1935-Jaguar burst onto the motoring scene

The first car to bear the Jaguar name was the SS Jaguar 2.5 Litre Saloon, unveiled at an exclusive event in London's Mayfair Hotel. It cost a mere £385. William Lyons' SS Cars company also produced a 1.5-litre version and a 3.5-litre model followed two years later.

1938-The first Jaguar sports car

The open-topped Jaguar SS100 had been released three years earlier but 1938 saw the launch of a 3.5-litre version that offered the

classic Jaguar combination of comfort, usability and powerful sports performance. With its sweeping profile and elegant detailing, the SS100 was designed for competition and won prizes in the Alpine Trial and RAC Rally.

1943-The engine that made Jaguar's name

The straight-six engine was first developed by engineers on night-time firewatch at the Jaguar plant during World War Two. The XK version, introduced in 1949, went on to power Jaguar cars for more than four decades.

1949-The Original XK

The XK120, designed by Jaguar's founder William Lyons, caused a sensation when it was launched at the British Motor Show. Although the name XK120 was a combination of its engine and its planned top speed, a model with no **windshield** was tested on the Ostend-Jabbeke motorway in Belgium and reached 132mph, making it the world's fastest production car.

1951-The winning begins

Jaguar's first success on the race track came with the C-Type, originally called the XK120C. Its beautiful rounded shape was inspired by the principles of **aerodynamics**. More powerful, yet 25% lighter than the XK120 it was based on, the C-Type claimed victory at its first appearance in the 24 Hours of Le Mans.

1954-A design triumph

With its distinctive stabilizing tailfin, the Jaguar D-Type, designed by Malcolm Sayers, was one of the most beautiful competition cars ever built. It also featured the first serious use in motorsport of a moncoque construction, still found in the majority of racing cars today. D-Types achieved remarkable success at Le Mans, finishing first, second, third, fourth and sixth in the 1957 race.

1956-Recognition for Jaguar's founder

William Lyons was knighted in recognition of his services to the British car industry, particularly Jaguar's export success. He had formed the company's forerunner, Swallow Sidecars, on his 21st birthday and excelled as a designer as well as an entrepreneur.

1957-Jaguar plant burns

In the evening of February12, 1957 a fire broke out in the service area of Jaguar's Browns Lane factory and swept through the production line. The blaze caused damage worth £3 million - a colossal sum at the time - but the plant was back in action, working at one-third capacity, just a fortnight later, thanks to the incredible efforts of the workers.

1961-A true automotive icon

The **iconic** Jaguar E-Type caused a sensation when it was launched at the Geneva Motor Show, leaving all its rivals in the shade. Described by Enzo Ferrari as "the most beautiful car ever built", it exuded feline grace, power and beauty, with its impossibly long, elegant bonnet.

1968-The birth of a legendary lineage

The XJ6 saloon was the last car designed by Sir William Lyons and became his longest lived creation, with more than 400,000 sales in the following 24 years. With its emphasis on comfort and a smooth, quiet ride, the car set standards of refinement that would lead the luxury car market for years to come.

1985-The end of an era

Sir William Lyons died at his home in Leamington Spa, 50 years after unveiling the first Jaguar and 13 years after retiring as Jaguar's chairman.

1988-Return to the winner's podium

The XJR-9 with a 7.0-litre engine proved unstoppable in the World Sports Car Championship, winning six of the 11 races and taking both the driver and team trophies. It also returned Jaguar to the top step of the **podium** at Le Mans for the first time since 1957.

1996-Jaguar's fastest-selling sports car

Jaguar's own design team beat off competition from other parts of the Ford group to create a new sports car for the company's first V8 engine. The XK8 took inspiration from iconic Jaguars of the past and blended them into a sleek shape that met the contemporary requirements of space, safety and luxury. The XK8 immediately exceeded all expectations and became the fastest-selling sports car in Jaguar's history.

2010-And beyond

There is no doubt Jaguar will continue to focus on innovative,seductive performance well into the future. It is already pushing the boundaries of design and sustainability. The C-X75 electric concept car, unveiled to universal acclaim at the 2010 Paris Motor Show, gave an exciting glimpse into what the future holds for Jaguar.

windshield ['windʃi:ld] n. 挡风玻璃

aerodynamics [ˌɛərəudai'næmiks] n. 气体力学

iconic [aɪ'kɒnɪk] adj. 标志性的

podium ['pəudjəm] n.领奖台

自1935 年 SS 捷豹 2.5 升轿车闪亮登场起，捷豹生产了数款著名跑车，并在新型发动机的开发上保持领先地位。

1935 年 —— 捷豹诞生

第一辆贴有捷豹标签的汽车——SS 捷豹 2.5 升轿车，在伦敦梅菲尔大酒店举行的奢华仪式上亮相，售价仅为 385 英镑。William Lyons 爵士的捷豹汽车公司还生产一款 1.5 升汽车，2年后捷豹又推出 3.5 升车型。

1938 年 —— 第一辆捷豹跑车问世

捷豹敞篷式 SS100 早在3年前便已推出，但集舒适性、易用性和强劲运动性能于一体的经典特色却始自1938 年问世的 3.5 升跑车。凭借流畅的弧线外形和优美的细节设计，SS100 成为竞技之选，并在阿尔卑斯山路汽车拉力赛和英国 RAC 汽车拉力赛中获奖。

1943 年 —— 令捷豹蜚声业界的发动机

直列六缸发动机于"二战"期间由工程师们在捷豹工厂借夜间防火时间开发而成。1949年推出的XK发动机，为捷豹汽车提供动力超过40年。

1949 年 —— 开启经典的XK

XK120 由捷豹的创始人 William Lyons爵士设计，在英国车展上推出时引起轰动。虽然 XK120 这个名称由该车的发动机和计划达到的最高时速组成，但一款无风挡的车型在比利时奥斯登至雅贝克的高速公路上试车时，速度竟达到每小时 132 英里，成为世界上最快的量产车。

1951 年 —— 胜利从此开始

捷豹在赛道上首获成功的车型为 C-TYPE，最初名为 XK120C。它优美、圆润的外形，深受空气动力学原理的启迪。C-TYPE 以 XK120 为基础，动力更强，重量却减少 25%，在勒芒 24 小时耐力赛上初次亮相即宣告成功。

1954 年 —— 设计典范

捷豹 D-TYPE 具有独特的稳定尾翼，由 Malcolm Sayers 设计，是史上最漂亮的赛车之一。同时，这是无大梁单体车身构造在汽车运动中的首次真正应用，直到今天这种结构仍为大多数赛车沿用。D-TYPE 在勒芒赛中大获成功，在 1957 年赛事中包揽前六名中的五个。

1956 年 —— 捷豹创始人获得殊荣

William Lyons 因其对英国汽车工业的贡献，尤其是捷豹出口所获的成功而被封爵。他在 21 岁生日那天组建了公司前身 Swallow Sidecars，是一位出色的设计师和企业家。

1957 年 —— 捷豹工厂火灾

1957 年 2 月 12 日的傍晚，捷豹 Browns Lane 工厂的维修区突发大火并席卷了整个生产线。大火造成 300 万英镑的损失，在当时这是个巨额数字，但在工人们的卓绝努力下，仅两周后工厂就恢复 1/3 的产能。

1961 年 —— 汽车美学典范

最具标志性的 E-TYPE 在日内瓦车展上推出时引起轰动。Enzo Ferrari先生称其为“史上最漂亮的汽车”。它的发动机盖不可思议的修长优美，散发出猫一般的优雅、力量和美感。

1968 年 —— 传奇车系诞生

XJ6 轿车是由 William Lyons 爵士设计的最后一款车，也成为经典，在之后 24 年里销售超过 40 万辆。这款车强调舒适及平滑安静的驾乘体验，确立了精致优雅的标准，引领未来豪华车市场。

1985 年 —— 一个时代的结束

首辆捷豹车诞生 50 年后，从捷豹董事长职位上已退休 13 年的 William Lyons 爵士在位于莱明顿温泉区的家中去世。

1988 年 —— 重返胜利者的领奖台

采用 7.0 升发动机的 XJR-9 在世界跑车锦标赛上势不可挡，赢得 11 项比赛中的六项，捧回个人和团队奖杯，同时也让捷豹自 1957 年以来再次重登勒芒最高领奖台。

1996 年 —— 捷豹销售最快的跑车

捷豹的设计团队打败了福特集团其他部门的竞争者，为公司首台 V8 发动机设计新跑车。XK8 汲取捷豹传奇车型的灵感，加以融

合，设计出线条流畅的外形，满足当代对空间、安全和奢华的要求。XK8 不负期望，问世后成为捷豹史上销售最快的跑车。

2010 —— 专注未来

毫无疑问，捷豹未来将会一直专注创新和卓越性能，不断扩展设计与可持续发展的极限。C-X75 电动概念车在 2010 年巴黎车展上一亮相即获得交口称赞，让人们得以窥见捷豹的未来，C-X75的诞生不仅为了庆祝捷豹75年的辉煌成就和夺目未来，更表明捷豹将在可持续发展之路上，继续坚持打造“优雅迷人而又动感激情”的汽车。

读书笔记

8.（英国）路虎 Land Rover

品　　类：车

标志风格：冒险、勇气、至尊

创 始 人：Spencer and Maurice Wilks

诞 生 地：英国

诞生时间：1948年

路虎的品牌标志以绿色为背景，“LAND ROVER”为主体。

品牌阅读

The first Land Rover made its debut in 1948. It was designed with brilliant simplicity for extraordinary ability and unrivalled strength and durability. In fact, seven decades on it is estimated that two-thirds of all these incredible vehicles are still at work - many of them in some of the most extreme conditions and **inhospitable** places on earth.

The original 1948 Land Rover was ingeniously designed and engineered for extreme capability and strength. With extremely robust construction and characteristics such as short front and rear overhangs, it drove off the production line ready to take on some of the world's toughest terrain. Today these qualities are as significant as they were 70 years ago, a part of what makes a Land Rover vehicle unique .

The Land Rover was the product of continuous evolution and refinement throughout the 1950s and 1960s with improved stability and a tighter turning circle. It was a period in which Land Rover took the lead in the emerging market for four-wheel drive vehicles.

In keeping with the **forward-thinking** philosophy that founded

Land Rover, a radical, entirely new product was introduced in 1970 and created its very own vehicle category. This overnight sensation was the original Range Rover. It had all the capability of a Land Rover with the comfort and performance of an on-road car.

This culture of innovation has developed ever since with both Land Rover and Range Rover vehicles: new models, more refinement, more innovative technology, more efficiency and fewer emissions. And it continues with initiatives such as e - Terrain Technologies (which improves the environmental performance of vehicles by reducing **CO_2 emissions**), Sustainable Manufacturing and CO_2 Offsetting. Land Rover will remain at the forefront of advanced design – the new small Range Rover is a testament to the vision that takes the company forward and keeps it at the cutting edge of technology and engineering.

inhospitable [ˌɪnhɒ'spɪtəb(ə)l] *adj.* 荒凉的

forward-thinking ['fɔ:wəd'θinkiŋ] *adj.* 前瞻的，有远见的

CO_2 emission 二氧化碳排放

1948年第一辆路虎车问世。其设计简洁而实用，功能神奇，且具有无与伦比的强度和可靠性。事实上，这70年来售出的路虎车中，预计2/3的车仍然在被人们使用，其中许多是在一些非常恶劣的条件及荒凉的地方使用。

1948年第一辆路虎车设计精巧，强度高，性能优异。它具有非常坚固的结构特点（如较短的前后悬挂系统），一下线就能投入到极端的地形环境。和70年前一样，现在这些特点仍是确保路虎车与众不同的重要因素。

20世纪50～60年代，路虎车不断创新和改进，可靠性得到提升，转向圆更小。在这期间，路虎在风云变幻的四驱车市场取得领

先地位。

秉承路虎高瞻远瞩的一贯宗旨，1970年推出全新车型，自有车系从此诞生。这款车一夜之间风靡全球，它兼具路虎的所有功能和公路汽车的舒适性与性能。

自此，路虎和揽胜车一直延续和发展这种创新文化：新型号、更加精致、更多创新技术、更加高效和更少排放。此外，路虎继续倡导未来科技（通过降低二氧化碳排放，提高车辆环保性能）、可持续制造和二氧化碳补偿等措施。路虎将始终引领创新设计潮流，全新的小型路虎揽胜证明，路虎公司将不断向前发展，并始终站在技术和设计的最前沿。

读书笔记

9.（德国）迈巴赫 Maybach

品牌名片

品　　类：车

标志风格：典雅、尊贵

创 始 人：卡尔·迈巴赫（Karl Maybach）
　　　　　威廉·迈巴赫（Wilhelm Maybach）

诞 生 地：德国

诞生时间：1909年

迈巴赫的品牌标志由2个交叉的M，围绕在一个球面三角形里组成，新的轿车将仍采用这个经典的标志，不同的是，以前双M代表“迈巴赫汽车”，现在，双M意味着“迈巴赫制造”。

品牌阅读

The Maybach marque has a remarkably distinguished heritage.

The company was originally founded in 1909 by Wilhelm Maybach with his son Karl Maybach acting as director and was known as “Luftfahrzeug-Motorenbau GmbH” based in Bissingen on the Enz. In 1912 the company moved to Friedrichshafen and changed its name to Maybach Motorenbau GmbH Friedrichshafen. Today, the marque Maybach Manufaktur is owned by Daimler AG and is based in Stuttgart.

More than 100 years ago, Wilhelm Maybach built a car that pointed the way towards the modern era. His Opus No.1 went down in history as the first Mercedes, and he is still remembered as the “king of the design engineers”.

Having set many standards in terms of size, technology and

performance by the end of the twenties, Maybach followed this up in the thirties with a surprise move: the introduction of a small model, known by the **abbreviation** SW, which stood for swing axle. These cars were notable for their six-cylinder in-line engines with 3.5, 3.8 or 4.2-litre displacement and were all lovingly handcrafted.Unique vehicles were built in accordance with the wishes of their owner.

"To create only the best from the best, a vehicle that is the ultimate in wish fulfilment, with a distinctive character of the finest elegance and power" — this is how a Maybach flyer from 1930 announced the company's aim, and it still applies at Maybach in its entirety to this day.

In 1996, for the celebration of his 150th birthday, Wilhelm Maybach took his deserved place in the Automotive Hall of Fame, together with other key figures in the automotive industry such as Gottlieb Daimler and Karl Benz. The following year, the foundations of the Maybach's marquee rebirth were laid: thc premises for a new, modern high-end luxury car were the combination of Mercedes's advanced development techniques and the exclusiveness and individuality that is a trademark of Maybach. The first stcp towards this new era **took place** in 1997, with the deployment of the Mercedes-Benz Maybach concept which was presented at the Tolyo Motor Show. The chauffeur driven limousine represented the basis for the realization of the Maybach for the new millennium. Together with the Maybach Zeppelin, presented in 2009, the aim of the founders was to create unique vehicles with a distinctive style capable of reinvigorating the soul. With a place in the new top luxury segment represented by Maybach, Daimler AG established its position at the summit of this highly exclusive market segment. To guarantee an

appropriate exhibition site for the Maybach vehicles and to illustrate the countless passibilities of **personalization** (an exclusive service made available by highly skilled specialists), the center of Excellence was established in Sindelfingen, Germany. In 2010, a superb facelift interested the actual range, defining new boundaries in term of luxury design, performance, consumption and emissions. All the Maybach models respect the Euro5 standard.

abbreviation [ə,bri:vi'eiʃən] n. 缩写；缩写词
take place 发生
personalization ['pə:sənəlaizeiʃn] n. 个性化

迈巴赫是汽车历史上一个充满传奇色彩的豪华品牌。

公司最初由迈巴赫父子（威廉·迈巴赫和卡尔·迈巴赫）于1909年成立，当时名为Luftfahrzeug-Motorenbau GmbH，地址在德国佛腾堡地区的比辛根（Bissingen）。1912年，公司迁至腓特烈港（Friedrichshafen），并更名为Maybach Motorenbau GmbH Friedrichshafen。时至今日，迈巴赫作为戴姆勒股份公司（Daimler AG）集团旗下的高端品牌，总部设在斯图加特（Stuttgart），继续闪耀昔日的辉煌。

早在一百多年前，威廉·迈巴赫制造了一架汽车，从此把汽车业带进一个全新的纪元。他设计的Opus 1号成为第一台梅赛德斯汽车，而他本人直到今日仍被公认为“设计之王”（King of the Design Engineers）。

20世纪20年代末，在车辆大小、技术及性能等方面奠定了新标准。30年代，迈巴赫做出了一个惊人的创举，推出采用摆动轴技术的小型车SW。这些轿车的6气缸引擎有3.5、3.8 以及4.2升的排气量，每一款轿车都经由人手工打造而成，震惊车坛。迈巴赫打造车主所想的独一无二非凡座驾。

迈巴赫的宗旨由1930年起始终如一：打造顶级轿车中的至尊，令客户梦想成真，成就无与伦比的典雅尊贵，非凡绝伦的澎湃动力。

1996年，为纪念威廉·迈巴赫诞辰150周年，他的名字和戈特利布·戴姆勒及卡尔·奔驰等汽车灵魂人物的名字被刻在汽车名人堂。次年，顶级豪华品牌迈巴赫获得重生，由奔驰的先进科技及迈巴赫非凡的尊贵独特联合打造的现代化顶级豪华轿车品牌诞生。1997年的东京国际车展上，奔驰迈巴赫概念车亮相，揭开了这个顶级豪华品牌划时代的新一页。这架需要司机驾驶的豪华轿车带领迈巴赫进入崭新的千禧世代。随着2009年迈巴赫Zeppelin的面世，迈巴赫这个非凡尊贵的顶级豪华轿车品牌再次于车坛焕发新生活力，重新在顶级豪华轿车市场占有一席之位，并帮助戴姆勒股份公司在豪华轿车市场确立地位。为确保迈巴赫拥有合适展出地方，并充分展示品牌的非凡个性，车厂特别在德国辛德芬根设立了迈巴赫卓越中心，并由经验丰富的专业精英提供贴身服务。2010年，一款顶级改装版豪华设计、出众性能同时低油耗及排气量的全新车型风靡万千迈巴赫迷，所有迈巴赫车型均符合欧洲五号标准的排放量要求。

读书笔记

读书笔记